Creative Onboarding Programs

Tools for Energizing Your Orientation Program

Doris Sims, SPHR

New York   Chicago   San Francisco   Lisbon   London   Madrid   Mexico City
Milan   New Delhi   San Juan   Seoul   Singapore   Sydney   Toronto

The **McGraw·Hill** Companies

1 2 3 4 5 6 7 8 9 10 QFR/QFR 1 5 4 3 2 1 0

ISBN 978-0-07-173679-4
MHID 0-07-173679-4

This publication is designed to provide accurate and authoritative information in regard to the subject matter covered. It is sold with the understanding that neither the author nor the publisher is engaged in rendering legal, accounting, or other professional service. If legal advice or other expert assistance is required, the services of a competent professional person should be sought.

—From a Declaration of Principles jointly adopted by a Committee of the American Bar Association and a Committee of Publishers

McGraw-Hill books are available at special quantity discounts to use as premiums and sales promotions or for use in corporate training programs. To contact a representative, please e-mail us at bulksales@mcgraw-hill.com.

This book is printed on acid-free paper.

To my Dad,
who continues to demonstrate a love
of teaching and lifelong learning

Contents in Brief

Complete Contents

PART 4—TOOLS, SYSTEMS, AND CHECKLISTS

PART 6—ONBOARDING LEADERS

Preface

The new talent you bring into your organization creates and drives your business results. The New Employee Onboarding process is a chance to start employees off on the right track—to build culture, attitudes, knowledge, and skill sets *right from the beginning* that will support and grow the company's business.

If you are responsible for orienting new employees, then you are the CEO of first impressions, as well as initial job satisfaction and accelerated new employee productivity. You represent the entire company to each new employee, so your job is critical. The organization has only one chance to create a first impression, and you have been chosen to deliver it.

Yet many companies have hundreds or even thousands of employees coming into their organizations every year without being properly welcomed and trained. Many other companies have onboarding processes that address the paperwork issues but do not include vital information about the company's products and services, culture, policies, customers, safety issues, and so forth. This book is designed to help those who are responsible for their organizations' onboarding processes by providing unique and creative ways to make your own process special, memorable, and effective.

In every other aspect of life, we know that preparation increases success. Prospective parents attend childbirth classes, engaged couples go through prenuptial counseling, new college students first visit campuses and then attend orientation programs. Leading companies understand that this concept applies to starting a new job as well, and they capitalize upon the moment to fully prepare the employee to be successful—because successful employees lead to a successful organization.

This book contains a wide variety of ideas for organizations of any size and shape. There are models and ideas from leading companies, as well as ideas from and for smaller companies, and ideas for companies that have small offices in remote locations. When I've given presentations on new employee onboarding, I have noticed that people are interested in benchmarking what others are doing in their orientation programs, and this book allows the reader to do that. It is designed to be a "conference in a book." Work to keep your material fresh by trying new activities from this book.

I thank the many contributors who put their time, energy, ideas, and advice in this book. They have provided a wealth of diverse options, so that anyone can find ideas that will work for their organization. I also thank the contributors who connected me to other contributors.

This book is designed to provide ideas, designs, and tools that you can use immediately on the job. I hope that you will find many uses for these resources, and I encourage you to keep trying new ideas on a frequent basis. This keeps the program fresh and interesting for you, the orientation facilitator, and it provides a forum in which to try new training methods to find those that best suit your style and your organization's needs.

Doris Sims

PART 1
Introduction

THERE IS A FIRST TIME FOR EVERYTHING . . .

. . . and the first time a new employee joins your organization is the one chance you have to make a great first impression with that employee, for the business purposes of:

- Accelerating the initial productivity level of new talent
- Increasing the retention of new employees in the first year of employment
- Enhancing the critical engagement level of new employees, which has been proven to increase business results for the organization
- Ensuring that all legal aspects of onboarding a new employee have taken place
- Providing a fair and equal opportunity for employees to learn about available employee benefits
- Enhancing your employee brand as your new employees tell their friends and business network associates about their positive experience with your company

ONBOARDING . . . USING MULTIPLE TOOLS AND A PHASED APPROACH

A traditional new employee orientation program often takes place on the first day of employment, or within the first few days or weeks on the job. The traditional program consists of survival information—a virtual data dump (also known as the "firehose approach") of procedures and policies.

Using a phased onboarding approach rather than a one-stop, one-time approach also helps to avoid the "information overload" problem, and enables employees to build relationships with other new employees and with those who teach, coach, and mentor them during the entire onboarding period.

To assist you as you create or update your New Employee Onboarding strategy, program, and processes, this book is filled with curriculum designs, checklists, evaluation forms, online tool ideas, games, and activities that engage the employee in the orientation process. These ideas will increase learning as well as increasing the motivational and engagement levels of the participants.

Today, we have so many new options and tools available to ease the new employee's transition into the organization. There is no reason for new employee orientation to be a series of boring lectures and tedious forms.

A Few Examples of New Employee Onboarding Tools

The tool . . .	Tool uses and benefits . . .
Company Web sites	Web sites provide a repository of forms, benefit information, contact information, etc., for new employees and their families.
Social Networking Sites	Such sites provide opportunities for new employees to learn about your job openings, connect with new employees, and receive updates and company news.
Video Materials (DVDs and CDs)	A CD or DVD with benefits information mailed to the employee's home prior to the first day of employment enables the new employee (and his or her family) to view at their own pace, and to make their benefit decisions with their spouse. Video materials can also provide segments of executive messages to employees, which communicate your company's vision, goals, culture, etc.
Sponsors or Mentors	Other organizations (i.e., self-help groups, churches, nonprofit groups, etc.) have long recognized the importance of assigning a sponsor to an individual who is joining the group, to provide that "personal touch" and to increase accountability. When new employees have a sponsor as they join the group, it helps them to feel more connected to the company immediately, and provides an additional contact person (other than the immediate supervisor) for questions as they arise.
Employee Handbooks, Safety Guides, Benefit Guides, etc.	These hardcopy tools are also helpful as quick reference guides for new employees to locate company policy and benefit information quickly.
Games and Activities	This book contains multiple ideas for activities for new employees to increase their interaction in the company, to enhance their learning, to integrate the new employee into the culture, and to energize the new employee.
E-learning	When presenting factual information (i.e., Harassment Training, Safety Procedures, Management Procedures, Benefit Information, etc.), E-Learning course materials provide an easy and inexpensive way to train volumes of new employees across multiple geographic regions.

COMMON ISSUES WITH NEW EMPLOYEE PROGRAMS

Many organizations design their New Employee programs with the best intentions to provide the most information to the new employee as soon as possible. As you are designing or updating your New Employee program, here are some common errors to avoid:

- Providing *too much information too soon* (the firehose approach)
- *Providing a "minimalist" program* that only provides tactical information
- Including *too much lecture* from one instructor or speaker
- Failing to prepare—the employee's *workspace, computer, and/or phone is not set up* for the first day
- Telling the employees *"I hope our orientation program is not too boring"*
- *Lacking a formal New Employee Onboarding Program* and process altogether
- *Feeling like a "cattle drive"* to the new employee

> What are other problems you have experienced as a new employee in your career that you want to address as you lead your organization's new employee program?

ENERGIZE AND ENGAGE YOUR NEW EMPLOYEES!

Most companies actually celebrate more when employees *leave* the company than when they *arrive*. When a valued employee leaves a company, often the workgroup takes the departing employee to lunch or buys a gift to remember the workgroup by. This is certainly a nice way to tell employees how much you appreciate what they did for the company. But why not learn to celebrate and appreciate the value of employees from the start?

Some companies build their orientation programs around a theme to keep the program interesting and cohesive. The theme can be related to the company's business or to the concept of a starting point, to represent the employee's starting point with the company. All of the program's games, visual aids, and training materials employ this theme.

DON'T FORGET TO COMMUNICATE THE UNWRITTEN RULES

Many companies do a good job of ensuring that new employees know the written rules of the organization, such as company policies, values, safety procedures, etc. But how well does your organization communicate the unwritten rules of the organization? Consider this story described by Diane Brown, founder of The Talent Journey, LLC:

> *A leader friend of mine just transitioned from a start-up organization into a large manufacturing organization. As you can imagine, she left a rapid-paced, feet-to-the-fire, everyone-does-everything type of work environment and transitioned into a slower-paced, more regulated, and role-defined organization. The change in dynamics was not a surprise and, by virtue of size, was expected.*
>
> *What **did** come as a surprise to her was the degree of cautious decision making in the organization. Within the first six months, she learned that the chain of command in the organization was a powerful force. When a senior-level leader made a decision, the leaders below that level of leader implemented the decision, often without much discussion or information. Mavericks were heavily frowned upon. After about eight months, she learned the rules of navigation within this system, got alliance and support, and successfully learned to manage up in this organization.*
>
> *My friend stated, "There are so many subtle patterns that I misread early in my transition. Had I understood this sooner, I could have generated significantly more positive contributions within my team. I'm just thankful that my peers were patient and forgiving while I learned the system."*

This story is an example of the importance of learning the "unwritten rules." Unwritten rules typically pertain to:

- Chain of command communications and decision-making norms
- "Normal" work hours in the organization
- The level of risk taking that is either encouraged or discouraged in the company
- The value of relationship building and friendships that exist in the organization
- The level of "fun" and energy that exists and is encouraged (or discouraged) in the organization

The ability to work within the culture and norms of any group is critical to making a successful transition into the group. As you are creating or updating your New Employee Onboarding program, work to identify your "unwritten rules" and include these in your program, and/or ensure that peers or official "new employee buddies" emphasize and teach these unwritten rules to the new employees. This is even more critical for new leaders in a company, who must obtain a high level of organization savvy early on to be successful in the new position.

ADDRESS "NEW JOB REMORSE" AND ENHANCE EMPLOYEE BRAND

Everyone has experienced buyer's remorse—that worrying, nagging guilt or concern that can occur after making a very large purchase, such as a new car, a piece of furniture, or a house. Many employees experience the same type of emotion when they make the decision to leave one company and join another. We could call it "new job remorse."

An effective new employee orientation program recognizes this emotion and works to create a dynamic motivational atmosphere that erases employees' doubts and concerns, leaving them confident that they made the right decision. The reality is that our customers are not the only population we must continually sell to; employees must also be initially and continually sold on the benefits of staying with and growing with the company, or they will be wooed elsewhere.

ONBOARDING . . . THE FIRST OPPORTUNITY TO COMMUNICATE CULTURE

The Mary Kay Corporation provides a 3-Day Quarterly New Employee Program that is designed to provide a deep dive into the culture, values, and products of the organization. The Mary Kay organization understands the value of this golden opportunity to make a distinct impression and to build company and brand loyalty within the employee population. Every company has its own culture and values. The question is, does the company have the culture and values it needs to be successful within its industry and market, or does the company have a culture that was created by accident?

If a company's orientation program does not include discussions and opportunities for employees to learn about the company culture, expectations, norms, and strategic plans, then a critical link in the process of creating a planned culture, with employees aligned with strategic goals, is lost.

New employees want to know what to do, what *not* to do, what to wear, and specific words or phrases that are valued either positively or negatively in the corporation. New employees desire to fit into the culture, avoid embarrassment, and be viewed as successful—and they want to know what is expected of them.

It is sometimes assumed that organizational expectations and social norms are consistent and universal in all companies, and that people should know them intuitively, but that is simply not the case. This can be verified by looking at even simple differences, such as the variety of dress codes throughout companies in the United States.

An effective orientation program helps new employees feel comfortable and confident by sharing this type of information and ensuring that employees know the strategic goals, and know how they can contribute to achieving those goals. In addition, orientation programs should include phone numbers, contact names, and titles of the company's human resource personnel, so employees know where they can go for help when they need it.

The orientation process should also include a discussion of the company's revenue sources. After all, if employees don't know how the company makes money, how can they help the company make more of it, to increase their own success and the overall success of the company? Some companies also include discussions of their products and services to help increase the size of the sales force by imparting to all employees the knowledge to help the company sell, no matter what position they may be in officially.

INCREASE NEW EMPLOYEE RETENTION

The jury is in, and the verdict is that an effective new employee orientation program is a measurable asset in the effort to retain talented employees.

Troy Van Houten, coordinator of Micron Technology's corporate new employee training program, credits its employee orientation and training programs for the company's lower employee turnover rate.

Like many other companies with superior orientation programs, Micron includes more than an initial first-day training. The program, called NET (New Employee Training), includes technical training, safety programs, reaching high performance, and an overview of the company's products and processes.

ACCELERATE NEW EMPLOYEE PRODUCTIVITY

New employee onboarding should be designed to help employees become productive more quickly on the job. To achieve this goal, the new employee (or the employee who is transitioning into a new role in the same organization), needs much more than just a one-day orientation session. To achieve accelerated productivity for new employees, the onboarding program should include

- Information and materials to "get a head start" *before* the employee's first day on the job; examples include the initial paperwork, benefits information, and company products and brand information
- All of the basics needed on the *first day* of employment—whom to meet, where to park, workstation information, etc.
- A *peer or buddy* assigned to the new employee, to provide an additional resource person to assist the employee, to answer questions, and to communicate the "unwritten rules" of the company
- A *full onboarding training session* that communicates company culture, values, products and/or services, clients, geographical information, the leadership of the company, etc.
- *Job-specific training*, which is typically a combination of formal training, such as workshops, e-learning, or procedure guides, and more informal on-the-job training, such as shadowing a current employee, observing others, participating on a new project team
- *Performance expectations and coaching* from the employee's immediate manager, to ensure clear communications regarding performance goals, productivity progress, etc.

PROVIDE NEW MANAGER ONBOARDING

New managers require more information regarding both the written and unwritten rules of the organization. If you are creating or enhancing a new employee onboarding program, be sure to identify the resources and methods that are needed to provide this additional information to new managers. Your new manager onboarding program should include:

- All required training components, such as harassment prevention, Sarbanes-Oxley, ethics, etc.
- Management procedures regarding hiring employees, obtaining contingent labor, performance appraisal processes, etc.

- Leadership development pertaining to coaching skills, developing others, strategic thinking skills, etc.
- Understanding the executive and leadership structure, culture, values, and competencies for leaders in the organization

CREATE CONNECTIONS AND TEAMWORK

I've conducted informal surveys with my audiences during speaking engagements to determine how many people think (in retrospect) that they stayed with a company longer because of the strong friendships and relationships they have built with their coworkers. The large majority of people indicate that coworker relationships and friendships in the workplace have played a major part in their decision to stay with a company.

Some onboarding best practice organizations extend this relationship factor to the new employee's family, and they include internal buddy systems to provide both a friend and resource for the new employee. Aneetha Rao, associate professor of Human Resources at Syndenham Institute of Management in Mumbai, India, worked with Firstsource (a leading global provider of business process management services) to incorporate both of these processes into the new employee onboarding program.

At Firstsource:

- Each person has a senior person who has worked for more than 18 months with the organization as a buddy.
- A family day provides an opportunity for families of the new employees to come to the office and view the work environment.

People spend a large amount of their lives at work, and forming strong and positive relationships with coworkers is critical not only for job satisfaction, retention, and effective teamwork, but is also critical for one's personal happiness and on-the-job engagement level. Companies that understand this include activities in the orientation program to foster the forming of employee relationships on the new employees' first day.

Many of the games provided in this book are designed to help new employees meet other new employees in the orientation program and to meet veteran employees in the workplace.

PROVIDE A CONSISTENT APPROACH TO COVER LEGAL REQUIREMENTS

Certain topics should be covered with all employees at some point during the orientation process to reduce potential lawsuits, to ensure the safety of employees, and to comply with employee law. It is impossible to provide an all-inclusive list here, because different industries and different geographic regions have different requirements. Topics to be covered may include the following:

- Harassment policies and reporting procedures
- Safety/OSHA topics
- Specific industry regulations
- Diversity topics
- The Employee Complaint Process
- Actions resulting in immediate termination

The delivery method and timing for this type of information varies by company; some of these topics can be delivered simply through e-learning courses, the company intranet, and an Employee Handbook, and others should be covered in live training sessions or online live virtual meetings to provide more of a personal touch, and to provide an opportunity for the new employees to ask questions.

Part 2

Program Development

If you are creating or updating a new employee onboarding, use the step-by-step process in this chapter to create a comprehensive strategy, plan, and program.

STEP ONE: CREATE A NEW EMPLOYEE PROJECT TEAM

Ideally, the organization's New Employee Onboarding Program is created (or enhanced) by a team consisting of both Human Resources participants and business leaders.

Considering the following ideas to create a Steering Committee or a Project Team, which might consist of participants such as:

- A group of High Potential employees from various departments in the company, which provides the additional benefit of developing the High Potential employees as they are working on the cross-functional project
- A group of employees who have been in the company for one year, enabling them to think back through the past year to identify what worked well for them as they joined the company, and what could be improved to better assimilate new employees into the organization
- Mid- to senior-level leaders who will serve as the strategic and financial sponsors of the new employee onboarding project team

STEP TWO: GATHER INFORMATION

First, you will need to review the current processes in your organization used to onboard new employees:

- The Employment Offer Process (review the company's Offer Letter, documenting the employee's acceptance of the position, notifying other applicants that the position has been filled, etc.)

- The New Employee Set-up Process (such as setting up the employee on the company's HR system, the company's Security system, etc.)
- The New Employee Welcome Process (review the Welcome Letter or Package sent to the new employee to make sure they know where to go on their first day, where to park, etc., and any materials and benefits information that is sent to employees prior to their first day)
- First day/week/month orientation programs and processes
- Onboarding training programs and resources currently available for new employees to help them develop job competencies
- Resources, checklists, and tools available to managers to onboard their new employees
- Tools, checklists, and online resources available for new employees

If you are updating your new employee notification process, check the list shown below to determine the part that each department plays in the onboarding process. Schedule a meeting with a representative of each department as needed to identify what is working well and what can be improved in each area.

It is amazing how many people it can take to set up a new employee in the organization. Examples of personnel who are part of this process (in addition to the training department) may include:

- Benefits personnel (insurance enrollment and 401(k) enrollment)
- Payroll personnel (payroll setup, direct deposit, and W-2 forms)
- HR/compliance personnel (I-9 forms and identification verification)
- Information systems personnel (computers, ID codes, and passwords)
- The company's intranet Webmaster (if the company keeps an employee phone and e-mail directory online)
- Receptionists (to update their phone listings)
- Administrative assistants (to order office supplies, prepare the workspace, order business cards, and update organizational charts)
- Facilities personnel (to determine where the new employee will sit, to order office furniture if needed, and to obtain such items as furniture keys)
- Accounting personnel (to keep head count and payroll accounts)
- Stock options personnel (to handle the administrative work associated with setting up stock options for new employees)

- Phone system personnel (to bring in a new phone if needed for the new employee, or to set up the phone number and voice mail system to reflect the new employee's name)
- Security personnel (to obtain a temporary or permanent badge, a parking sticker or card, and building access keys or cards)

When you conduct this meeting, use the chart on the following page to determine the information each department needs and when they need it, to obtain feedback regarding how well the process is currently working, and to obtain ideas regarding how the process should work.

STEP THREE: DEFINE THE GOALS OF YOUR NEW EMPLOYEE ONBOARDING PROCESS

When you are creating or updating any Human Resources program, you will want to define your current situation, the strengths and weaknesses of your current program, your goals, and the actions needed to achieve the goals.

After gathering all of the information shown in step two, use the outline below to plan your onboarding strategy:

Describe the overall current state of our New Employee Onboarding Strategy.	
Approximately how many employees do we plan to hire annually?	
Where will new employees be located? Do we need an onboarding process for virtual employees?	
What issues have we uncovered during our data-gathering processes that need to be addressed?	
What strengths were discovered about our program that we want to continue?	
What does a "best practice" new employee onboarding program look like in our organization?	
How will we measure our results?	

STEP FOUR: PLAN AN ONBOARDING OUTLINE

Use the following sample basic outline of a "phased approach" to onboarding a new employee to create your own customized onboarding outline that meets your company's business needs, size, and hiring rate.

For each action that you select for your own onboarding program, identify who is responsible for executing that action.

Prior to the employee's first day …		
Action	How Will We Customize This?	Who is Responsible?
Provide access to the company's Web site		
Provide a benefits video and package		
Send a Welcome Letter that explains the orientation process		
Activate the workspace setup process (computer, phone, office supplies, etc.)		
Activate the internal security processes (User IDs, parking, security badge, security entrance requirements, etc.		
Set up the employee on the HRIS system/payroll system		
Send "Onboarding Your New Employee" information to the new employee's manager		

On the employee's first day		
Action	How Will We Customize This?	Who is Responsible?
Greet new employees and acquaint them with security access to the building		
Meet new work peers		
Conduct a facility tour		
Complete forms and all legal requirements		
Provide any safety training and/or point out safety stations and fire extinguishers		
Assist the employee in navigating the company's intranet site and accessing e-mail for the first time		
Assist the new employee with the selection of benefits as needed		
Take the new employee to lunch and/ or provide other ways to help the employee feel welcome within the new workgroup		

In the first weeks or first month on the job ...		
Action	How Will We Customize This?	Who is Responsible?
Provide an Orientation workshop		
Provide job-specific training (i.e., customer service, systems, etc.)		
Provide a mentor, sponsor, or buddy for the new employee		
Provide the structure for the new employee to meet with leaders and key contacts within the organization		
Provide management orientation (or executive onboarding) to new employees in leadership positions		
Provide performance goals and acquaint the new employee with the performance appraisal process and philosophy		
Provide any application training guides, employee handbooks, etc., for reference		

In the first 90 days on the job …		
Action	How Will We Customize This?	Who is Responsible?
Obtain onboarding feedback from the new employee for continuous improvement to the onboarding process		
Provide 90-day performance feedback to the new employee (this may be a formal review or informal feedback)		
Ensure all 90-day training requirements have been completed		

In the first year on the job …		
Action	How Will We Customize This?	Who is Responsible?
Obtain onboarding feedback from the employee at the one-year anniversary point to measure the engagement level of these employees		
Provide additional job-specific training to the employee as needed		
Ask the one-year employee to serve as a buddy or a mentor to newly hired employees		

A SAMPLE PHASED ONBOARDING CURRICULUM

The following table shows a sample onboarding program that includes actions and resources provided prior to the employees' first day, as well as first-day, first-month, and 90-day onboarding activities.

Orientation Events	Actions	Resources Available
Phase 1: **Before the First Day**	Welcome Letter outlining orientation process New Employee, Supervisor, Sponsor, and Logistics Checklists sent to employee Before the First Day Web site Welcome from CEO First Day Forms, Security, Policies, Tax Documents, and Harassment Training Local Community Information	Welcome Letter Sample New Employee Checklist Supervisor Checklist Sponsor Checklist New Employee Website
Phase 2: Welcome!	Required forms and documents	Forms Administration Guidelines HR Generalist
Onboarding Session	Orientation Curriculum: Company Overview, History and Values Performance Management Policies and Ethics Products and Services Who We Serve Where We Are	Employee Handbook Ethics Web Site Onboarding Workshop Materials New Employee Director
Meet Your Colleagues	Meet with your supervisor and peers and discuss the New Employee Checklist items	New Employee Checklist
Orientation to Benefits	Lunch with Sponsors Live Benefits Presentation or E-learning Module (based on location)	Benefits E-learning Module
Phase 3: **Department** **Orientation**	Orientation to Department Goals, Procedures	Department Orientation Guidelines

(*continued on next page*)

Orientation Events	Actions	Resources Available

Phase 4:
  Follow Up
  Orientation
	90-day Feedback Survey
	90-day Performance Check
	Quarterly Meet-the-New-Employees
	  Breakfast
	Skills Training Modules
		Corporate University
		Local HR Generalist
		Manager
		Feedback Survey
		90-day Performance Check

STEP FIVE: IDENTIFY YOUR AUDIENCE(S)

Depending on your company's needs, your budget, and your resources, you may want to develop one general orientation program, or you may want to have additional, specialized programs for:

- Executives
- Managers
- New college graduates or interns
- Professional, salaried employees
- Technical employees
- Customer service and/or call center employees
- Retail store employees
- Franchise owners

Develop specific training programs for these employee populations as needed; typically, these training programs will be offered to new employees in addition to the general orientation program, rather than in place of the general program.

STEP SIX: PROVIDING RESOURCES FOR VIRTUAL NEW EMPLOYEES

Very few organizations are able to offer new employee onboarding workshops and training in one location—most must reach out to new employees in multiple cities and countries. Some employees work alone out of a home office, and others work in remote small group office locations.

Reaching all new employees in an organization and ensuring that they feel welcome and receive the information they need is an important and sometimes very challenging part of setting up an effective new employee onboarding program.

- Use virtual "what it is like to work here" online videos
- Use the new employee Web site (i.e., new employee portals)
- Design new employee e-learning modules
- Don't lose sight of the "people connection"
- Make use of multiple onboarding facilitators and mentors
- Use management tools such as guides, flip books, videos, and checklists
- Make use of today's communication tools such as PSP and iPhones

- Institute larger periodic employee welcome sessions
- Hold department orientation
- Evaluate onboarding success
- Ask the facility manager to greet new employees
- Remember to use "old fashioned" side-by-side training methods

STEP SEVEN: DESIGN YOUR LIVE ORIENTATION WORKSHOP

Most, though not all, organizations hold one or more central facilitator-led workshops to provide more information to new employees about the company culture, values, products, and services.

In addition, this type of live venue (which may be offered monthly, quarterly, or even annually) works to engage new employees and provides an opportunity to build company loyalty and relationships between new employees, which in turn increases employee retention.

Best practice onboarding programs also serve to continue the "employment branding" that begins with the recruiting process. Examples include:

- Be sure to use your company brand and logo on all materials provided to the new employee
- Provide promotional materials (i.e., shirts, cups, pins, etc.) with the employee brand, logo, and vision to new employees
- Show any marketing advertisements in the onboarding program—television ads, magazine ads, etc.
- If applicable, let new employees experience your products and services
- If applicable, have all new employees work in a storefront situation to gain an experience facing customers
- If you provide any employee discounts on your company products and services, communicate this to new employees (or provide a coupon to ensure that new employees use the company's products)
- Name your onboarding program in a way that defines it; for example, Red Lobster refers to their orientation as "New Crew Onboarding"
- If you have a live onboarding workshop, make sure the room reflects the company brand, with wall posters, pens with the company logo, etc.

STEP EIGHT: OBTAIN FEEDBACK AND MEASURE RESULTS

Within this book, several human resource practitioners have shared their evaluation forms, feedback questions, and processes to obtain feedback from employees about their onboarding experience.

Typical metrics used to measure the success of a New Employee Onboarding program include:

- The retention rate of new employees at the 90-day point
- The retention rate of new employees at the one-year point
- Accelerated "up-to-speed" productivity time for new employees who have completed all onboarding components, as compared to employees who did not participate in onboarding activities
- The engagement level of new employees (measured through employee engagement survey results)
- Time and cost savings achieved through streamlined and standardized onboarding processes
- Time and cost savings achieved by moving "manual" onboarding processes and training online
- Reduced employee calls to the company's human resource complaint hotline, and/or reduced employee calls to employees in the benefits department, the IT department, etc., that typically must handle a large volume of new employee questions
- Measurement of compliance with all legal requirements and paperwork required from all new employees

IT'S TIME TO GET STARTED!

Now that you have prepared your basic onboarding strategy and outline, read the ideas for additional design models, tools, and activities that will make your onboarding program unique to your company's business needs and culture.

Part 3

Design and Process Models

Whether you are creating a new employee orientation program for the first time or updating your current program, one of the first things you will need to do is determine the objectives and topics to be covered in (or added to) your program. It is often difficult for a seasoned employee to think of all the things new employees need to know when they come into the company. Therefore, this section can be used, in addition to your internal needs assessment, to shape the outline and the goals of your own program, by using the New Employee Learning Topics List and the sample onboarding programs written by multiple contributors throughout the book.

THIS SECTION PROVIDES THE FOLLOWING TOOLS:

THE NEW EMPLOYEE LEARNING TOPICS LIST

This is a comprehensive checklist of potential topics for a new employee orientation program. Simply review the list and check the topics that pertain to your company. Then use the customized list to form the basic outline for your program.

PROGRAM DESIGNS

Review the sample onboarding designs for new employees, new college students, and new nonprofit volunteers in this section to obtain ideas about the content, preparation, facilitation, and evaluation of an effective program. Sample curriculums, project plans, and evaluation forms have been provided by the internal practitioners as examples to assist you as you create or update your own new employee onboarding program.

In this section, you'll find ideas for orienting employees, volunteers, and students in:

- A Global Organization
- A Large Organization with Virtual Employees
- A Small Business
- A College Environment
- A Nonprofit Organization
- A Start-Up Organization
- Multiple Industries, such as Healthcare, Restaurant Service, Wealth Management, Cosmetics, Automotive, Semiconductors, and more!

Chapter 1

Identifying Your New Employee Learning Topics

Contributed By: Doris Sims, SPHR, President of Succession Builders, LLC

Doris's Contact Information:

Succession Builders, LLC
www.successionbuilders.com
doris@successionbuilders.com
214-906-3155

About the Author: Doris M. Sims, SPHR is the Founder and President of Succession Builders, LLC, a talent management, succession planning, and new talent onboarding consulting firm. Her experience in organizational development spans over 20 years working in Fortune 100 and Fortune 500 companies. Doris received her master's degree in Human Resource Development from Indiana State University. Doris is the coauthor of the talent management books *Building Tomorrow's Talent: A Practitioner's Guide to Talent Management and Succession Planning; The 30-Minute Guide to Talent and Succession Management;* and *The Talent Review Meeting Facilitation Guide.* Doris is also the author of the McGraw-Hill book *Creative New Employee Orientation Programs,* and has contributed articles to many other McGraw-Hill books and multiple periodicals, including *Training Magazine, Talent Management Magazine, Professionals in Human Resources,* and *The Consultant's Toolkit.*

New employee onboarding is often the most customized training program in any corporation; it must be geared to your company's specific culture, policies, procedures, and values, so it is very important to conduct a thorough needs assessment process to determine the objectives of your own program.

This new employee learning topics list can help accelerate your orientation needs assessment process by providing a checklist of potential topics that have been used in the orientation programs of other companies. Use the checklist in needs assessment interviews, focus groups, or surveys. If you are in the process of updating your orientation program, use the shopping list to identify any potential objectives that should be added to your course.

The New Employee Learning Topics List

Check the topics that are appropriate to include in your company's orientation program, orientation materials, and/or employee handbook:

- ❑ The Company's Mission Statement
- ❑ The Company's Vision Statement
- ❑ Company Strategy/Goals
- ❑ The Company's History
- ❑ Company Leaders/Executives
- ❑ A Facility Tour
- ❑ Organizational Chart(s)
- ❑ The Company's Quality Program(s)
- ❑ Group/Individual Photographs
- ❑ Lunch with Company Leaders
- ❑ Parent Company Information
- ❑ Company Subsidiary Information
- ❑ Company Locations/Size(s)
- ❑ Executive Presentations
- ❑ Company Growth—Past and Future

- ❑ Industry Awards/Recognition
- ❑ Top Market Niches
- ❑ Company Values
- ❑ The Company's Products/Services
- ❑ The Company's Customers
- ❑ Company Logo(s) and Marketing Plans
- ❑ The Company's Competitors
- ❑ Diversity Training and Cultural Awareness
- ❑ Customer Service Training
- ❑ NYSE Symbol/Information
- ❑ Business Partners of the Company
- ❑ Press Releases
- ❑ Company Stories/Case Studies

COMPANY BENEFITS

- ❑ Medical Insurance Benefits
- ❑ Vision Insurance
- ❑ Short-term Disability
- ❑ Life Insurance
- ❑ Flexible Spending Accounts
- ❑ Stock Option Programs
- ❑ Free or Discounted Meals
- ❑ Tuition Reimbursement
- ❑ Dental Insurance Benefits
- ❑ Vacation Benefits
- ❑ Personal Accident Insurance
- ❑ Concierge Services

- ❑ Floating Holidays
- ❑ Pension and Retirement Programs
- ❑ Child-care Assistance
- ❑ Paid Volunteer/Charity Time
- ❑ 401(k) Programs/Investment Options
- ❑ Employee Discounts
- ❑ Sick-child Assistance
- ❑ Employee Assistance Program
- ❑ Accidental Death/ Dismemberment Insurance

(*continued on next page*)

- ❏ Cafeteria Location
- ❏ Directory of Local Restaurants
- ❏ Compensation/Bonus Policies
- ❏ Profit-sharing Benefits
- ❏ On-site or Near-site Day Care
- ❏ Holiday Schedule
- ❏ Long-term Disability

- ❏ Business Travel Accident Insurance
- ❏ On-site Health Services
- ❏ Workout Facilities
- ❏ New- hire Referral Bonus Program

COMPANY POLICIES AND PROCEDURES

- ❏ Work Hours/Work Schedules
- ❏ Telephone Procedures
- ❏ Telephone Directory
- ❏ Emergency Procedures
- ❏ Computer/Internet Use Policies
- ❏ Payroll Schedule
- ❏ Inclement Weather Policy
- ❏ Environmental Issues
- ❏ Purchasing Forms and Procedures
- ❏ Breaks and Meal Periods
- ❏ Weapons Policy
- ❏ Alcohol and Drug Abuse Policies
- ❏ Insider Trading Policies
- ❏ Family Leave Policies and Procedures
- ❏ Smoking Areas and Policies
- ❏ Sending Interoffice and U.S. Mail
- ❏ Visitor Policies
- ❏ Company Courier Services
- ❏ Worker's Compensation
- ❏ Conflict-of-interest Policy
- ❏ Ergonomics
- ❏ Performance Appraisal Policies
- ❏ Jury Duty
- ❏ Gum-chewing Policy
- ❏ Uniforms

- ❏ Travel Policies and Procedures
- ❏ Sick-Time Policies and Procedures
- ❏ Performance Appraisal Periods
- ❏ Corporate Credit Card Policies
- ❏ Ethics Policies
- ❏ Code of Conduct Policies
- ❏ Locations of Fire Extinguishers
- ❏ Bereavement Policy
- ❏ Overtime Policies
- ❏ Expense Report Procedures
- ❏ Reserving a Conference Room
- ❏ Break Room Locations/Policies
- ❏ Union Policies
- ❏ Attendance and Tardiness Policies
- ❏ Flextime Policies
- ❏ Serving Customers with Disabilities
- ❏ Risk Management Policies and Procedures
- ❏ Gross Misconduct
- ❏ Confidentiality Policies
- ❏ Solicitation Policies
- ❏ Policy on Radios and iPods in the Workplace
- ❏ Copier Locations and User Codes
- ❏ Office Furniture Requests and Keys

(continued on next page)

- ❏ Employee Suggestion Box/Policy
- ❏ Appropriate Grooming Guidelines
- ❏ Dress code
- ❏ Parking Policies
- ❏ Purchasing Policies/Procedures
- ❏ E-mail Policies
- ❏ Timesheet Procedures
- ❏ Sexual Harassment Policies
- ❏ Harassment Reporting Procedure
- ❏ Recycling
- ❏ Voicemail Procedures
- ❏ Company Property Policies
- ❏ Proprietary Information Policy
- ❏ Security Services and Contact Information
- ❏ Handling Customer Complaints
- ❏ Equal Opportunity Employment Policy
- ❏ Solicitation Policies
- ❏ Employee Complaint Resolution

COMPANY PROGRAMS AND SERVICES

- ❏ Safety Programs/Sanitation
- ❏ ATM Location
- ❏ IT Help Desk
- ❏ Charitable Initiatives
- ❏ Volunteer Opportunities
- ❏ Corporate Travel Services
- ❏ On-site College Courses
- ❏ Wellness Programs
- ❏ Internal Job Transfer Program
- ❏ Technical/Computer Training
- ❏ Sick Bay Area and First Aid Supplies
- ❏ Security Services and Policies
- ❏ Training Programs
- ❏ Employee Sports Teams
- ❏ Ergonomics Products/Services
- ❏ Company Toastmaster's Club
- ❏ Company Weight Watcher's GROUP
- ❏ Family Services and Events
- ❏ Career Planning Services
- ❏ Company Newsletter
- ❏ Prenatal Programs
- ❏ Company Store—Physical or Virtual

OTHER ACTIVITIES OR TOPICS

- ❏ Have employees sign I-9 forms and provide appropriate identification
- ❏ Take photos of employees for security badges
- ❏ Conduct tours of laboratories, assembly lines, and manufacturing areas
- ❏ Plan team-building and icebreaker exercises
- ❏ Demonstrate the company's intranet site
- ❏ Hold breakfast or lunch for new employees
- ❏ Prepare taped or live CEO presentation
- ❏ Explain mentor or buddy programs

(continued on next page)

- ❏ Provide a package of basic office supplies
- ❏ Obtain information for business cards
- ❏ Obtain a completed nameplate order form
- ❏ Have employees complete an emergency contact form
- ❏ Issue vehicle identification or parking stickers
- ❏ Have employees complete automatic paycheck deposit forms

Chapter 2

Onboarding in a Start-Up within a Global Group

Contributed By: Jean Pfeifer, Director, UBS Business University, as relayed in an interview with Doris Sims

About the Author: Jean (French equivalent of John) is a seasoned learning professional. He worked 10 years in UBS's core business (Wealth Management) before starting a 10-year career in Learning & Development, where he served as Director in the UBS Global Learning Strategy, as well as Project Manager at the UBS Wealth Management Campus Asia-Pacific in Singapore, the local CLO of UBS Japan in Tokyo, and currently the Talent Manager in the Business Area LAMMA (Latin America, Canada, Europe, Middle-East, and Africa).

Jean's Contact Information:

Jean.pfeifer@ubs.com
+4179 758 02 22
UBS Business University
Max-Hoegger-Strasse 81
CH-8048 Zurich, Switzerland
www.ubs.com

In 2004, Jean founded the Geneva Learning Managers Roundtable, an organization of approximately 25 learning managers to share hands-on best practices. He is also a member of the Advisory Board of the Global Council of Corporate Universities (Paris). Jean holds a BBA (Lausanne) followed by postgraduate studies in Business Economics (UC Berkeley), and received a second MA in Human Systems Engineering (University of Applied Sciences, Lausanne, Switzerland) and the Swiss Advanced Federal Diploma in Corporate Education.

ONBOARDING AROUND THE WORLD

UBS is a premier global financial services firm offering wealth management, investment banking, asset management, and business banking services to clients around the world. With more than 65,000 employees worldwide, UBS has developed several onboarding best practices designed to effectively integrate employees. The UBS onboarding program includes multiple components for the new joiner, the new joiner's buddy, and the joiner's manager.

These best practice onboarding components are illustrated in more detail in this article as examples. But the real story lies in the unique challenge that occurred as UBS (a Swiss company) as the organization expanded operations in Japan. This expansion offered a new opportunity to work with the Japanese UBS employees to plan and implement a program that would incorporate UBS time-tested best practice onboarding components while also aligning with the Japanese culture and meeting the business need to teach new technology as new employees are hired in the Japanese branch.

UBS EXPANDS INTO JAPAN

When the Wealth Management division of UBS opened a new branch with new technology in Japan, the branch was hiring up to approximately 10 new employees every month, starting from zero employees in 2005, with no formal onboarding or training program in place to integrate and prepare the new employees for success. The new joiners required too long to become fully productive, they were not obtaining enough information about UBS internal values, tools, and structure, and the new employee integration process was fragmented and stretched over multiple weeks.

The new branch needed a new joiner onboarding program immediately. To achieve this goal, multiple challenges and opportunities were addressed:

- The intercultural challenges of the project were very high—not only did the content of the current UBS onboarding materials need to be translated into Japanese, but the content and approach also needed to be aligned with Japanese culture and the new technology in the Japanese branch, which was very different from the wealth management environment in Swiss banking (and even that in the rest of Asia).

- UBS Japan was a small but fast-growing start-up organization within a mature, large global financial services group.

- In Japan, in contrast to other geographic markets, UBS was relatively unknown, with minimal branding, making it more difficult to attract top talent.

- The program had to be created and implemented quickly in order to meet the business need of the rapid growth of the Japan branch and the need for the new branch to quickly demonstrate strong business results.

THE STRATEGY AND APPROACH

In 2007, Jean Pfeifer relocated from Switzerland to Japan for one year to serve as a local chief learning officer, with his first priority the implementation of a new employee onboarding program that would create a common culture across the organization and of training courses to teach the new technology and processes. This was a unique approach—many companies would have hired a local human resources professional to simply "plug in" the corporate UBS onboarding program.

But UBS felt that it was important for Jean to move to Japan to work in person with the Japanese UBS employees, in order to build the trust, relationships, and credibility that are needed for this type of change management initiative.

Jean started his new position in Japan by listening. He listened to the company leaders to learn about their successes and challenges, and he met with employees in various positions in the Japanese branch. Jean spent more than a month building relationships with the leaders and employees of the branch, listening, observing, asking for advice, and gathering information. He felt it was important to show that he genuinely wanted to help the branch to be successful and that he wanted to work in a cooperative and collaborative manner with the leaders and employees of the Japanese branch.

Jean's next step was to develop and execute a pilot onboarding program. Although existing onboarding materials from the UBS Swiss corporate office were used (and translated) where appropriate, most of the materials for the Japan branch were created "from scratch" in order to meet the specific business and cultural needs of the branch. After delivering the pilot program, Jean observed the results and made changes to enhance the final onboarding program.

With all of the time needed for Jean to relocate, to listen and build relationships, to run a pilot and make enhancements, one might form an impression that this approach takes too long to achieve results—why not just implement the corporate office program and fly back to Switzerland? But within three months of Jean's arrival in Japan, a new seven-day onboarding program was finalized and implemented, with very successful results.

The new program provided a standardized integration process with the following components:

- Two "off-the-job" booster programs: A one-day Welcome Program, a five-day induction training program, and a one-day follow-up
- A one-hour meeting with the local CEO in the first session of the welcome day; the CEO also discussed the vision, mission, and strategy for the company
- Regular coaching sessions by Line Managers
- On-the-job support from an assigned buddy for the new employee

- Standardized tools—a Starter Kit, Guides, Task List, and a New Joiner Navigator tool
- A "Swiss Evening" session, held on the first day of the Orientation Program, which provided an understanding of Swiss culture for the local Japanese employees; this indirectly acted as an intercultural course in a fun and friendly atmosphere and created bonds between locals and expatriates. All executives and speakers from the induction program were invited to join this "party."

THE RESULTS

When the new onboarding program was implemented at UBS Japan, the results were so positive that additional sessions were requested for "old employees" who did not have this program to attend when they were new employees, because the current employees felt that they did not know as much as the new employees! UBS has been named the "Best Private Bank in the World" for six consecutive years by *Euromoney*.

Additional results of the UBS Japan New Employee Onboarding include:

- New employees who completed the program gave it a high level-one evaluation (average ratings of 9.2 on a scale of 1 to 10).
- The program includes employees who are making an internal career move, in addition to employees who are joining the company for the first time.
- The program effectively integrated the best practice onboarding components of the corporate program while including the Japanese cultural values and the new business needs of the branch.
- All content and materials are delivered to new employees in the local language (Japanese) by internal Subject Matter Experts.
- Learning logs were provided to new employees to use in a dedicated session with the line managers to:
  - Increase the learning transfer to the job
  - Discuss, debate, and clarify the learning from the onboarding program with managers
  - Strengthen the manager's relationship with the new employee
- Content from new employee learning logs was also consolidated to provide a feedback loop for the business leaders to provide ideas and perceptions from these employees regarding multiple business topics for continuous improvement.

- A high level of consistency in the program delivery has been achieved, even though the program is delivered 100 percent of the time by local subject matter experts.
- The program quickly became a recruiting tool for UBS Japan; potential candidates interviewing with the company were very impressed by the way the company integrated a new joiner, which also served to dissipate the fears potential employees had about joining a foreign capitalized company.

Examples of the onboarding curriculum and tools used at UBS are shown on the following pages.

New Joiner Integration at UBS

We work together to facilitate the integration of New Joiners

Objective: Helping New Joiners to prepare and assimilate much quicker

Accelerating business performance delivery

Roles of Stakeholders

Line Manager

Discuss the integration program

Regular coaching meetings with New Joiner and Buddy

Review meeting with New Joiner and Buddy

Define Follow-up measures after 90 days

Human Resources

Support Line Manager to select Buddies

Sending Buddy's and Line Manager's guide to respective persons

Coach Line Managers and Buddies

Support Line Manager to capture role as PMM objective

Review meetings with New Joiner

Buddy

Help with settling in

Introductions to the team

Organize team lunch on the first day of the New Joiner

Day-to-day on-the-job training

Act as a role model

Education & Development

Providing comprehensive training modules during entire integration process (starting with Welcome Day and 4 days Induction Training)

Supports on-the-job learning through processes and methodologies

Learning Logs Coupled with Action Plans

Please use this learning log to write down interesting ideas that you collect during this training and that you can put into practice. These ideas will be shared with your colleagues at the end of the day and discussed with experienced Desk Heads. Your line manager will also be asked to discuss it with you after the training.

Session	Key Idea/Key Learning	How to put it into practice
Example: Client Experience (Speaker: Tani-san)	Clients want us to understand more. It will make a big difference with the competition and bring me more business	Before each client meeting, I will take time (at least 20 min) to analyze the client's profile and I prepare a list of questions that would be relevant to better know and serve my client.
Using Best Practices Prospecting pipeline (Speaker: M.Eckart)	Referrals are the best way to get new clients. Introduction to the next gener ation is an excellent source of prospects.	For the next Client event next month, I will tell my prospects and clients to bring their children and grand children.
Core-satellite approach Speaker: Mishina-san	The core-satellite approach is a win-win solution that brings stability, opportunity and flexibility to my clients	I will select 10 clients from my portfolio and, within the 20 next days, will call them for a meeting where I explain them the core-satellite approach.

Session	Key Idea/Key Learning	How to put it into practice
例： Client Experience（スピーカー：谷さん）	顧客は我々にもっと理解して欲しいと思っている。そのことが、競合との差別化に繋がり、更なるビジネスの獲得を生む	顧客とのミーティングの前に、必ず十分な時間をとって（最低20分）その顧客のプロファイルを分析し、より良いサービスの提供・ニーズの理解をするために適切な質問リストを準備する
Using Best Practices Prospecting pipeline（スピーカー：）	紹介は新しいクライアントと会うための ベストな手段である。	来月に行われるクライアントイベントでは私の顧客や彼らの子供や孫を連れて くるよう促す。
Core-satellite approach（スピーカー：みしなさん；もしくはミシナさん）	コアサテライトアプローチは両者に利益をもたらすもので、安定性・チャンス・フレキシビリティを与えるソリューションである。	自分のポートフォリオから10名のクライアントを選びこの20日間にミーティングをセットアップし、コアサテライトアプローチを説明する。

Off-the-Job Integration Programs

All New Joiners receive an introduction to UBS within the first week ...

Welcome Day

Time	Module	Owner	Speakers
9.00-10.00	Vision and Strategy & WM In Japan	WMI	Humair/ Tani-San
10.00-10.45	Corporate Value / Client Experience	WMI	Humair/ Tani-San
10.45-11.00	Break	all	
11.00-12.00	Branding	COO	Yamashita/ Aodai
12.00-13.00	Lunch	all	
13.30-14.30	Compliance / Legal	CFO	J. Akama/ E. Sawano
14.30-15.30	Due Diligence	CFO	J. Akama/ E. Sawano
15.30-16.00	Break	all	
16.00-16.30	HR (incl. Internal referral system)	HR	Niitsu-San Nakashima-San
16.30-17.00	E&D (WM induction / integration)	E&D	Pfeifer Ito-San

Welcome Day

Five-Day Induction Training

Day I: Business Areas of UBS

Time	Module	Owner	Speaker
9.00-10.30	Living our Strategy	WMI	DH / Business Mgmt
10.30-10.45	Break		
10.45-11.30	WMI introduction (WM global/region, legal entity set-up...)	WMI	DH / Business Mgmt
11.30-12.00	Key Clients Solutions	WMI	Abe-San
11.30-13.00	Lunch	all	
15.00-14.00	RCOO	COO	
14.00-14.45	CFO	CFO	
14.45-15.00	Break	all	
15.00-15.45	MS&D	MS&D	
15.45-16.30	Introduction IE / AM	?	Niitsu-San
16.30-17.15	Human Capital Mgmt (RDM/PMM)	HR	

Day II: Products Day

Time	Module	Owner	Speaker
9.00- 9.45	Outline P&S SJ	P&S SJ	Wakayama-a-San
9.45-10.00	Break	WMR	B.Rose
10.00-10.30	Investment Philosophy (tbd)	WMR	B. Rose
10.30-11.00	WM Research	WMR	B. Rose
11.00-11.30	Funds and portfolio planning	P&S SJ	Wakayama-a-San
11.30-12.00	TP-Structured Notes	P&S SJ	Watanabe-San
12.00-13.00	Lunch	all	
13.00-13.30	TP-Equity Solutions	P&S SJ	Yamanash-San
13.30-14.00	TP-Other TP Products	P&S SJ	Mori-San
14.00-14.30	Lending Products	P&S Bank	Miyawaki-San
14.30-15.00	FX&Structured Deposits	P&S Bank	Miyawaki-San
15.00-15.15	Break		
15.15-15.45	Credit Risk Framework	CFO	Shingu
15.45-16.30	Round up, Target Achievements, Closing	E&D	J. Pfeifer Y. Ito

Day III: Applications and Tools

Time	Module	Owner	Speaker
9.00-10.00	Account Open ng & CPAC creation (iCRM)	COO	Uno/ Watanabe
10.00-10.15	Break		
10.15-12.00	Transaction Processing (eTrader) CI Statement (e-Portfolio) Suitability framework & process		Tanai / Watanabe
12.00-13.00	Lunch		
13.00-14.30	SIB Transaction processing		Wantanabe/ Kino
14.30-14.45	Break		
14.45-16.45	iFOP ePortfolio iCRM e-trader / OMS		Obara
16.45-18.00	FX Option Trader*		

Day IV: Client Experience

Time	Module	Owner	Speaker
9.00-13.00	Client Experience Follow Up		
13.00-14.00	Break		all
14.00-15.00	UBS BP Prospect mgmt Client Mgmt		J.C. Humair / ?

Legend:
- All employees
- Focus on CAs, CAAs optional for other BAs
- CA, CAAs only

... and attend the Induction training within the first two months with UBS

Chapter 3

Onboarding Volunteers in the Nonprofit Sector

Contributed By: Gary Henderson, CEO, and Dana Smith, Director of Community Investments and Volunteerism, Communities in Schools of North Texas

To Contact Gary or Dana:

www.cisnt.org
ghenderson@cisnt.org
dsmith@cisnt.org
972-436-6377
P.O. Box 295543
Lewisville, Texas 75029-5543

About the Authors: Gary Henderson joined CISNT and the nonprofit sector after a 17-year business career as a Senior Manager at Price Waterhouse and a Senior Vice President at Bank of America. Gary led Bank of America's Private Bank Technology and Operations team. With a bias for growth, Gary has a passion for helping at-risk children and a deep desire to leverage the skills and experiences he has gained throughout his business career to impact the North Texas community.

Dana Smith received her Master's in Social Work from Baylor University. She helped start a nonprofit organization in Waco, Texas, before coming to CISNT in 2005. She has experience in counseling, program management, and grant writing. Her background enables her to be effective in the community sharing the needs of our programs across all age groups. Dana is responsible for building relationships within the communities we serve to increase the financial and human resources at CISNT through fundraising, special events, and volunteer management.

OUR KEY GOALS—RETENTION OF VOLUNTEERS AND CHILD SAFETY

The mission of Communities in Schools of North Texas (CISNT) is to provide and coordinate community based solutions that equip at-risk students to overcome barriers, succeed in school and prepare for life. In an effort to help at-risk students overcome barriers and achieve their goals, CISNT believes that every child deserves five basics:

- A one-on-one relationship with a caring adult
- A safe place to learn and grow
- A healthy start and a healthy future
- A marketable skill to use upon graduation
- A chance to give back to peers and community

Volunteers are a critical resource in our dropout prevention programs. In fact, in 2009 more than 1,000 volunteers donated over 11,500 hours helping CISNT's at-risk students. As a result, 91 percent of the at-risk students participating in our dropout prevention programs promote each year to the next grade level or graduate from high school.

CISNT views our volunteers as the "unpaid staff" of our organization. Their donated time leverages the effectiveness of our CISNT staff and programs and increases the impact we have in our community. As is true with recruiting any type of staff members, there is an actual cost and an opportunity cost associated with recruiting volunteers. So the more effective we are at retaining volunteers, the more effective our dropout prevention programs will be.

Our new volunteer "onboarding process" is the first and most critical experience a potential volunteer has with us. New volunteers have an expectation of rapid deployment. However, to protect the assets of the organization and, more important, to protect children, we must thoroughly screen, check, train, and match new volunteers with the children they mentor.

CISNT serves students who are at risk of dropping out of school and who come from economic and cultural backgrounds that are very different from those of most typical CISNT volunteers. CISNT volunteers are drawn to work with at-risk students for a variety of reasons, but regardless of the reason, their passion drives them to make a difference. Our job is to provide the most effective level of training in the most efficient amount of time to give them the highest probability of success.

High probability of success for CISNT mentors means high retention of new volunteers, more effective volunteer experiences, and higher academic outcomes for at-risk students in CISNT programs. There are several key components of the CISNT new volunteer training program that drives our results. In the program we provide:

- An overview of the dynamics of a child living in poverty (we use Dr. Ruby Payne's book *A Framework for Understanding Poverty*)

- A background for the new volunteer on the benefits of building assets in at-risk children (we use the Search Institute's *40 Developmental Assets* framework)

- A clear and concise volunteer job description with roles and responsibilities

GROWTH OF THE CISNT VOLUNTEER PROGRAM

In 2003, CISNT had around 100 volunteers in our dropout prevention programs. In an effort to leverage our limited staff resources and increase our services to at-risk students CISNT made a strategic decision to develop a robust volunteer management process. In 2008, over 1,000 CISNT volunteers donated more than 12,000 hours. This tremendous growth is the result of focused effort to recruit, train, and nurture members of our community who have a passion for helping at-risk students succeed in school.

Strategic recruitment of volunteers is as much a factor in successful volunteer management as is training. Much like recruiting outstanding staff, recruiting outstanding volunteers is an ongoing challenge to a nonprofit organization committed to growing a strong volunteer base. In 2009, CISNT volunteers served in a variety of roles, but CISNT volunteers are primarily mentors or tutors to at-risk students. Therefore, it is critical that we prepare and train our volunteers in a consistent and thorough manner before they begin to work with children; each volunteer is serving as a representative of CISNT and as a caring partner and a key to the success and growth of each child.

RECRUITING AND TRAINING NEW VOLUNTEERS

Successful orientation of volunteers at CISNT is foundational to our success. There are several steps in the process of recruiting, screening, onboarding, training, and ongoing communications with each volunteer, as outlined below:

Application. We attract a wide range of people to volunteer at CISNT. It is important that we offer multiple channels for them to express their interest in becoming a CISNT volunteer. Our primary avenue begin the new volunteer onboarding process is our online application on our website at www.cisnt.org.

Because CISNT programs are funded through a variety of private, corporate, and public funds, there are several attributes of our volunteer application that help us achieve grant reporting requirements. Senior adults are an outstanding volunteer pool for CISNT. It is important that we offer these high-potential future volunteers an avenue of application that meets their needs.

As a result, many senior adults choose to apply to become CISNT volunteers through our paper-based process. It is worth noting that the vast majority of CISNT volunteers utilize our online application process.

Our volunteer application form and process can be viewed on our Web site at www.cisnt.org.

Criminal Background Check. Protecting children served by CISNT is our highest priority at CISNT. As a result, we perform a criminal background check on EVERY volunteer applicant. In addition, each CISNT volunteer must agree to submit annually to a criminal background check. Processing the criminal background check is critically important, and this step must not be missed. CISNT's criminal background check form is located on our Web site for CISNT volunteers to download, print, and bring to the new-volunteer orientation.

New Volunteer Orientation. Every CISNT volunteer attends a New Volunteer Orientation before they are deployed and begin their CISNT volunteer experience. A successful volunteer orientation at CISNT is the result of several factors.

First, CISNT is committed to small group volunteer orientation. This allows for open and direct dialogue between the trainer and the new volunteer. Having a number of new volunteers attend training together creates a comfortable environment (more comfortable than a large group setting and more comfortable than one-on-one training). The basis of the training is the *CISNT Volunteer Orientation Handbook.* This handbook is the result of years of experience training volunteers, including feedback from volunteers and our campus staff who supervise CISNT volunteers daily. The Table of Contents (which provides the outline of our *Handbook* content) is included in this article.

We know that a new volunteer orientation session has been successful when the new volunteer has a clear understanding of the expectations of a CISNT volunteer (many of our expectations are described in the "Volunteer Code of Conduct" section of our *Handbook*) and a clear idea of where they want to spend time volunteering at CISNT. There are many places and ways that a new volunteer can make a difference at CISNT. The perfect match is one where we optimize CISNT's greatest needs for volunteerism and a volunteer's passion and interest. It is in the New Volunteer Orientation that we have the greatest opportunity to learn enough about each other to achieve this perfect match.

Board of Directors Orientation. Our Board of Directors is also a group of volunteers who require information and preparation to serve most effectively. A special Board Orientation program and materials are also provided to new board members, to discuss the CISNT mission and values, information about Board Committees, responsibilities of Board Members, and so on.

Campus Orientation. At CISNT, once a new volunteer has completed orientation, their next step is to attend Campus Orientation at the school where they will be serving as a CISNT volunteer. The Campus Orientation covers basic information like accessing the school, security procedures, and the layout of the school. In addition, much more critical information is exchanged between the new volunteer and the CISNT program manager at the school who will be supervising the volunteer—this critical information will be the basis for matching an at-risk student to the new volunteer and establishing the role and nature of the volunteer experience.

Information about interests, hobbies, life experiences, motivations for volunteering, and expectations are all valuable in training the new volunteer. The Campus Orientation training culminates when the CISNT program manager introduces the new volunteer to the at-risk student they will be working with each week. Not all volunteers work one-on-one with an at-risk student, but most do.

Some CISNT volunteers serve in other ways that support dropout prevention programs at CISNT like *Food 4 Kids, Dressed to Learn,* as well as a number of resource development and administrative volunteer roles. Regardless of the type of volunteer work they are planning to do, all new volunteers attend orientation and training to understand the mission, programs, and needs of CISNT.

Ongoing Training. Deploying a new volunteer at CISNT is only the beginning. A growing number of CISNT volunteers have been in their role for more than three years. Increasing volunteer retention and the average tenure of CISNT volunteers is a strategic imperative. Ongoing training is an important way to increase retention and grow volunteer tenure.

With each year of service, CISNT volunteers want to know more, do more, and increase their passion for working with at-risk students in CISNT dropout prevention programs. For some, this means deeper training about families in poverty. For others, this means practical activities and strategies for increasing the academic benefit in their volunteerism with at-risk students. Regardless of the motivation of the volunteer and the needs of the student, it is clear that we must continue to develop the knowledge and skills of our volunteers, much as a company develops its staff.

The multiple steps and components of the CISNT orientation and training process work together to ensure that each volunteer has received all of the information, resources, and materials necessary to work effectively with students, and with the CISNT paid staff, to achieve the CISNT mission.

TRAINING MATERIALS, FACILITIES, AND TRAINERS

Clearly, the *CISNT Volunteer Orientation Handbook* is a critical resource for successful new volunteer training. However, the trainer and the training room play a significant role in the success of a CISNT new volunteer orientation.

As a nonprofit organization, we have limited resources. However, we have an abundance of community partners who want to help CISNT succeed, and many CISNT new volunteer training sessions take place in bank buildings, CPA offices, university classrooms, or chamber of commerce meeting rooms—each room offered to us free of charge! It is a creative way to bring partners into the success of the program but even better, the environments offered are professional, quiet, and very conducive to a learning environment.

The trainers who provide the onboarding and training workshops for CISNT volunteers are a variety of staff members, volunteers, or CISNT board members. CISNT volunteer trainers are passionate about our programs, our volunteers, and the success of our at-risk students. CISNT volunteer trainers are school principals, social workers, counselors, and highly experienced current CISNT volunteers. The common bond is a competence for training and hands-on experience working with at-risk students. CISNT training sessions are scheduled at times and locations that are convenient to a wide variety of people—lunchtime training sessions, evening training sessions, and Saturday training sessions.

CONDUCTING THE CISNT VOLUNTEER ONBOARDING PROGRAM

New volunteer orientation sessions are offered on a weekly basis throughout the year on a variety of days of the week and times of day to reach a large number of scheduling needs.

Training sessions range from 60 minutes to 2 hours, depending on the time available and the needs of the volunteers.

CISNT views the volunteer management process as an "onboarding process." We monitor volunteer pipeline time carefully because we believe that the initial impression we create in the mind of a new CISNT volunteer deeply influences the probability for long tenure and retention. Entry into the pipeline begins with an application, and exit of the pipeline is the first volunteer hour of the new volunteer.

The metrics we track include:

- The number of volunteers currently serving CISNT, and the growth in our volunteer staff
- The number of volunteers at each stage of our pipeline process
- The number of hours of volunteer work provided for CISNT students
- The number of orientation sessions provided for volunteers
- Statistics pertaining to our Criminal Background Check results
- E-mentoring statistics of our volunteers (E-mentoring is one of the tools provided to CISNT volunteers to work with their students)
- E-newsletter statistics that provide information about the communication tools and information volunteers receive on an ongoing basis

A sample Volunteer Metrics page, as found in the CISNT CEO Report, is shown below:

CISNT CEO Report - December 2009
Customer Perspective - Volunteer Management

Volunteers & Volunteer Hours		FY 2007-08 Actuals	FY 2008-09 Actuals	FY 2008-09 Actuals - as of 12/31/08	FY 2009-10 Goals	FY 2009-10 Actuals as of 12/31/09	Scorecard Measurement/Comment
Volunteers:	Volunteer Mentors/Tutors	938	886	592	975	567	Target 10% growth in volunteers
	Non-Recurring Volunteers	250	54	46	250	91	Maintain target of Non-Recurring volunteers
Total Campus Volunteers		1,188	940	638	1,225	658	
	Administrative	33	83	37	83	65	Maintain target of Administrative Volunteers
	Interns (SW, DFEC & LPC)	8	15	7	15	6	Maintain level of Interns
	Directors & Advisory Council	49	52	47	50	116	Target full and diverse board of 30 and advisory council of 20 (or more)
Total Volunteers		1,278	1,090	729	1,373	845	
Volunteer Hours:							
	Volunteer Mentor/Tutor Hrs	11,585	8643.25	2801	10,238	4,769	Target growth in average annual hours per volunteer to 10.5 hrs
	Non-Recurring Vol Hrs	627	169	146	625	276	Maintain level of Non-Recurring volunteer hours
Total Campus Volunteer Hours		12,212	8812.25	2947	10,863	5,045	
	Administrative Hours	404	779	122	780	873	Maintain level of Administrative Volunteer hours
	Interns Hours	1,880	1791	1075	1,800	1,233	Maintain level of Intern volunteerism hours
	Board & Adv. Council Hours	450	535	85	720	138	Target growth in total volunteer hours for board and advisory council
Total Volunteer Hours		14,946	11,917	4,229	14,163	7,289	

Volunteers Pipeline Analysis	
Days from Application to	
First Student Meeting	
Pre-enrollment	n/a
0-30 Days	27
31-60 Days	39
61-90 Days	58
91+ Days	0

Volunteer Orientation Sessions	
Dec-09	11
2009-12 YTD	45
December 2008	2
2008-09 YTD	31

Criminal Background Checks	2008-09	YTD 2009-10
Total Number of Applicants	974	1,040
Applicants Failing Criminal Background Check	31	21
Registered Sex Offenders Caught in Process	5	1

e-Mentoring Activity	Nov 09	Dec 09
eStudents	296	296
eMentors	337	337
Messages Sent	8	9

In-Kind Donations	Dec-08	Dec-09
	$50,756	$ 91,406

CISNT Constant Contact (eNewsletter) Statistics						
Date	Purpose	# Sent	# Bounces	# Opt Out	# Open	# Clicks
12/15/09	Partners Press	3678	748	12	596	28
11/30/09	Partners Press	3621	1001	12	652	18
10/28/09	Partners Press	3531	722	6	642	33
9/25/09	Partners Press	3466	691	11	624	60
8/27/09	Partners Press	3349	701	17	593	75

STORIES ABOUT CISNT VOLUNTEER TRAINING

CHANGING STEPHEN'S LIFE

Stephen earned one-half credit his freshman year of high school. He was clearly on a track that would lead to his dropping out of school. Many would have written Stephen off, but the CISNT volunteer who was his mentor did not. Neither did the CISNT Program Manager at his high school. Stephen's mentor came to CISNT with a passion to give back to his community; he wanted to serve his city and make a difference in someone's life. That someone would be Stephen.

First, it was important that Stephen's mentor learn enough about the socioeconomic cultural differences between them. Otherwise, all of the passion would be wasted on efforts that simply would not be successful. Stephen's mentor also needed to understand what success for Stephen would look like and the possible path that would lead to Stephen's success. Finally, Stephen's mentor needed to understand the boundaries of this new relationship.

Being a mentor is complicated enough, but being a mentor to an at-risk student who has earned less than one credit his freshman year of high school is not for the faint of heart. So, how did it work out for Stephen and his mentor? Stephen graduated from high school, and his mentor was there to support him. He was a young man who, according to all the research and statistics, would have dropped out of school. In fact, that is what his mother told him to do his senior year.

Many people are responsible for the interventions, resources, and support that enabled Stephen to get back on track and graduate. But his volunteer mentor made the difference. The power of this trained, equipped volunteer changed Stephen's life forever.

CHILDREN IN BURMA

The population of refugees from Burma (Myanmar) increases every week in one of the communities served by CISNT. Children who were living in tents in the jungle just weeks before enter an elementary school with only the clothes on their backs. CISNT springs into action immediately, leveraging a wide range of resources made available by our donors and community partners—clothing, food, school supplies, and, most important, a volunteer who tutors and mentors the new refugee immigrant.

Training a volunteer to work with a recent immigrant is a richly rewarding experience. Volunteers who are assigned to work with CISNT Burmese refugees spend vital time helping to accelerate the acculturation of the children. The vast majority of their time together each week will be on vocabulary building. Not only are volunteers teaching the art of learning a new word, they are also helping children comprehend what that word means. This can be a real challenge when the word doesn't exist in the language and culture of the refugee—*refrigeration* is a great example of this type of word.

But even more important than the language acquisition tutoring is the mentoring relationship that will be built over time between the volunteer and the refugee student. Imagine the anxiety and emotions that result from fleeing a country, living in the jungle, and coming to a new world. This is the pinnacle in preparing a volunteer to work with a student from a difference socioeconomic background!

Communities In Schools of North Texas is a 501(c)3 nonprofit organization committed to dropout prevention through a mission of providing and coordinating community based solutions that equip at-risk students to overcome barriers, succeed in school and prepare for life. To learn more about CISNT, visit www.CISNT.org.

The CISNT Volunteer Handbook: Contents

The CISNT Volunteer Code of Conduct

1. Honor your commitment. Be dependable and on time for your weekly visits at the school. Your mentee looks forward to this mentoring time. Please contact the CISNT campus staff if you need to miss a week or need to change the meeting time.

2. Sign in and out at the school office (unless otherwise directed). Be sure to wear an identifying name badge.

3. Proceed to designated mentoring area. (i.e., cafeteria, library, classroom, CISNT office, etc.) All mentoring areas must take place in rooms with open doors on the school grounds in sight of school personnel or CISNT staff.

4. Students must remain on the school campus. Exceptions may include activities that are promoted through the school or CISNT.

5. Respect cultural, social, and religious differences. Respect students' diversity.

6. The law requires any person who believes that a child is being abused, neglected, or exploited to report the circumstances to Texas Department of Family and Protective Services (1-800-252-5400).

7. Mentors are discouraged from giving students gifts. Mentors may, however, give the student books, pencils, pens, magazines, posters, etc., as rewards and incentives for academic/behavior achievement or birthday recognition. Value should be kept under $10.

8. Mentors are role models. Please dress and speak "kid friendly."

9. Mentors may wish to become involved in school events with students. Participation is encouraged, but not required.

10. Mentors will refrain from any of the following activities with students/families served in the CISNT mentoring program:
    - Selling products or marketing of any kind
    - Distributing literature not provided to you by CISNT

11. Volunteers must appreciate the diversity of the students and be respectful of the U.S. Constitution's prohibition of establishing or sponsoring any religion in the schools. All volunteers'/mentors' efforts during the school day must be non-sectarian in nature.

12. In the event that a physical altercation breaks out in the presence of a CISNT volunteer, their first responsibility is to contact the school security or administration. It is the policy of this agency that its volunteers will not jeopardize their safety by attempting to stop the fight themselves.

13. Mentors will treat all information about a child or family as strictly confidential.

(*continued on next page*)

14. In regards to the issue of human sexuality, it is CISNT's intention to follow Texas law, laid out in Senate Bill 1: We will promote abstinence from sexual activity as the preferred choice of behavior in relationship to all sexual activity as it relates to our students.

15. Don't share personal information. Mentors should never share personal information nor take personal information from a mentee such as phone number or e-mail address. If you have an account on a site such as "MySpace" or "Facebook" please keep those accounts private.

16. Don't talk with your mentee about financial status.

I agree to abide by the CISNT Volunteer Code of Conduct to the best of my abilities. I agree that breaking the code of conduct is grounds for dismissal as a CISNT volunteer.

_____   _____
Print Name   Signature

_____
Date

Chapter 4

Onboarding Employees in a University Workplace

Contributed By: Stacy Doepner-Hove, Onboarding Program Director, University of Minnesota Office of Human Resources, with co-author Jennifer Rosand, University of Minnesota student in the Master of Education in Human Resource Development program

About the Author: Stacy Doepner-Hove began work on New Employee Orientation at the University of Minnesota when the position of Onboarding Director was created in 2007.

Stacy's Contact Information:

doepn002@umn.edu
UMN Office of Human
Resources
B20 Donhowe
318 15th Avenue SE
Minneapolis, MN 55455
612-624-5866

Since then her team has taken the program from a three-hour benefits explanation to a year-long series of training and social modules that span the breadth of the University.

Stacy and her team continue to grow and improve the program and are excited to expand its reach to provide some new programming for current employees as well. Stacy has a bachelor's degree, a law degree, and a master's degree in human resources and industrial relations all from the University of Minnesota.

ONBOARDING AT THE UNIVERSITY OF MINNESOTA

The University of Minnesota takes pride in hiring a talented, innovative, and productive workforce. Training and retaining this workforce—especially during times of economic hardship—is a critical component of helping the University achieve its mission of teaching, research, and outreach.

As an employer, the University of Minnesota aims to provide a supportive and welcoming environment to its new employees. Designed for the employee who is unfamiliar with the culture of the University, the New Employee Orientation (NEO) program consists of a series of courses that cover different facets of an employee's understanding of the University, how business is done here, relevant policies and procedures, but also fun and exciting elements that make the University feel like home to so many students and employees.

The training sessions and modules for new employees are held throughout each individual's first year on the job in a phased approach, keeping each individual's overall employee development in mind. Each training activity covers a new topic, opening up a new opportunity for learning and development for the employee.

There are three main sessions that take place in the first, sixth, and twelfth months of the employee's tenure. Additional training modules and social events are also scattered throughout the year for new employees during this first year of employment.

Different components of the year-long program include a focus on and history of the University, diversity training, professional and personal development opportunities, job-specific trainings, communications trainings, networking and social interaction opportunities, and more.

The New Employee Onboarding program at the University of Minnesota is run with one full-time employee, three employees who have new employee orientation as part of their job description, and student interns in human resources development.

The following outline provides an overview of the University of Minnesota's New Employee Curriculum:

Session 1—Overview of the U

THE U: WHO WE ARE, WHERE WE'RE GOING

Conducted: Within first month of employment at the University

Length of time: 3 hours

Description:

This session provides a quick introduction to the University, giving an overview of the mission and strategic vision of the University as a whole. It also provides a warm-up to the culture found here and equips new employees with basic University knowledge, which is not typically learned on the job or at the departmental level.

During this session, participants hear from senior leadership, learn about the University's "Driven to Discover" branding campaign, hear about the five different campuses, and develop an understanding of the University's Code of Conduct. They learn about the different classifications of employees at the University and meet with their employee group representative. This training session also provides broad access to different programs on campus, in a casual information table atmosphere.

The session consists of the following topics:

- Overview of the U
- History of the University of Minnesota
- Strategic positioning of the U
- Five University campuses and many outreach centers
- Driven to Discover campaign, including the TV ads
- Learning about the four employee groups (union, civil service, professional academic and administrative, faculty)
- Overview of senior leadership
- Guest speaker who is one of the senior leaders of the University
- Maroon & Gold Trivia (with University of Minnesota branded prizes)
  - Some serious topics, some not (e.g., What are the University's "Firsts"? How many bike racks are there?)
- Code of Conduct and compliance
- Video and policy discussion
- Meeting with employee group representatives
- Information Fair
  - 25 tables of different organizations throughout the University (e.g., Benefits, Student Union)
- Photo opportunity with Goldy Gopher (University of Minnesota Mascot)

Session 2—Diversity Training

INCLUSION, DIVERSITY, EQUITY, & ACCESS (IDEA)

Conducted: After six (6) months of employment at the University
Length of time: 2.5 hours

Description:

This session is the second in a three-part series. The focus of this session is on diversity, equality in the workplace, access to everyone, and inclusiveness. Conducted primarily by the Office of Equity & Diversity, this session discusses the University's commitment to diversity and provides resources available to employees.

This session is participatory. Employees get an opportunity for self-reflection on their experiences in diverse settings and a chance to share those experiences. Simulated work-based scenarios are conducted, offering the employees a chance for discussion on different issues of equity in a safe and controlled setting.

In session two, employees are also guided through a facilitated discussion on topics of diversity and inclusion. In the end, employees take a self-quiz, which is not reported back to their supervisor, but allows for each employee to see how inclusive they are being in their daily work activities.

The session consists of the following topics:

- Introduction on "Diversity Drives Discovery"
- Presentation by representatives from the Office of Equity and Diversity
- Discussion topics:
  - University's commitment to diversity
  - Resources available
  - Participation questions (e.g., When was the first time you traveled outside the U.S.? When was the first time you met someone of a different ethnicity?)
- Six (6) workplace scenarios dealing with different topics of equity and diversity. Topics include:
  - Hierarchy, religion, transgender, hiring, disability, speech patterns
  - Presentation on becoming an "ally"
    - o Inclusive language use
    - o Issues and topics
  - Self-quiz (non-reported). Topics include:
    - o How inclusive is your work? Is it accessible to all? Do you have presentations available in alternative formats? How in tune are you with diversity topics and issues?

Session 3—Personal & Professional Development

DEVELOPING YOUR WHOLE SELF

Conducted: One (1) year after beginning employment at the University
Length of time: 2.5 hours

Description:

This is the final session in the series of three (3) sessions and is conducted at the end of the first year an employee has been with the University. With a reception style and flair, this final session focuses on the employee's professional and personal development, as well as providing recognition for the employees who have completed the full training series during their first year of employment at the University.

Topics covered in this session include professional development, technology, public engagement, and employee wellness.

The session consists of the following topics:

- Presentation videos of real employees and how they have used the University's programs to develop themselves both personally and professionally.
- Professional development
  - Opportunities available for employees
- Technology
  - Where to get additional training
  - Technology resources to help in doing work at the U
- Public engagement
  - What the University does
  - How employees can get involved, both on-campus and off-campus
- Employee Wellness
  - What is this
  - What programs are available to employees

Module 1—Job-Specific Training

JOB-SPECIFIC TRAINING

Conducted: Ideally, every four months or three times per year. Currently, these modules are held whenever there is a "critical mass" in each job field to do a training session.

Length of time: Varies by training session and position. Two (2) days of training is required for the supervisory session, which includes those who are new to supervising at the University or are new supervisors altogether.

Sessions:

- Human Resources
- Communications
- Research
- Teaching
- Information Technology
- Student Services
- Supervision

Description:

The focus of these training modules is job specific. The New Employee Orientation employees create curriculum in partnership with offices from around the University who are specialists in the field. For example, the New Employee Orientation employees work with the University Relations office (the people who handle both internal and external communications and marketing for the University) to develop curriculum and carry out the training for any new employee who does communication work on campus.

Module 2—General Topics Training

THE LIBRARIES AND U

Conducted: Every month
Length of time: One hour

Description:

This training module is a general module that is offered to new employees but can be taken by anyone at the University. It occurs every month and rotates around to the different libraries housed throughout the Twin Cities campus.

The purpose of this module is to foster a working knowledge of the extensive library system, including its resources and search engines, so that employees gain an understanding of resources available to them for their job positions or their own personal edification.

COMMUNICATING AT THE U

Conducted: Twice a year
Length of time: Three two-hour sessions

Description:

This module series focuses on communication at the University, including the hidden dynamics between communications of different types of employees and different stakeholders.

The modules will include the following:

PART I: COMMUNICATING THROUGH DIFFERENCES

The ability to effectively communicate across differences and conflict is critical to working in a large and complex organization like the University. In this submodule, participants gain a deeper understanding of the nature and value of conflict, increase their awareness and knowledge of how we manage and resolve differences, and learn strategies and skills for effective communication in conflict situations.

PART II: COMMUNICATING WITH STAKEHOLDERS

This submodule covers the basics of stakeholder service training for all employees. It addresses the vast array of stakeholders that a new employee may come into contact with on a daily basis. Higher education settings not only have customers, colleagues, and vendors, they have students, alumni, and parents to communicate with as well. This session provides tools to identify and work effectively with key stakeholders for any new employee.

(*continued on next page*)

PART III: COMMUNICATION AT THE U

The University has a unique culture that can pose exceptional communication challenges. This submodule helps new employees to explore the organizational culture of the University and of its many and varied units. The session provides tools to new employees to enable them to work effectively across departments, across unit, and across the hall. It also addresses acronyms and the many other nuances of University culture that new employees must learn to successfully adapt to the University environment.

Module 3 — Social Topics

BROWN BAG FUN LUNCHES

Conducted: Monthly
Length of time: Over lunch hours

Description:

Purely fun lunches, this module is designed to be all about socializing over the lunch hour. Along with the "Brown Bag" theme, this module includes various topics of guided discussion that focus on different elements of the University. Past topics have included an astronomy lecture by a faculty member, a visit to the University's Raptor Center, a tour of the dairy lab, a lecture on being a "locavore" (eating locally), and a talk about and tour of the library archive caverns.

CULTURE CRAWLS

Conducted: Monthly during the school year
Length of time: Varies by event

Description:

This module is designed to introduce the University's cultural side to our newer employees. Each module includes two different cultural events, usually with an arts theme. Examples might include a tour of the Weisman Art Museum followed by a play performed by the theater department. New employees can bring a guest to promote networking among the new employees as well as establishing a connection to the University for the new employee's guest.

GOPHER GO

Conducted: Monthly during the school year
Length of time: Varies by event

Description:

Designed in tandem with the Athletics Department, this module is designed to offer newer employees an opportunity to meet with the Gophers Athletics coaching staff and also get an opportunity to see different sporting venues, which is a tremendous asset in a Big Ten university. Employees are given discounted rates or free tickets to different sporting events and sit together at those events. They are encouraged to bring family and friends as well.

TIPS FOR SUCCESS

Communications for the entire program are delivered monthly to new employees and quarterly to the supervisors of the new employees. This way the new employee knows what is coming up and the supervisor can help to decide what would be the most important things for a new employee to attend. The program is required, but that requirement is adapted to the specific needs of a new employee.

The University of Minnesota also provides a separate Web site specifically for new employees that lists all upcoming modules and sessions, provides links to on-campus professional organizations, and houses a social networking opportunity so the new employees can communicate with each other if desired.

The New Employee Orientation (NEO) staff also works with each department at the University to coordinate with the overall orientation program. Each unit will often host its own one-session new employee orientation, in addition to sending the new employee through the main orientation program. The NEO staff has provided "best practices" information and ideas to departments to help them build their own programs and avoid repetition in content. NEO staff also provide direct training to supervisors on their important role in the life of a new employee and on ways the supervisor can make the transition to the new job as easy and efficient as possible.

The University of Minnesota understands the necessity of a strong start for all of its new employees. As the University pursues its goal of being one of the top three public research universities in the world, the vital importance of a well-trained and dedicated group of employees is clear. The New Employee Orientation program strives to be that first link in a new employee's understanding of how the University environment works.

Chapter 5

Orientation and Onboarding in a Small Business

Contributed By: Kellie Auld, CHRP, Founder of Now You're Talking Business Consulting

Kellie's Contact Information:

kpauld@telus.net
hrscoops.wordpress.com
250-318-1068 (cell)
604-447-1701 (res)

About the Author: Kellie has been in human resources for 10 years and has 15 years of training and facilitation experience in an assortment of industries, including the federal government, a crown corporation, manufacturing, pulp and paper, and the financial and banking industries.

Kellie's consulting practice provides recruitment and selection services, development and instruction of courses to assist job seekers in résumé and cover letter writing techniques, interviewing skills for job seekers and recruiters, and career coaching. She has also developed and instructed leadership and management coaching, conflict resolution, employee relations, onboarding processes, policy and procedure development, and particularly management coaching and managing change. Kellie has also developed and delivered New Employee Onboarding programs for several clients. Check out Kellie's blog at: hrscoops.wordpress.com.

IN A SMALL BUSINESS, EACH EMPLOYEE MUST BE A STAR!

As a small business owner you may question whether you can take the time or wonder if you have the resources to provide an effective process—*don't make that mistake!* Research has repeatedly proved that the first impression your employee has of your company will determine the degree of engagement. Ultimately, engaged and happy employees are what will make your business successful, and the costs of employee turnover and the costs of disengaged employees working with your customers are higher than any of the costs associated with a solid orientation program in a new business. These are the people who work with your clients and represent your integrity, products, and services every day.

In small businesses, it is likely going to be the owner who will create the steps for implementing and creating an orientation to the business. Of course, there is always the option of hiring an HR professional to provide this service; however, you will need to be very clear in your own mind as to how to manage the process realistically once it has been developed.

The following information represents a brief description of the differences between the orientation process and onboarding—with some tips on successfully managing each. First, it is important to recognize the difference between orientation and onboarding; both are crucial processes in facilitating the success of a new employee's working relationship and fulfillment of job expectations.

> **Definition of "orientation":** *"an introduction, as to guide one in adjusting to new surroundings, employment, activity, or the like: New employees receive two days of orientation."* . . . *"An adjustment or adaptation to a new environment, situation, custom, or set of ideas."* (Dictionary.com)

This is your opportunity to create a positive experience, instilling pride in the new staff member who is joining your company. An effective orientation should begin on the employee's first day on the job and last approximately to the end of the first week. Its purpose is to introduce the employee to your work environment *and* your work culture.

Remember, as a small business owner, it will be entirely up to you to determine what is needed to introduce the new employee effectively and in such a way that he or she is able to understand your vision and expectations. You may also want to hire an external consultant to handle your orientation and training processes so you can focus on your business and your customers.

ORIENTATION PROCESSES IN A SMALL BUSINESS

While small businesses may not have the multitude of policies that larger organizations do, at a minimum, all organizations should communicate policies concerning hours of work and overtime, code of conduct policies, leave administration, workplace safety protocols, and expectations relating to performance.

Depending on the size of your business, your company is subject to many of the same employment laws and legal requirements that a large business is required to follow, so it is important to have some documentation and a standard process to ensure that all legal and safety requirements and employment practices are followed consistently with each employee.

An easy way to manage new employee orientation in a small business is by using a checklist to ensure that each employee receives the identical information and that all items are covered consistently. The responsibility for completing the checklist items can be placed on the new employee, with accountability to ensure completion resting with the business owner or the manager of the new employee.

It is also a good idea to require each employee to document and date the completion of their new employee actions and to turn in a signed copy of the completed checklist to keep on file. This action increases accountability for both the new employee and the manager and provides a record of the training actions that were completed for each employee.

As a small business owner, you will probably be using a hands-on approach to your orientation and onboarding processes as opposed to an electronic system to manage and track these procedures. If much of your process is computerized, be sure that there is ample opportunity for personal discussion along the way.

A computerized checklist system can automate the process of orienting new employees and enable the employee to move through a "self-serve" training program to complete specific orientation and training tasks. Many small businesses also use computer "kiosks" for new employees to complete online training modules on a self-serve basis to obtain knowledge about the company's procedures, products, services, and policies.

Much of the way you handle the orientation speaks to the culture of your business, and if you are in a service or sales industry of some sort, you certainly want the culture to be one that illustrates your mission and values. As the company representative, you do not want to be one who "talks the talk" but "doesn't walk the talk."

There are distinct differences in the way a larger organization would probably manage or implement the orientation/onboarding process. The following table illustrates who would have responsibility for each phase of the process as well as demonstrating the differences between a larger and smaller company in the onboarding process:

Process or Procedure	Larger Organization	Smaller Organization
Hiring documentation	HR Officer (Administrator) [†]	Manager/Supervisor/ Owner
Letter of offer/Welcome	HR Officer (Administrator) [†]	Manager/Supervisor/ Owner
Copy of handbook/Policies	HR Administrator [†]	Manager/Supervisor/ Owner
Job description	HR Administrator [†] Manager [*]	Manager/Supervisor/ Owner
Assignment to trainer/coach	Manager [*]	Manager/Supervisor/ Owner
Provide tour & work schedule	Manager [*] Coach	Coach [‡]
Provide introductions	Coach	Coach [‡]
First day breaks together	Coach	Coach [‡]
Explain training program	Coach	Coach [‡]
Explain workplace culture	Coach	Coach [‡]
Review checklists	Coach	Coach [‡]
Questions from the day	Coach	Coach [‡]
Job shadowing	Coach	Coach [‡]

[*] "Manager" is interchangeable with Supervisor in some companies.

[†] HR administrator may manage distribution of paperwork, but the content responsibility is with the HR officer.

[‡] "Coach" is a term used interchangeably with "trainer." It should be noted that in a small company, this may well be the owner if there is no one to whom to delegate the task.

A small business will typically use a checklist to ensure that all steps of the orientation process are covered. The sample below is provided as an example of this type of checklist:

Sample Checklist

FIRST DAY:

- ❑ Make sure the manager or a designated employee is there to greet the employee.
- ❑ Introduce the new employee to the mentor or trainer (if this person is another employee that she will work with once the orientation is complete).
- ❑ Introduce the employee to any other staff members who are on site that day.
- ❑ Provide the employee with a small tour of the workplace—be sure to include such areas as the photocopier location, the mail room, mailboxes, and lunch area (if applicable), and mention what employees typically do for lunch.
- ❑ Make sure that the employee knows where to hang up her coat; where to put her personal property; and where her work area is (if relevant).
- ❑ Provide the employee with a copy of her job description or duties list.
- ❑ Review the schedule for the training week.
- ❑ Provide any legal documentation and policies that must be completed (income tax forms, offer of employment letter, policies for sign off).
- ❑ Review computer sign-on, password set-up, etc.
- ❑ Review telephone procedure and expectation of how to answer—include call transfer, hold, long distance dial-out, etc.

Other items, such as a discussion of work hours, could most definitely be added to the checklist (Are hours posted ahead of time? Do shifts rotate? Are there split shifts?).

Your checklist will depend on the amount of information you wish to cover, but—*a word of caution*—do not inundate the employee with too much information on the first day. Furthermore, be sure to allow time for questions about policies or paperwork that is being signed off by the employee.

Before the employee leaves for the day, do a check in. Give him an opportunity to tell you what he liked about the day and ask if there is anything else he feels he needs. Provide him with a brief overview of what you will expect on the second day and reaffirm that he will probably be performing some of the job tasks with you or a coach over the course of the next few days.

Reiterate and confirm what your expectations are in terms of his being able to start on his own—a sense of autonomy can add a level of excitement to his future with your company.

Each day can include a simple checklist. In fact, I would recommend one so that not only is there consistency, as previously mentioned, but you will have the added advantage of the paperwork/checklist in the employee's file to support what information was actually received. *Note: I used to have employees initial the checklists and provided copies for their records as well. While you want the absolute best opportunities for success, you must also be mindful that if things do not work out, you can demonstrate the steps you took to provide the best chance of success.*

An example of a checklist for additional days of the onboarding process might be as follows:

Sample Checklist

THE FIRST WEEK:

- ❑ Partner up the coach and the new employee and review the previous day's discussion and respond to any questions that remain.
- ❑ Make sure some work assignments are ready for the new employee so that he can feel productive and the coach can see how he handles the tasks assigned.
- ❑ Review the job duties and explain the work as it's being done—this is important as it's the perfect opportunity to help the new employee align with the " 'way you do and want your business to work.' "
- ❑ Consider having lunch together at least one day as an opportunity to discuss things other than work (this indicates an interest in employee as a person and helps to build relationships).
- ❑ Share unwritten rules, traditions, and practices with the employee (such as casual Fridays).
- ❑ Review what the business connections are (for instance, who your clients are, what community involvement the company has).
- ❑ Review expectations concerning attendance, communication, and routines to be followed.
- ❑ Assist the employee in building his own " 'how to' " manual (this can be something as simple as note taking during training sessions).

Again, this type of list will be very dependent upon the business itself, but make it something that reinforces how you want the employee to function in your company. The goal is to provide clear expectations of the employee's role, to make her feel welcome, to make her feel a part of the team, and to be able to contribute confidently as soon as possible.

One of the main complaints that new employees have is that they haven't been given a clear picture of what they are expected to do! Not too many of us are mind readers ... so, be clear right from the get-go ...

The purpose of onboarding is to finalize the integration of the employee into the workplace. This is a longer-term process that typically lasts for the period of time the employee is on probation; however, that is a guideline rather than a hard and fast rule.

It is also more common in a larger organization; although, it doesn't mean that a small business can't also adopt some of the "'best practices'" that have proved successful in the workplace.

Onboarding ensures that the employee still feels there is support to help him succeed during his "learning curve." It is also an opportunity to measure how well he is integrating into the culture of the company and forging effective work relationships. The employee needs to become self-sufficient and know where to find the resources he needs to do his job.

Onboarding will help to solidify the fact that you have the "'right fit'" for your company: an employee who represents your values and vision.

THE ONBOARDING PROCESS IN A SMALL BUSINESS

Throughout the entire process of onboarding, you should be making sure that the employee truly is a fit. The true intention is to help him be successful; however, if the person doesn't fit in and if there is a lack of success in integrating the person, it is during this time that you may need to make a decision as to whether or not you wish to retain this staff member.

For the small business owner, this may feel like quite an onerous task; but in the long run, it will definitely improve the opportunity for success—for other employees as well as for the business venture itself.

Once again, checklists will certainly aid in making the integration successful and clearly articulating the company's goals and vision.

THREE TO FOUR WEEKS AFTER THE START DATE

Check in with the coach as to how things are going with the new employee. *Note: The owner could very well be the trainer, in which case there will already be awareness for some of these questions.*

The first "appraisal" meeting should include the business owner, the coach, and the employee. Again, this should typically occur at about the 3–4 week mark. The timelines are not set in stone, but according to "'best practices,'" it is typically at about this time that the employee can give you some honest feedback as to how he feels he is managing. This meeting should involve an exchange of information with feedback available from the employee as well as the coach. When you meet with the employee and the coach together for the first session, take some notes and ask questions.

Questions for the Employee

- Do you have any concerns or issues at this time?
- Do you feel as if there is any additional training you might need, and if so, in what areas?

Questions for the Manager

- What is your perception of her progress to date?
- Do a quick review of the job description with the employee. Has she had an opportunity to do or at least see the majority of the required duties (this will help to identify training needs she may have that she's not aware of)?

Provide clear, accurate, and timely feedback on how the employee is doing at this stage.

If the employee is managing well, this could be a very brief exchange, but don't let it slide. Remember, this is still a new employee and there will still be areas of his job that he is not familiar with.

You could even consider providing a quiz to the new employee about some of the duties if that provides a greater level of comfort around his acquired knowledge to this point.

It is also at about this stage that there may be benefit in asking the employee's coworkers how they feel he is managing. Always include the positive feedback. If there is any criticism, be mindful of how this is communicated and ensure that what you relay is for constructive purposes—the goal should always be to make the employee successful.

Note: If this is a one- or two-person operation, asking coworkers may not be relevant—but don't exclude your customer feedback if it is appropriate.

EIGHT WEEKS AFTER THE START DATE

As mentioned, onboarding is a longer process than orientation, but don't forget that it is connected to the orientation in that its purpose is to further integrate the employee into your way of doing things. It's easy to forget at this stage that the employee is still relatively new.

As above, review what concerns there are, if any, what his progress is to date, and any feedback you feel he needs to hear. Document this conversation as well. Please, don't forget the good feedback along with the concerns (if there are concerns).

It is important to note that if your new employee does have concerns or identifies learning opportunities, provide the assistance you can. This is where you can build trust in the relationship—extremely important in employee engagement!

THE END OF THE EMPLOYMENT PROBATION PERIOD

In a small business, the onboarding process typically ends at the 90-day period of employment, often referred to as the probationary period of employment. During this 90-day time period, it is very critical to continue to engage in open conversations with the employee, and to provide extensive feedback in order to help ensure that the employee starts off on the "right track" and integrates well into the company.

The end of the probation period is where most organizations make the determination as to whether or not the employee will stay with the company, and it is at this point that the company can state, with some level of confidence, that the employee has been given the best possible opportunity to succeed.

For a small business owner, it often feels like a lot of work to hire, orient, and train new employees, but remember that your employees are part of the investment in your company. Just as you carefully manage the finances in a small business, you will want to manage the performance and engagement of your employees to ensure success. Long-term, engaged, successful employees will ensure that you have a competitive edge in your business.

There is nothing more satisfying for a business owner than to know that you have the best people! The best way to make sure that's true is to coach and guide them throughout the first months of their employment.

Chapter 6

Onboarding Employees in a Start-Up Company

Contributed By: Don Barkman, President of The Business Center

About the Author: Don Barkman worked for three Fortune 500 firms for 15 years and operated his own training and consulting business for more than 20 years. He has helped numerous clients design start-up organizations and trained their workforces to operate in highly participative team systems.

Don's Contact Information:

The Business Center
www.bizcenter.com
120 Westview Lane
Oakridge, TN 37830
865-220-0774

Don is the author of *"START-UP!, A Guide to Getting Off on the Right Foot"* and *"Skill-Based Pay: Design and Implementation."* Both books have proved to be invaluable guides to start-up organizations. He is a certified Scanlon Plan consultant and has been a speaker at national conventions for the Ecology of Work, ASTD, and so on. Don holds a BA from the University of Notre Dame and an MBA from Ohio University.

HOW IS ONBOARDING UNIQUE IN A START-UP ORGANIZATION?

Starting a new operation like a store, a restaurant, or a plant means bringing together many new people and orienting them to their new jobs. Some of these people may be internal transfers while many are external hires. While the internal transfers are already familiar with the organization's existing culture and procedures, the new people don't have a clue. However, if the start-up unit will be significantly different from the culture of the existing organization, then the internal transfers may need as much orientation as the new hires.

Start-ups are unique opportunities to do things differently. Expectations for success and "good things" run high across the board. Orientation needs to maintain this positive "can do" attitude, while tempering it with the reality that not everything will go as planned or hoped for. Orientation is as much about control-ling psychological expectations as it is about acquainting people with how the organization works and what their responsibilities are. Traditional orientation techniques can be employed to convey information about the organization and each employee's responsibilities, but it is the issue of expectation management that makes start-ups unique.

The entire leadership team from the human resources staff through the first-line leaders must understand and present the same picture of how the organization will operate. This is especially true if employees are promised the opportunity to participate in decision making as is often the case in team systems.

One great pitfall of orientation is for the human resources' staff to present one version of participation to new hires only to have either a much more restrictive or more liberal description given by line managers when employees arrive at their work stations. Having line managers conduct orientation briefings about the "management system," while human resources staff members assist, helps to keep the message consistent. Periodic random visits with employees on the job by top managers and human resources staff can check to see if mixed signals are being sent after initial orientation.

What makes a start-up organization so susceptible to expectation issues? It has to do with how well things go according to plan. We all know that "Murphy's Law" pessi-mistically predicts "Things will go wrong at the worst possible moment." Start-ups tend to believe in the optimistic opposite, Yphrum's Law: "Everything that can go right will go right at exactly the right time." According to this outlook:

- There is a plan for everything and there are no surprises.
- All the money needed is available to build everything the best way.
- Only the newest and best tools and equipment are purchased.
- Everyone who applies for work is fully qualified and eager to work.
- All the equipment that is ordered arrives on time and works perfectly the first time.
- No one misunderstands anything anyone says.
- The wages, benefits, and working conditions are the best in the country.
- All jobs are always interesting and never hard or boring.
- All the training is interesting and useful and everyone remembers all of it.
- No one displays irritating behaviors after they are hired.
- Customers and other company groups never change their minds.
- The economy chugs along positively—just as forecasted.

If you are lucky enough to have this type of start-up where everything is planned and all the plans come true, count your blessings. If, on the other hand, you suspect there's a possibility the unexpected will happen, that communications will get messed up, or that reality may fall a bit short of the ideal, then you appreciate why careful orientation is essential for start-ups.

New hires usually recognize that "You never get a second chance to make a first impression!" Companies are in the same position. The impression created by the firm during orientation and throughout start-up lasts a long, long time.

Most new hires will give a new employer the benefit of the doubt at the beginning. In fact, they may be overly optimistic and expect they are being hired into the best of all organizations. Expectations that cannot be met need to be adjusted during the hiring process. Orientation actually begins prior to a job offer.

There are several ways to incorporate aspects of orientation into the hiring process:

- Describe the expected organization culture during the interview process. This is particularly important if the culture is very different from what employees were accustomed to in their previous jobs.
- Give applicants an opportunity to visit the job site and perhaps perform a sample of the job duties they will perform (sometimes called a "realistic job preview").
- Show a video of the working conditions and job duties from a similar operation.
- Show a video of interviews with company employees working in a similar culture and operation describing what it is like from an employee's viewpoint.
- Provide written materials for prospective hires to read, and question them about the material in later interviews.
- Provide a time for potential hires to ask questions about the culture and job duties.

MANAGING EXPECTATIONS IN A START-UP ENVIRONMENT

Because start-ups are often fast-paced, there are loose ends and incomplete plans that will be resolved as the start-up progresses. Leaders must be very cautious not to overextend their explanations and "promise" things that have not been decided. Pay scales, advancement ladders, and work schedules are especially sensitive items.

Here is a true story to illustrate this point of the importance of managing expectations of new employees in a start-up environment:

A human resources staff member was responsible for part of pre-employment orientation. He had the job of explaining to new hires what the new company intended to do with its participative management programs. He was an honest, well-intentioned person. He did his best to paint an accurate picture based on what he knew at the time.

During one orientation session, he compared his company's innovative pay system to that of another local firm using a similar system. He intended to illustrate the features of the system, not the pay rates (the other company's pay rates were much higher). What did people remember?

You guessed it—the pay rates, not the structure of the system. When the new company did not pay as much as the firm he used in the example, who got blamed for missed expectations about the pay program? He did, and by proxy, so did the new employer. The sender almost always takes the blame if the message doesn't get across.

Most new hires come from companies that have been in business for more than a few years. Some are just out of school—but that school has been around for a while.

Those are "stable systems." Stable systems have had the time to plan, try, change, and adjust how they operate. Eventually, most of the common problems have happened and people know what to do about them. Organizational life is more routine. Policies and procedures don't change very often. Events are predictable. Maybe employees there didn't like the way things were done, maybe they did, but at least they knew what to expect.

Start-ups are organizations that are in the process of being formed. Many systems and practices are only on the drawing board. They are concepts, ideas, plans. All the pieces may not be put together yet. Some of the pieces may be missing altogether. The company may be waiting for equipment to arrive and be installed. There may be a need to write policies on how to call in for illness, or to write training manuals on how to run and repair equipment. An Employee Handbook and Company intranet site may not be available or fully formed yet.

Because of the evolving nature of start-ups, orientation is a continuing process. Planning to check with employees all the way through the start-up and stabilization of the organization will help issues surface and enables you to manage them proactively. Orientation may begin with many explanations, but it progresses to a sensing and responding mode as things swing into action.

Start-up is tough because you are trying to do work when the systems for doing the work aren't ready yet. Even simple decisions can take a long time while the organiza-

tion figures out who should be involved, what should be considered, how the decision should be communicated. Nearly everything is a "first time" event.

After a while, a pattern develops and systems are created in the new organization.
In the meantime, there's the double workload of doing the work while systematiz-
ing the way it is to be done. *Getting new hires to understand this aspect of start-up is part
of onboarding. It is one of the major contributors to high levels of overtime prevalent in start-
ups and usually affects the professional and leadership staff.*

New employees join start-ups because they see the adventure and promise of a
better life. Many are young and often inexperienced in the demands of the
workaday world. Older workers may have a more tempered view. A few may be
downright cynical but join anyway. Start-ups attract people just as the pioneers of
early America were attracted to the West. Some sought opportunity, some had a
vision of a new future, others were leaving behind a bad situation.

All employees bring along baggage from their previous employers. They may
project that employer's practices and behaviors onto your new organization. If
they worked for good firms, they will expect good things. If they were mistreated,
they may expect you to do the same. The lenses through which they view your
actions will color their perceptions. What does each of your new employees bring
to your start-up? You will need to address those experiences and perceptions during hiring and orientation.

In start-ups, expectations for good treatment, good work, good opportunity,
good pay, and good security are all high. This is the "halo effect"—when a few
things look good, everything looks good. "Young love" also has this same wonderful feeling to it.

Reality, however, has a way of disappointing people. Organizations can't always
live up to everyone's great expectations. Onboarding must give employees a "realistic yardstick" instead of an "idealistic yardstick" for measuring success. It can
also help to address the fact that different people have different expectations.
Meeting one person's expectation may mean not meeting someone else's. For
example, not everyone can get promoted to the same job.

Here is an example to illustrate that different employees (or groups of employees)
have different needs and situations, causing a potential problem with expectations.

*The first group of employees hired into a company was sent to Japan for extensive
training. Traveling to a foreign country was both exciting and scary because some had
never flown before. This first group got the inside track for future leadership positions
because of their early selection and special training. Employees who came later had to
wait much longer for the opportunities that were available to the first group. On the*

other hand, the first group had to cope with much more uncertainty regarding who would be doing what.

Sometimes companies can't deliver on the expectations they knowingly or unknowingly created. When people are first hired to start up new organizations, some details aren't completely finalized. What gets presented to new employees is what the company and its managers *intend* to happen. Unfortunately, the best plans sometimes don't materialize. Sometimes they get delayed—what was supposed to happen in one year takes three.

Is that somebody's fault? Did people lie about the plans? No, not really, but it can be perceived that way. Things don't always happen the way we want them to. Patience and charity help to make some of these developments easier to handle. Nurturing these virtues during orientation can prove beneficial.

People who don't like change may not adapt well to start-ups. They may have picked the right company, but at the wrong time. Start-ups are full of changes (and changes, and more changes ...). Some of these changes people will like, some they may not. Some they may have influence over, some they may not.

Start-ups often include a lot of experimentation. Something is tried and checked. It may be modified. The new way may be abandoned and the original way re-adopted. Employers need to help employees think about how they will respond to changes. People who want simple, black and white answers, or a lot of rules, will find start-ups frustrating. Orientation can't cure this problem, but selective hiring may prevent it.

Professionals who study start-ups describe an unavoidable "let down" sometime after the start-up gets up and running. This post–start-up dip is like the postpartum depression some mothers experience after delivering a newborn. Routine replaces discovery. The small "family" atmosphere present when there are fewer people and everyone knows everyone drifts away as the organization grows. Don't be surprised if it happens to your new organization. Orienting new hires to the start-up environment is replaced by a follow-on orientation to regular operating mode.

There's an excitement in joining and working in a start-up organization. There's more challenge in a start-up than at almost any other time in an organization's life. Enjoy it while it lasts. Plan your orientation to help employees "go with the flow," and sailing through both the advantages and challenges associated with a start-up organization will be much easier for everyone, resulting in increased employee retention, productivity, and engagement.

Chapter 7

Onboarding Employees at Ford Motor

Contributed By: Kristopher Kumfert, Human Resources Business Partner, Ford Motor

About the Author: Kristopher has 13 years of experience with Ford Motor, with a background in Security, Health and Safety, and Lean Manufacturing.

Kristopher's Contact Information:

Ford Motor of Canada
Oakville Assembly Complex
905-845-2411, ext. 3626
kkumfert@ford.com

Kristopher has obtained a Six Sigma Black Belt. Kristopher earned his BS degree in Administrative Studies from York University. He is currently an HR Business Partner of Salaried Personnel and Organizational Development at Ford Motor.

ONBOARDING NEW EMPLOYEES IN AN ASSEMBLY OR MANUFACTURING WORKPLACE

Ford Motor Company of Canada's Oakville Assembly Complex is the world's only producer of the Ford Edge, Ford Flex, Lincoln MKX, and Lincoln MKT crossover utility vehicles. The site encompasses 410 acres of land, and the six buildings cover over 6 million square feet of state-of-the-art flexible vehicle manufacturing. The 55-year old site includes its own daycare center and emergency response (fire and medical) department.

With over 3,500 employees on site, the orientation of new employees is a critical element of the operation's success. The New Employee Orientation program was developed after a series of focus groups. In our focus groups,

- **Current Employees** discussed their experiences and conveyed what went well, and what they wished their orientation had included.
- **Senior Management Leadership** discussed the critical knowledge required for their own employees as well as internal suppliers and customers.
- **Senior Union Leadership** discussed the orientation elements that would support an ongoing productive relationship.

With the feedback received from the focus groups, the current orientation program was developed. Some of the critical elements included:

- **Staggered learning between the classroom and the manufacturing floor.** Focus group participants explained that many training courses were specific to the local manufacturing operation, and were best understood after seeing the operation for a short period.

  Consequently, certain programs such as lean manufacturing and quality processes are taught in a classroom setting only after the new employee has had a prescribed amount of time on the manufacturing floor. This staggered learning enables the new employee to understand the training course in better context. This has led to increased training effectiveness.

- **Total understanding of the site's operations.** A flexible manufacturing assembly line that spans a 410-acre site is dependent on several functional areas and operations working together, and this is dependent on understanding one another.

  As an example, Paint Operations is most successful when employees understand their internal supplier (Body Welding) and their internal customer (Trim Shop). Therefore, part of the new hire orientation includes a tour of the whole site's operations, and a short time (1/2 day) working in each area. This has proved to be very effective in helping employees to understand the total system and how actions in one department affect others.

A FOUR-WEEK ONBOARDING PROGRAM

Week 1:

- Onboarding paperwork
- Corporate policies regarding harassment and discrimination
- Computer resources training
- Mandatory pedestrian, chemical, and general safety training

Week 2:

- Total site tour
- One-half-day work experience in Body, Paint, Trim, Chassis, Pre-Delivery, Material Handling, Quality Control, and Finance

Week 3:

- In-class training (lean manufacturing, quality processes, scrap handling, proprietary information systems, safety auditing)

Week 4:

- On-the-job shadowing
- Focus group session with Human Resources to review orientation and readiness
- Skip Level meeting with Plant Manager to obtain high-level leadership vision

OUR RESULTS

After the 4-week session, employees are ready to begin their jobs. Our program provides the opportunity for the newly hired employees to understand the total operation and learn the new skills required to be successful. Ford Motor has experienced a 24 percent improvement in Training and Development scores as measured by our corporate Pulse dimension. The success of the program is due in large part to the fact that it was designed by employees and senior leadership.

Chapter 8

New Crew Members "On Board" at Red Lobster

Contributed By: Krista Rice, Manager of Crew Training and Development, and Janice Shanahan, Senior Trainer at Red Lobster

Krista and Janice's Contact Information:

Krista Rice
krice@darden.com
Janice Shanahan, MBA
jshanahan@darden.com

About the Authors: Krista Rice is manager of crew training and development at Red Lobster. She holds a BS in Hospitality Management from Florida State University. She has several years of experience in food and beverage operations with a focus on training. Krista began teaching hospitality management in a private technical college before she returned to school for graduate studies. She joined the Red Lobster People Development group just before earning a master's degree in Human Resource Management with an emphasis on training.

Janice Shanahan is senior trainer of crew training and development at Red Lobster. She holds a BA degree in Psychology and a master's degree in Business Administration. She has more than 25 years' experience in the field of training and development in diverse industries including banking, insurance, and hospitality. Her responsibilities at Red Lobster include designing new crew training, new crew orientation, and facilitating Managers-in-Training and New General Managers training programs.

DELIVERING A CONSISTENT ORIENTATION MESSAGE ACROSS MULTIPLE LOCATIONS

The new employee onboarding challenge for Red Lobster is to provide orientation to thousands of employees each month in over 650 locations! In the past five years, we have redesigned our new crew orientation and training programs (along with much of our management training) to better align and support each other and Our Core Values.

Red Lobster employs 60,000-plus employees in the USA and Canada, and hires approximately 4,100 new employees each month, averaging approximately six new employees per restaurant monthly.

Our need for new orientation was triggered by a need for consistent onboarding to our company culture and a "first stop" before position-specific training begins for each employee. We explored several options for delivery (from video to read-only materials), and we decided to use a manager-facilitated program. We wanted personal involvement from managers without losing consistency or creating distance, and we didn't want new crew members oriented by someone they would not be dealing with daily in their own restaurants.

The result of our research into the best orientation delivery mode for hundreds of different locations is a consistent message delivered in a program we call "New Crew Orientation," which is presented to every crew member by the highest-ranking manager on-site. The materials support the message while allowing each manager to customize his or her own presentation.

The method and content of the program were presented to and approved by our executive team, who then fully supported the program development and implementation. The program was piloted in several local restaurants (those near our Restaurant Support Center) to best determine the sequence of content material.

The orientation program was launched at our annual General Manager Conference. General Managers first attended sessions as participants viewing the New Crew Orientation program. The General Managers (who are responsible for facilitating the program at their restaurant(s)) worked through questions and practice to prepare to teach the program.

New Crew Orientation covers the Red Lobster Brand, Our Core Values, and the crew handbook. The format allows managers to set out their expectations clearly while letting new crew members know what to expect as members of the crew. New Crew Orientation usually lasts two hours, and is provided within one week of joining the restaurant crew.

MATERIALS PROVIDED TO THE GENERAL MANAGER FACILITATORS

To help each General Manager facilitate the New Crew Orientation program, we provide the following materials:

- A facilitator guide with talking points for the manager/facilitator, to guide the manager through the key points of the program

- A DVD that discusses our brand, culture, and information about our restaurants, to help the new crew member become better acquainted with Red Lobster

New Crew Orientation is reviewed annually by Red Lobster Crew Training and Development personnel. Any needed changes are made, and new materials are sent to each restaurant.

THE RED LOBSTER NEW CREW ORIENTATION CURRICULUM

The new crew orientation program is designed to allow on-site managers to conduct the program based on the restaurant's schedule. Therefore, the program components include the recommended steps for managers to follow, and a guide with talking points for the manager to use as a delivery outline.

The primary components of the New Crew Orientation Program include:

1. The New Crew Orientation Manager's Guide

2. The Red Lobster Brand

3. Our Core Values

4. Crew Handbook (Red Lobster's Crew Guidelines).

After completing the New Crew Orientation curriculum with their manager, new employees receive job-specific training from a certified trainer in the restaurant.

Individual restaurant managers determine the frequency of orientation based on their hiring schedule. The program is held as often as once per week. Red Lobster will hold orientation for one new crew member or as many as a dozen new crew members at once.

Our orientation program is held in our restaurants, usually in the dining area before it is opened to guests for the day. Red Lobster delivers orientation in over 650 Red Lobster restaurant locations.

OUR RESULTS

All in all, our New Crew Orientation is hitting the mark by providing necessary information to our crew in an easy, friendly environment with a high-impact presentation. The fact that our general managers present the program is a strong indicator to our new crew of their value and of the importance Red Lobster places on keeping our promises to crew members and guests.

New Crew Orientation was the most recognized program when we polled our restaurants. Managers were aware of the complete process and could clearly provide detail on the schedule they followed to ensure orientation presentations to their crew.

Executives and managers of Red Lobster are very supportive of our New Crew Orientation program. Here is what they have to say about the value it provides for the company:

Karl Schiner, Director

"As they say, the speed of the leader determines the rate of the pack. The New Crew Orientation program gives the GM the opportunity to make the best first impression of Red Lobster possible, and to really set the pace and the standard to live by. If we didn't do this orientation, we'd lose people simply because they didn't understand the job. New Crew Orientation starts the Red Lobster experience off on the right foot."

Steve Weigel, Senior Vice President

"One thing that sets really great organizations apart from the others is the time they invest in dealing with the people who take care of the organization's customers and guests. Our New Crew Orientation program really helps managers bond with their new crew members from the beginning. It's a powerful tool that makes new crew members feel at home and helps them become productive quickly. It also provides an opportunity to clear up any questions about the job, and sets out a clear vision for new crew members when they start."

Chapter 9

Developing Consistent Onboarding Procedures

Contributed By: Brad O. Casemore, New Employee Orientation Coordinator, Children's Hospitals and Clinics of Minnesota

About the Author: Brad began his career at Children's Hospitals and Clinics of Minnesota in 2007. After participating in a Lean project he was asked to take over the responsibility of the organization's orientation program. Some of his other responsibilities at Children's include strategic conference planning, appointed member of the Welcoming Environment steering committee, and Service Standards Ambassador program coordinator.

Brad's Contact Information:

Brad.casemore@
childrensmn.org
casmoreb@gmail.com
linkedin.com/in/
bradocasemore
Phone: 612-813-5128

CREATE PROCESS FLOW DIAGRAMS TO STANDARDIZE ONBOARDING PROCESSES

Children's Hospitals and Clinics of Minnesota is a nonprofit organization with over 4,500 employees. Children's has two hospitals, one located in St. Paul, and the other in Minneapolis. In addition to the two hospitals, Children's has several out-patient facilities across the Twin Cities metro area.

At Children's it is important to us that we provide a Welcoming Environment for everyone, including patients, families, guests, delivery drivers, employees, providers, and so on. Over the past couple of years Children's has made major changes to our onboarding program. One of the things we have done is create process flows for many of our onboarding processes. We then established metrics to measure the effectiveness of each process. The metrics are reported on a monthly basis at the HR leadership meeting and operations meeting.

Prior to the creation of the process flows, there was a lot of confusion and inconsistency regarding who was responsible for each action associated with onboard-

Sample New Employee Process Diagrams at Children's Hospitals of Minnesota

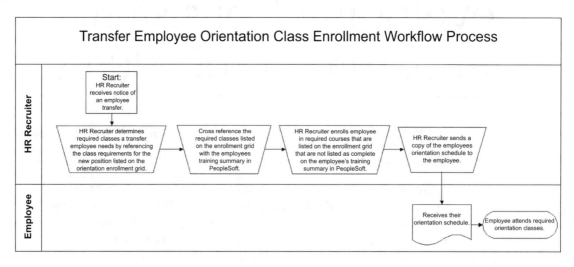

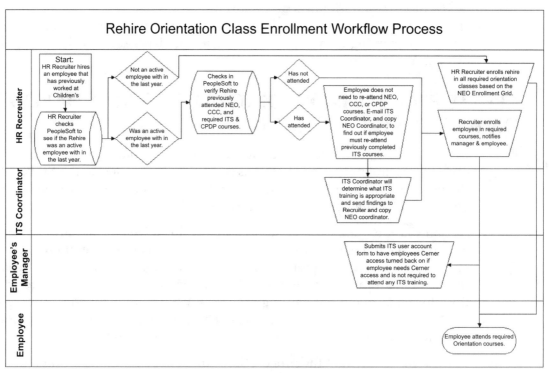

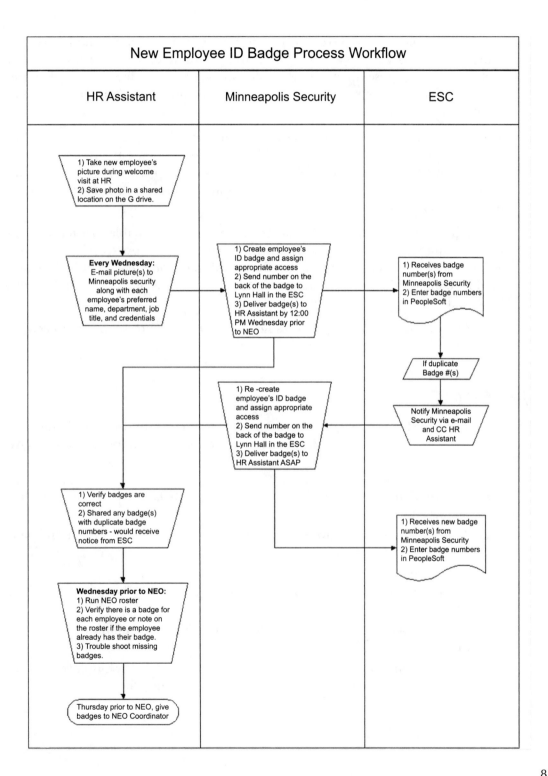

New Employee ID Badge Process Workflow

HR Assistant	Minneapolis Security	ESC

HR Assistant:

1) Take new employee's picture during welcome visit at HR
2) Save photo in a shared location on the G drive.

Every Wednesday:
E-mail picture(s) to Minneapolis security along with each employee's preferred name, department, job title, and credentials

Minneapolis Security:

1) Create employee's ID badge and assign appropriate access
2) Send number on the back of the badge to Lynn Hall in the ESC
3) Deliver badge(s) to HR Assistant by 12:00 PM Wednesday prior to NEO

ESC:

1) Receives badge number(s) from Minneapolis Security
2) Enter badge numbers in PeopleSoft

If duplicate Badge #(s)

Notify Minneapolis Security via e-mail and CC HR Assistant

1) Re -create employee's ID badge and assign appropriate access
2) Send number on the back of the badge to Lynn Hall in the ESC
3) Deliver badge(s) to HR Assistant ASAP

1) Verify badges are correct
2) Shared any badge(s) with duplicate badge numbers - would receive notice from ESC

1) Receives new badge number(s) from Minneapolis Security
2) Enter badge numbers in PeopleSoft

Wednesday prior to NEO:
1) Run NEO roster
2) Verify there is a badge for each employee or note on the roster if the employee already has their badge.
3) Trouble shoot missing badges.

Thursday prior to NEO, give badges to NEO Coordinator

ing a new employee. We were also having difficulty measuring some human resource metrics because we didn't have the standard process documented. In addition, having these documents enables anyone to come in and complete the processes for a new employee ensuring a Welcoming Environment for every employee.

New employees have a better experience when they begin their career at Children's in orientation on the first day. Thus, we require new employees to attend orientation their first day of employment. If this is not possible, the hiring manager must submit a request for an off-cycle start along with the business case to the NEO coordinator.

If, because of extenuating circumstances, an employee is unable to attend orientation within the first 30 days of employment we have developed an online interactive e-learning module we have the employee complete. The e-learning module contains the same content as orientation but it is provided in a different format, including several videos.

Examples of our onboarding process flow diagrams are shown on the preceding pages.

OUR METRICS

At Children's Hospital, we track multiple metrics to ensure the completion and the consistency of the onboarding process for each new employee. We measure to:

- Ensure that all employees complete their 30-day requirements within 30 days.
- Track how many employees actually start on a day that they can attend New Employee Orientation on their first day—we do NEO twice a month on every other Monday.
- Ensure that that a new employee comes into HR 10 days or more before orientation.
- Track for occurrence of any schedule errors in the new employee's orientation schedule.
- Track orientation "no-shows," and follow up with the new employee's manager to ensure compliance and to increase accountability.

- Track orientation logistics such as a classroom change, which is a huge inconvenience for the new employees, the recruiters, and the HR coordinators.

- Report on new hire satisfaction based on a survey pre-hire, at orientation, and at 30 days.

- Track the number of employees who complete the facilitator-led program and the number of employees who complete the new employee e-learning module, as assigned.

- Ensure that all licenses and certifications of the employee are entered into our human resources system prior to the employee's first day.

We use a Training Grid that lists every position in the organization by job code, title, and department, with the required classes and requirements listed for each of these positions. We track how fast the grid is updated with the position requirements when a new job is created.

The recruiter enrolls the new employee into the courses required for their position, based on the listings on the Training Grid. New employees also receive a Welcome Letter during their welcome visit to HR that lists the courses and the dates they need to attend orientation. In the manager's portal, the manager can view the classes their new employees will attend. The recruiters use a checklist as they complete all of their action items for each employee; this is done in the HR system for tracking and reference.

ACHIEVING NEW EMPLOYEE ONBOARDING ACCOUNTABILITY

Following through with all new employee onboarding and training activities is a part of our culture that starts at the top and includes Lean principles. In addition, everyone has been able to see that as we have documented these processes and streamlined them, it has saved everyone time and work. Our metrics help to increase accountability and show the business reason for complying with these processes. We are also able to recognize when a process is not working and needs to be reviewed and updated. It has taken some time to obtain this level of buy-in and accountability; it takes at least two years to accurately document these processes, work out issues that arise, increase accountability, etc.

Examples of the Children's Hospital of Minnesota New Employee Onboarding evaluation forms are shown in the following pages.

New Employee Orientation Day 1—Evaluation

 Children's HOSPITALS AND CLINICS of Minnesota

New Employee Orientation
Day 1 - Evaluation

Today's Date MM/DD/YY

Your feedback about the New Employee Orientation Program (content, structure, and hosts) is very valuable.
Thank you for helping us improve the effectiveness of these sessions.

Prior to arriving at orientation today:

1. Received and understood orientation schedule in advance............................ ___Yes ___No

2. Know where to go after completion of orientation...................................... ___Yes ___No

3. Had picture taken at HR and received name badge on day one of orientation ___Yes ___No

4. Understood how to set up parking prior to orientation. .... ___Yes ___No

5. Overall rating of your experience prior to day one of orientation...... ___Excellent ___Good ___Fair ___Poor

Hosts / Speakers: Please state your agreement or disagreement:	Strongly Agree	Agree	Disagree	Strongly Disagree
6. I feel welcome at Children's	☐	☐	☐	☐
7. The hosts answered my questions	☐	☐	☐	☐
8. The guest speakers were effective	☐	☐	☐	☐

Program segments:	Strongly Agree	Agree	Disagree	Strongly Disagree
9. Executive Presentation – Mission, Vision, Values	☐	☐	☐	☐
10. Service Standards	☐	☐	☐	☐
11. Patient Safety	☐	☐	☐	☐
12. Employee Safety	☐	☐	☐	☐
13. Parking	☐	☐	☐	☐
14. Family Centered Care (parent panel)	☐	☐	☐	☐
15. Hospital Tour	☐	☐	☐	☐
16. Population specific	☐	☐	☐	☐
17. Payroll	☐	☐	☐	☐
18. Benefits	☐	☐	☐	☐
19. Kronos (timecard) & Self-Service	☐	☐	☐	☐
20. Lean	☐	☐	☐	☐
21. Fair Booth Material/Representatives	☐	☐	☐	☐

Overall:	Strongly Agree	Agree	Disagree	Strongly Disagree
22. The printed materials enhanced my orientation	☐	☐	☐	☐
23. The breakfast/lunch was satisfactory	☐	☐	☐	☐
24. The room was comfortable	☐	☐	☐	☐
25. I am glad I decided to join Children's	☐	☐	☐	☐
26. I understand how I contribute to the mission	☐	☐	☐	☐
27. I learned what I needed to know on my first day	☐	☐	☐	☐

Thank You Page

How was your experience with Children's prior to orientation?

Are there any ways in which the organization, or your manager, could be more helpful to you as a new employee?

Do you have any suggestions for how we can improve the hiring and/or orientation process for future new employees?

If you are willing to be contacted to discuss your experience, please provide your name and phone number below.

Name _____

Phone Number _____

30-Day Orientation Follow-Up Evaluation

30-Day Orientation Follow-Up Evaluation

Please answer the following questions using the below scale.

	Strongly Agree	Agree	Neutral	Disagree	Strongly Disagree
I understand my job duties and what is expected of me.	O	O	O	O	O
The job I was hired for was accurately described during the hiring process.	O	O	O	O	O
I feel comfortable asking my manager or supervisor if I have questions.	O	O	O	O	O
I feel comfortable asking my coworkers if I have questions.	O	O	O	O	O
I have received feedback from my manager about how I am doing.	O	O	O	O	O
I have made a friend at work since I have begun working at Children's.	O	O	O	O	O
My unit/department was prepared for my arrival.	O	O	O	O	O
The information and resources in orientation prepared me to do my job.	O	O	O	O	O

Please answer the following questions using the below scale.

	Strongly Agree	Agree	Neutral	Disagree	Strongly Disagree
I feel appreciated and understand the importance of the work I do.	O	O	O	O	O
I am glad I made the decision to join Children's.	O	O	O	O	O
I would recommend Children's as a good place to work.	O	O	O	O	O
I would recommend Children's to family and friends who need care.	O	O	O	O	O
I know where to find the information and resources I need to do my job.	O	O	O	O	O

I have received a Service Star.

O Yes
O No

(continued on next page)

At Children's we are committed to providing a welcoming environment for all new employees. It is important for us to ensure our employee's needs are met before and during orientation. Please answer the following questions so we know what you liked and areas that we can improve to enhance the experience of our new employees.

1) What did you like about orientation?

2) What could be improved in orientation?

3) What suggestions do you have for future orientation sessions? Topics?

Additional Comments:

Chapter 10

Orienting and Retaining a Technical Population

Contributed By: Troy Van Houten, Training & eLearning Manager, Micron Technology Inc., Information Systems.

About the Author: Troy Van Houten has over 20 years of broad-range experience in the training and development field in both the manufacturing and business environments.

Troy's Contact Information:

Troy Van Houten
mail@troyvanhouten.com
8000 S. Federal Way
Boise, Idaho 83707
208.484.4334

Troy has been recognized as a leader in his field sharing best practices throughout the United States, Singapore, and Japan. Troy has received numerous industry certifications and education from Boise State University in Boise, Idaho.

THE MICRON TECHNOLOGY, INC. NEO AND NET ORIENTATION TRAINING PROGRAMS

Micron Technology, Inc. has established itself as one of the leading worldwide providers of semiconductor memory solutions. Micron has approximately 5,000 employees at its main location in Boise, Idaho, and approximately 15,000 employees worldwide.

Micron's orientation program accommodates approximately 25 to 50 new employees per month. Many of these new employees are in technical positions. A challenge for any organization with a high number of technical employees is to retain employees with highly desired technical skills. Micron credits its orientation program with helping to keep its employee turnover rate low. *Micron's turnover rates are below both state and industry averages.*

Micron Technology has divided its new employee program into two parts. Each new employee hired into the Micron team attends:

- A one-day New Employee Orientation (NEO) and . . .
- A one-day New Employee Training session (NET)

These are back-to-back agendas on Mondays and Tuesdays of each week. The outline included in this article provides an overview of each day of our new employee program.

On average, Micron hires and orients about 8–12 people a week. This is an ideal size for our program. Variances in head count affect breakout classes in the training portion of the program.

The Micron program is held on-site, in various rooms dedicated for meetings and training. These rooms can be modified to seat audiences of varying sizes depending on the new employee volume for a particular week.

DEVELOPING THE MICRON NEW EMPLOYEE PROGRAM

Micron internal resources have been used for the development, implementation, and maintenance of its programs. Multiple curriculum developers throughout the corporation have built the program and keep it maintained.

Different departments may contribute to our course curriculum, based on subject matter. (For example, the Human Resources Department developed Harassment-Free Workplace, the Micron Fitness Center Physical Fitness Trainers developed Safe Work Practices, and Information Systems developed Information Security.) The course content is maintained and modified by subject matter experts and instructors, with a final edit completed by curriculum developers.

An example of the Micron Technology, Inc. new employee curriculum is shown on the following pages.

Micron Technology, Inc. Orientation Agenda

8:00–8:30	Security Registration
	✓ Employee identification badge preparation
	✓ Vehicle parking decal registration for Micron on-site parking
	✓ Verification of employment form (I-9 Form)
	✓ Personnel files distributed to be taken back to area supervisor
	✓ Coffee, tea, and water available
8:30–8:45	Welcome to Micron and introductions
8:45–9:00	Introduction to Micron video
9:00–9:15	Training & Education department presentation
	✓ Map of Micron training facilities
	✓ Training resources at Micron
	✓ Core required classes
	✓ Micron education assistance program
9:15–9:30	Security
	✓ Vehicle tracking
	✓ Employee tracking
	✓ Property tracking
	✓ Workplace violence prevention and reporting
9:30–9:45	Health Services
	✓ Location of Health Services
	✓ Health Services coverage, hours of operation, and cost
	✓ Ergonomics, injury prevention, and health/wellness
9:45–10:00	Break (A Micron product table is available to review)

(continued on next page)

10:00–10:30	Micron Officer Presentation
	✓ Micron company history
	✓ Company core values and philosophy
10:30–10:45	Micron Officer Questions and Answers
10:45–11:00	Stock Overview
	✓ Employee stock purchase plan
11:00–12:15	Micron Benefits
	✓ Insurance
	✓ Time-off plan
	✓ Retirement at Micron plan
12:15–1:00	Lunch (Provided by Micron)
1:00–1:15	Afternoon Facilitator Introduction (different from the morning facilitator) & Basic PC Pre-assessment
	(The PC Pre-assessment is designed to identify basic PC skill competencies for all new team members. Employees who fail to meet assessment expectations will attend a basic PC class the morning of NET.)
1:15–1:30	Micron Workforce/Equal Employment Opportunities
	✓ EEO policies
	✓ Harassment policies
1:30–1:50	Payroll
	✓ Direct deposit
	✓ W-4 information
1:50–2:00	Department-Specific Training Schedule
2:00–2:15	Break
2:15–2:45	Personnel Paperwork Wrap-Up
2:45–3:45	Plant Tour
3:45–4:00	Q & A and Closing

(*continued on next page*)

7:30–8:00	Basic PC Training

(This class is only for new team members who failed to meet expectations on the assessment during NEO. The audience size is typically about 10 percent of our total group size, or about 2 to 3 team members a week.)

Supporting Objectives:

✓ Define the PC and its common uses at Micron

✓ Practice using the mouse to left/right click, double-click

✓ Practice opening, closing, moving, and resizing a window

✓ Discuss the most commonly used keyboard keys

8:00–10:00	Harassment-Free Workplace

(Separate groups of no more than 30 employees)
Supporting Objectives:

✓ Define what harassment and discrimination are

✓ Recognize behaviors that may be perceived as illegal harassment

✓ Understand Micron's harassment policy

✓ Understand the complaint process for reporting

✓ Identify additional resources to help prevent harassment

10:00–10:15	Break
10:15–12:45	PC/VAX for New Hires

(Separate groups, with no more than 16 employees per group)
Supporting Objectives:

✓ Log on to the Micron network

✓ Discuss and identify desktop terminology

✓ Discuss Windows buttons using the Internet Explorer (I.E.) browser window

✓ Change passwords using password maintenance

✓ Log onto H.R. Online and enter personal data

✓ Practice using Timesheet in H.R. Online

(continued on next page)

✓ Discuss and identify basic I.E. features and links

✓ Log on to Outlook and practice using e-mail and calendar

✓ Log onto the VAX and use Phone and the TRAIN program

12:45–1:45	Lunch
1:45–2:15	Information Security

(All new team members, large-group setting)

Supporting Objective:

✓ Identify how you can protect Micron information to maintain our competitive position in the semiconductor industry

2:15–3:00   Safe Work Practices

(All new team members, large-group setting)

Supporting Objectives:

✓ Reduce injuries and claims related to work injuries

3:00–4:00   Electrostatic Discharge—ESD

(All new team members, large-group setting)

Supporting Objectives:

✓ Define electrostatic discharge

✓ Explain how ESD is generated

✓ List four ways ESD can be prevented

LESSONS LEARNED ALONG THE WAY

Developing an orientation program sooner rather than later is highly recommended. Once a company starts to grow and gets comfortable without a program, it can be difficult to implement a full-fledged program. We found many of our departments were reluctant to join the new orientation program when it was first developed.

OUR RESULTS

The Micron new employee program results at a high level include

- Communication of Micron's culture, values, and business strategy
- Consistent content delivery through subject matter experts
- Lower turnover rates compared to state and industry averages

Chapter 11

Orienting New College Students on Campus

Contributed By: Megan Miller, Director of the Students Activities Office at the Maryland Institute College of Art (MICA)

Megan's Contact Information:

memiller@mica.edu
MICA Student Activities
1300 Mount Royal Avenue,
Baltimore, MD 21217

About the Author: Megan Miller has been in the Student Activities Office at the Maryland Institute College of Art (MICA) for seven years, first as Assistant Director and now as the Director. Megan obtained her Bachelor of Arts degree from Florida State University in Studio Art. While at FSU, she was an Orientation Leader and discovered her passion for student affairs. She went on to complete a post-baccalaureate degree in Photography from Studio Art Centers International (SACI) in Florence, Italy. While in Florence, she assisted with new student orientation as a side project and decided to apply for her master's degree in Student Affairs. She earned her master's of science in Student Affairs in Higher Education from Colorado State University, and was the graduate assistant for Orientation for two years.

Megan found her calling working as a student affairs professional at an art college, merging her love of art with student services. Megan has written articles such as "Using Art in Collegiate Settings to Encourage Moral and Intellectual Development" (*NASPA Journal of College and Character*) and "Finding Their Niche: Union Galleries on College Campuses" (Association of College Unions International, *The Bulletin*, Volume 74, Issue 4, July 2006).

ONBOARDING NEW STUDENTS AT THE MARYLAND INSTITUTE COLLEGE OF ART (MICA)

MICA has always felt strongly that Orientation is the key to a successful transition for students, going from their high school lives into the more autonomous environment college life demands. For parents, Orientation is a "letting go" process, and for students, it's about harnessing that newfound freedom and learning to be successful as an independent college student. Because MICA is a specialized art institution, we have to take the transition to college one step farther in sharing what it means to be at an art college (which is very different from the average collegiate experience).

Additionally, many students are moving from all parts of the country and the world to come to MICA. Some students have never been to the campus before they arrive on the first day of Orientation. Unlike regional colleges, we feel we also have a great responsibility to orient students to Baltimore and the surrounding area, as well as the campus. Our primary goal is for students to feel that they have made the right choice in coming to MICA. This requires that they make new friends and feel that MICA is their new home.

In order to meet these goals, we developed a four-day program that balances the "nuts and bolts" of campus life with the social engagement and the orientation to the city of Baltimore. Our *Day One* Orientation program encompasses the move-in process, parent orientation, and necessities like student ID cards, parking permits, opening a bank account, and more.

On *Day Two* we ensure that the formal (but necessary) academic assessments are completed in the morning. In the afternoon, we begin the more structured social norming programs such as our diversity, campus safety, and Baltimore presentations. By the end of Day Two, the students are breaking out into smaller groups, taking walking tours of the surrounding area and attending sessions about sexual heath and campus life.

On *Day Three* of the Orientation program, we move into topics pertaining to academics and campus expectations. In the afternoon, students can participate in optional tours into the city of Baltimore, including group activities such as shopping, hiking, visiting local music and theater venues, and a museum trip.

By *Day Four* of the Orientation program, we want to ease the students into even more optional and autonomous programs based on their interests. Therefore, on Day Four we provide options such as volleyball games, service trips, visits to area churches, involvement workshops, and more shopping (there can never be enough shuttles to Target and Ikea for new college students). Each night we host a large social program to end the day and let loose. These events gradually increase in their "fun level," and students become more involved in campus action as the nights go on.

DEVELOPING THE MICA STUDENT ORIENTATION PROGRAM

Our four-day MICA Orientation schedule has developed over time. Each year, we review data from multiple assessments of our program, including two evaluations from the students, and two from our Orientation Leaders. Using this data, we have been able to add or take away programs to form the best possible schedule.

The foundation of our planning process takes place in our Orientation Committee. We involve Student Affairs Division staff members, our Parents Council staff person, and two student Orientation Coordinators. The committee begins in March, when we determine the theme for the upcoming year. MICA is an art college, so creativity is expected as we are working to develop a theme, colors, and a logo!

The committee and the Orientation staff work during the spring to develop our Orientation welcome packet, which is mailed to all admitted students the first week of July. We do our best to make the mailer student friendly, but we recognize that parents are likely to be the ones who are reading this information, so it is designed to meet the needs of both audiences. In addition, our Orientation Web site is designed to match the mailer.

Next the committee focuses on the Orientation schedule. This includes bringing in various campus partners such as our Academic Advisers, Admissions Counselors, our Graduate Studies staff, and our International Affairs Director for consultation and decision making. The scheduling typically takes four months to complete. We also ensure that our budget is developed to include the costs associated with the resources required for the Orientation events, such as tents, table and chair rentals, catering, speaker fees, transportation, tours, promotional items, staff training, and so on.

FACILITATING ORIENTATION EVENTS AT MICA

The Office of Student Activities at MICA is responsible for making sure the entire program runs smoothly. Our office includes four professional staff members who focus most of their time on the Orientation planning during the summer. We use a detailed project plan to keep the team on track and to identify internal and external partners and vendors we will be working with to execute the program.

A major partner in the MICA Orientation program is our Events Office, which has four staff members who are dedicated to assisting with logistics. With the committee's input, they arrange the master plans for seating, tables, tablecloths, signage, AV/Tech for each event. Their work is critical to the success of the program. Our facilities and building services crews take their direction from the Office of Events on everything from setting up and breaking down spaces to trash removal. Our AV/Tech crews manage sounds and video equipment, and our on-campus caterer manages all of the food orders.

It is also important to consider safety and security when planning any college campus Orientation program. At MICA, we have campus safety officers on hand throughout the four-day Orientation program to ensure the safety of all students, and to manage the traffic for move-in and parking.

BEST ORIENTATION PRACTICES AT MICA

One of the things we are proud of at MICA is that we strive to prepare students and their parents so they know what to expect before they arrive at Orientation. We have generated a *Parent Handbook* that gives parents an in-depth look at the college and answers as many questions as possible prior to their arrival. In a nutshell, one of the best practices for a student Orientation program is comprehensive "frontloading"—providing information to new students and to their parents in multiple formats prior to their arrival on campus.

Another best practice in the MICA Orientation program is the dedicated team of student Orientation Leaders. The Orientation Leader small groups are vital to the Orientation experience for so many of our students. Once students arrive at MICA and see the diversity of the student body combined with the shared element of artistic ability, they immediately feel at home. Parents often share this experience too, and breathe a sigh of relief that their student has found a place where his or her creative thoughts, ideas, and artistic works are encouraged.

Our Diversity Presentation also helps many students understand and embrace their differences, while celebrating their likeness as artists. We bring in a nationally recognized speaker to facilitate a step-in circle activity that asks students to step into the circle if they feel a part of a specific group, which may pertain to race, ability, sexual orientation, gender, etc. It is a program about respect, and if students can hold that respect for each other throughout their time at MICA, they learn much more from their peers than they might have otherwise. Students often tell us how awesome this program was for them, and how accepted they felt afterward in the MICA community.

At MICA, we hope that our new students and parents feel that they are individuals from the minute they arrive on campus, and that we've been waiting for them. One way we do this is by personalizing their folders and their nametags. We have their keys ready to go, and our student Orientation Leaders are there to help carry the belongings of the new students to their rooms. These little things make parents and students feel important. We pride ourselves at MICA on being a close community, a caring and nurturing place, and these details helps to extend that feeling. We paint many welcome banners for each building that even in a subconscious way say, "We're excited that you are here!"

Another MICA best practice is to provide multiple motivators to encourage full participation in the Orientation program. Our Orientation Leaders do everything they can to make sure each student comes to every event. We "dangle carrots" like ID cards, or finalized course schedules that we know students want and need, and give them to them at the end of the session. It doesn't work 100 percent of the time, but the majority of our students appreciate the push afterward. We provide a continuous message to "Join us!" at MICA.

On the following pages you will find a sample page of our Orientation optional events, a sample page of our Orientation Leader Project Timeline, a sample page of our Orientation Staff timeline, and our Student Evaluation form.

Sample MICA Orientation Activities

7 A.M.–8 A.M.: SWEATING AT SUNRISE!

Join us for some early morning exercise to start the day off right!

Running and Walking Groups—Departing from the Commons Gatehouse

8 A.M.–8:45 A.M.: CONTINENTAL BREAKFAST

9 A.M.–1 P.M.: TRANSFER STUDENT CONNECTIONS AND LUNCH

Begin your morning in the Brown Center with a welcome from our Undergraduate Dean. Then break out with other transfer students to review your academic degree plan, meet your advisor, and get tips on successfully transitioning to MICA. Orientation Leaders will take you on a campus classroom tour, pointing out key offices and resources along the way. Finish up the morning with a presentation by Career Development and a lunch with current students and faculty members from your department.

9 A.M.–11 A.M.: NEW STUDENT ACADEMIC REGISTRATION

Begin your morning with a welcome from our Undergraduate Dean. Then meet the Academic Affairs and Foundation staff members to get your class schedule and discuss the registration process. Ask them questions and get helpful insight for how to be successful in your first year.

11 A.M.–NOON: TRUE SCOOP PART II — NEW STUDENT CAMPUS AND CLASSROOM TOURS

After registration, OLs will lead guided tours of campus to help you find your way to class and locate key offices you will need to use during your first year.

NOON–2 P.M.: LUNCH

During lunch, be sure to sign up for a "Choose Your Own Adventure" tour during the afternoon. This is your chance to get off campus and explore Baltimore!

(If you do not have a meal plan, you may purchase lunch.)

2 P.M.–6 P.M.: CHOOSE YOUR OWN ADVENTURE!

Pick one of the following adventures to develop your knowledge of Baltimore:

- The Music and Performing Arts Adventure
- Hiking and Outdoor Merriment Adventure
- The Baltimore Collegetown Shuttle Tour and Shopping Adventure

(continued on next page)

- Inner Harbor Adventure
- Vintage Shopping in Hampden Adventure
- Walking to The Walters Adventure
- Mt. Washington Adventure

6 P.M.–7 P.M.: DINNER

(If you do not have a meal plan, you may purchase dinner.)

9:30 P.M.: EXTREME BINGO!!!

Meet MICA's bingo gods and goddesses and play to win some fabulous prizes! A MICA tradition you have to see to believe.

10 P.M.: BOARD GAMES AND HOT COCOA

Join us for a cozy and relaxing evening of board games and hot cocoa! A variety of games will be provided, but feel free to bring along your own games to share with the group.

New and Transfer Student Orientation: "The Groove"

Sample Page from the Project Timeline for the Orientation Leader

Activity	Person Responsible	Date Due	Date Completed
Research sites for ropes course/ retreat	Assistant Director	January	
Obtain a Gwynn Falls Trail Park Permit	Director	January	
Visit Foundation classes to discuss leadership opportunities on campus	All	Late January	
Update the Orientation Leader application and upload it on the Web site and in the office as hard copy	Assistant Director	Late February	
Communicate, communicate, communicate! Design Poster, Tables, etc.	Orientation Team	Late February	
Students applying for the Orientation Leader (OL) roles sign up for interviews	Director	Mid March	
OL interviews are conducted	All	Late March	
Notify OL applicants who were not selected	Assistant Director	Late March	
Select OLs and send a congratulatory letter	All	Late March	
Send "invitation" to attend the April Welcome Activity	Assistant Director	Late March	
Coordinate RSVP List for the April Welcome Activity	Administrative Assistant	Early April	
April Welcome Activity	All	April 13	

(continued on next page)

Activity	Person Responsible	Date Due	Date Completed
Prepare OL Summer mailing information	Assistant Director	April 13	
Send letter to OL's to get them excited to come back and to provide relevant dates and exercises to prepare	Assistant Director	June 15	
Schedule Transportation ❑ Buses to Ropes Course ❑ Scavenger Hunt Vans	Assistant Director	June 15	
Update the Campus Resource Document	Workstudy Assistants	June 30	

Sample Page from the Project Timeline for the Orientation Staff

Activity	Person Responsible	Date Due	Date Completed
Finalize contracts with the Orientation Guest Speakers	Director	January	
Finalize Health & Wellness Contract	Director Assistant	January	
Facilitate Workgroup Meeting 1–4/17 ❑ Overview of Evaluation/Special Concerns/Theme Ideas	Workgroup Assistants	4/17	
Order MICA Folders from Communications	Director	5/1	
Meet with Designer to Determine Publication Schedule	Director	5/15	
Send copies of brochure sections to relevant department for updates/revisions	Director	5/17	
Contact vendor about summer mailing and contact information for booklet	Director	5/17	
Workgroup Meeting 2–5/27 ❑ Theme/Logo options, schedule overview	Workgroup Assistants	5/27	
Revise Orientation Leader Training	All	6/1	
Get text and graphic changes back to Designers and Communications. Go to press.	Director	6/1	

Activity	Person Responsible	Date Due	Date Completed
Workgroup Meeting 3–6/3 ❏ Theme/Logo options, schedule overview	Workgroup Assistants	6/3	
Workgroup Meeting 4–6/10 ❏ Schedule overview ❏ Finalize mailing/logo/ t-shirt color/lanyard	Workgroup Assistants	6/10	

MICA Orientation—Student Evaluation

 ## MICA Orientation—Student Evaluation

Here in the Student Activities Office, we would greatly appreciate your feedback on what we could do to improve our Orientation program. Take a few minutes to complete this form and tell us what you think. We will be collecting evaluations on Sunday, August 30th at the BBQ & Band Night from 6–8 pm. We will have a drawing with all of the completed evaluations at the end of the evening, so please complete them and you will be rewarded!

First Name _____ Email _____

Tell us about yourself: Live on Campus/ Residential _____   Live Off-Campus/ Commuter _____
(check all that apply)   Transfer _____   Freshman _____   International _____   Exchange _____

Please circle the response that best matches your experience at Orientation, and add comments if applicable.

Additional Comments	Strongly Disagree				Strongly Agree

Correspondence concerning Orientation was adequate prior to my arrival at MICA.
_____   1   2   3   4   5

Check-in was efficient and well organized.
_____   1   2   3   4   5

My family members and guests felt welcomed and had their questions answered.
_____   1   2   3   4   5

Small group sessions with my Orientation Leader were informative and helpful in helping me adjust to my new living environment and the culture at MICA.
_____   1   2   3   4   5

My Orientation Leader _____ was welcoming, knowledgeable, and resourceful.
_____   1   2   3   4   5

As a result of Orientation, I have a better understanding of the on-campus resources available to me.
_____   1   2   3   4   5

After Orientation, I feel more comfortable and familiar with the city of Baltimore, and know where to acquire items I may need throughout the year.
_____   1   2   3   4   5

The Orientation program as a whole answered many of my questions and made me feel welcome at MICA.
_____   1   2   3   4   5

What did you enjoy most about Orientation?

Comments or suggestions to improve Orientation:

Comments or suggestions for your Orientation Leader/ Orientation Staff:

If you could add one thing to our program, what would it be? If you could remove something, what would it be?

(continued on next page)

Please rate the sessions below based on the extent to which you agree or disagree that they were worthwhile:	Strongly Disagree				Strongly Agree	NA

Thursday, August 27

Office of Diversity Welcome (3-4 pm)...1	2	3	4	5	NA
*Welcome Games in the Commons (6-7:15 pm).........................1	2	3	4	5	NA
*Transfer Student Orientation Session (6-7:15 pm)................1	2	3	4	5	NA
*Community Meetings (7:30-9 pm)...1	2	3	4	5	NA
*Off-Campus & Commuter Student Meeting (7:30-9 pm).......1	2	3	4	5	NA
Tiki Party (9-11 pm)...1	2	3	4	5	NA

Comments: _____

Friday, August 28

Writing Assessment (8:45-10:45 am)..1	2	3	4	5	NA
Guest Speaker (11 am-12:30 pm)..1	2	3	4	5	NA
All About Baltimore! Charm City! (2-3:30 pm)......................1	2	3	4	5	NA
Neighborhood Walking Tours (3:30-6 pm).................................1	2	3	4	5	NA
Sex Rules Presentation (7-8:30 pm)...1	2	3	4	5	NA
True Scoop Groups (8:30-9:30 pm)..1	2	3	4	5	NA
Kickin' It, Karaoke Style (9:30-11 pm).....................................1	2	3	4	5	NA

Comments: _____

Saturday, August 30

*Transfer Student Connections & Lunch (9am-1 pm)...............1	2	3	4	5	NA
*New Student Registration (9-11 am)..1	2	3	4	5	NA
*New Student Campus Classroom Tours (11 am-Noon) 1	2	3	4		NA
*Choose Your Own Adventure Tours (2-6 pm)					
Music & Performing Arts...1	2	3	4	5	NA
Hiking & Outdoor Merriment......................................1	2	3	4	5	NA
Collegetown & Shopping..1	2	3	4	5	NA
Inner Harbor 1	2	3	4	5	NA
Vintage Shopping in Hampden...................................1	2	3	4	5	NA
Walters Art Museum 1	2	3	4	5	NA
Mt. Washington 1	2	3	4	5	NA
Extreme Bingo (9:30-Midnight)..1	2	3	4	5	NA
Board Games & Hot Cocoa (10 pm-Midnight)...........................1	2	3	4	5	NA

Comments: _____

Sunday, August 31

*Local Opportunities for Worship (9:30am-1 pm)....................1	2	3	4	5	NA
*Ready, Set, Spike Fest Volleyball (1-4 pm) 1	2	3	4	5	NA
*The Art of Critique (2:30-4 pm)...1	2	3	4	5	NA
*Mo' Money, Mo' Problems! (4-5 pm)..1	2	3	4	5	NA
*Finding Your Groove-How to Get Involved at MICA! (5-5:30 pm)..1	2	3	4	5	NA
*MICA Fitness Center Open House (6-7 pm)..............................1	2	3	4	5	NA
Concert & BBQ (6-8 pm)..1	2	3	4	5	NA

Comments: _____

*Starred items indicate multiple programs happening at once; please evaluate only those you attended.

Thank you for your feedback and continuing to make our Orientation program even better!

Chapter 12

Mary Kay's Three-Day Orientation Program

Contributed By: Linda G. Duebner, Senior Employee and Organization Specialist, Mary Kay Inc.

About the Author: Linda's experience in education, training, and development spans twenty years. Her training and development background includes both technical training and employee development programs. Linda holds a BS degree in Education.

Linda's Contact Information:

Linda.duebner@mkcorp.com
P.O. Box 799045
Dallas, Texas 75379-9045

A DEEP DIVE INTO MARY KAY CULTURE AND PRODUCTS

The Mary Kay three-day New Employee Orientation program is designed to enculturate and welcome new corporate employees (not independent Beauty Consultants) within the first three months of their start date. Another primary goal of the program is for new employees to be able to "find" themselves within the product/sales cycle and understand the importance of their job to the company's overall mission of Enriching Women's Lives. The program is used to give new employees exposure to critical business areas that impact product development, our supply chain, and our sales force support functions. In addition, participants have an opportunity to meet and get to know company executives and culture committee members.

The three-day program is designed around three basic themes:

- **Day 1—Make Me Feel Important**: Named after one of our Company's values, this day focuses on the benefits of working for Mary Kay, career development, our Corporate Social Responsibility efforts, why it's different to work for a direct sales company, why it's different to work for a privately held company, and Employee Communications, among other topics. For many people, this day brings their first glimpse of Mary Kay Ash, our founder. In videos, the participants are greeted by Mary Kay, and then they watch a dramatic reenactment of her life story and what led her to become the founder of the company.

- **Day 2—Our Products**: The topics of Day Two of the program include product strategy, manufacturing processes, and tours of our manufacturing and distribution facilities.

- **Day 3—Our Sales Force**: This day focuses on the people and groups that support our sales force. From public relations to sales development (the "coaches") to an actual sales force member sharing her experiences, this day helps new employees understand our central mission of supporting the sales force.

The program serves new employees well because it gives them a broader view of the Company. Many are surprised that we have people talking to customers and sales force members on the phone, while there are also scientists in the lab looking at skin cells in a test tube. Participants are often astounded at the breadth of the business. It also creates bonds and relationships between the individuals that come to each program. There are groups that have "reunions" with their New Employee Orientation session members, sometimes years after they were "new."

Without fail, the short-term results of the program are emotional and strong. Participants become attached to the company in a deeper way than "it's just my job." They come to appreciate the difference between Mary Kay and other companies they've worked for. Often, at the conclusion of the program, someone in the group will ask for a group photo. Long-term benefits include such successful bonding that we've historically had very low turnover.

PREPARING THE THREE-DAY PROGRAM

Our three-day program requires a lot of preparation, mostly on the part of our department coordinator, who schedules rooms, speakers, catering, and A/V support, as well as transportation for tours of our manufacturing facility and distribution centers. She also sets up for our product demonstration and prepares all necessary materials for the participants.

Historically, we offer this program once a quarter, but the schedule fluctuates as hiring levels fluctuate.

MATERIALS AND RESOURCES

We use the following resources to prepare for and to facilitate the three-day program:

- Media Room, with projector and A/V support
- Subject matter experts (speakers)
- Tour guides
- Branded materials, including folders, agenda for the three days, helpful information, and so on.

Our 3-Day Orientation Curriculum and Evaluation Form are shown on the following pages.

The Mary Kay Three-Day Orientation Curriculum

Day 1: Make me feel important		Day 2: Our Products		Day 3: Go-Give* spirit	
8:30-9:00	**Welcome** *Employee & Organization Development*	8:30-8:45	**Welcome** *Employee & Organization Development*	8:30-8:40	**Welcome** *Employee & Organization Development*
9:00-9:15	**Mary Kay Message** *Video*	8:45-10:00	**Branding/Products** *Speaker – Chief Marketing Officer*	8:40-9:15	**U.S. Marketing** *Speaker – VP, US Marketing*
9:15-9:55	**Company Overview** *Speaker -Chief People Officer*	10:00-10:10	**Break**	9:15-9:45	**Legal** *Speaker – Chief Legal Officer*
		10:15-10:30	**Manufacturing History** *Speaker – Chief Supply Chain Officer*		
9:55-10:10	**Break**			9:45-10:00	**Break**
10:10-11:10	**Traditions** *Speaker – Tenured employee*	10:30-10:50	**Research & Development** *Speaker – VP, Research and Development*	10:00-10:15	**Corporate Public Relations** *Speaker – Corporate PR Representative*
11:10-11:30	**Culture Committee** *Speaker – Culture Committee Member*	10:50-11:10	**Contract MFG/International** *Speaker – VP, Contract Manufacturing*	10:15-11:30	**Golden Rule Service**
11:30-12:30	**Lunch with Culture Committee** *Glass Dining Room*	11:15-11:30	**Clinical & Consumer Evaluation**	11:30-12:30	**Lunch with Executive Team** *Glass Dining Room*
		11:30-12:30	**Lunch** *Glass Dining Room*		
12:30-1:00	**International** *Speaker – International Leader*	12:30-12:45	**Break**	12:30-1:00	**e-Business** *Speaker – Director, e-Business*
		12:45-1:15	**Travel Time to MFG** *Tour Bus*		
1:00-1:30	**Corporate Social Responsibility** *Speaker – Director, CSR*	1:15-1:30	**Skin Care Research**	1:00-1:45	**Sales Development**
1:30-1:45	**Break**	1:30-1:50	**Product Quality & Good Manufacturing Practices**	1:45-2:00	**Break**
1:45-2:15	**Employee Communication/ Recognition** *Speacker – Employee Communication and Recognition Manager*	1:50-3:00	**MFG Tour**	2:00-2:45	**Sales Force Experience** *Guest Speaker*
		3:00-3:15	**Bus Travel Time to ASRS** *Tour Bus*	2:45-2:50	**Break**
		3:15-4:15	**ASRS Tour**	2:50-3:50	**Product Demonstration**
2:15-3:15	**Managing Your Mary Kay Career** *Speaker – Employee & Organization Development Specialist*	4:15-5:00	**Travel time to TMKB** *Tour Bus*	3:50-4:30	**Closing Wrap-up** *Employee & Organization Development*
3:15-4:00	**Thinking Like a Woman** *Video*				
4:00-4:30	**MK Tour** *Mary Kay Ash's office and the Mary Kay Museum*				

Mary Kay's
New Employee Orientation Program

December 02 - 04, 2008

EVALUATION FORM

Please fill out this evaluation in order to be entered in a drawing at the end of the program for a special prize!

Please rate the following program segments:	Not Effective at all	Somewhat Ineffective	Effective	Very Effective
Day 1: Make me feel important				
Company Overview				
Traditions				
Culture Committee				
International Strategy and Direction				
Corporate Social Responsibility				
Learning About Mary Kay				
Managing Your Mary Kay Career				
Day 2: Our Products				
Branding / Product Development / Product Line				
Manufacturing / R&D Topics				
Manufacturing / R&D Tours				
ASRS Tours				
Day 3: Go-Give® spirit				
U.S. Marketing				
Legal				
Corporate Public Relations				
Golden Rule Service				
e-Business				
Sales Development				
Sales Force Experience				
Skin Care Class / Product Sampling Table				
What did you find most valuable about this program?				

(continued on next page)

What would you have liked to spend more time on in this program?

What did you find least valuable about this program?

Please give examples from the three days of ways you were able to:

Network:

Learn:

Share:

Grow:

Please include any feedback for improvement on content or facilitation:

General Comments:

Chapter 13

Designing a Buddy Program

Contributed by: Julie Wilson, Organizational Development Consultant and Coach

About the Author: Julie Wilson is an organization development consultant and coach at Harvard's Center for Workplace Development and a founder of Impact Consulting

Julie's Contact Information:

Impact Consulting Partners
www.juliemwilson.com
Julie@juliemwilson.com

Partners, a consulting and coaching practice dedicated to helping managers improve the performance of their team.

She is a contributor to the 2001 ASTD Training and Performance Yearbook and coauthor of *The Complete Guide to Orientation and Reorientation.*

Julie graduated with honors from Queen's University, Belfast, and from the Harvard Graduate School of Education with a master's degree in Education, specializing in adult development and behavioral change.

BUDDIES ASSIST WITH THE UNWRITTEN RULES

Orientation and retention are all about making your new employees feel at home. Along the way, that also means helping them understand your organizational culture and politics. A buddy program is a great tool to assist in achieving both of these objectives.

It's tough being a new employee. You're not too sure what lies behind each door, there are enough acronyms and buzzwords to fill a book, and somebody keeps moving the photocopier!

These concerns pale into insignificance, however, when compared with the sheer confusion of not knowing what's "normal" in the organization: What's right and wrong here? What's expected of me? What's the company's culture? Not knowing the answers to these and similar questions makes every new employee feel like an outsider, at least for a while.

Consequently, the typical new employee is less confident and somewhat insecure when it comes to relating with colleagues—senior, peer, or junior. Not knowing what's right or what's accepted here can make the new employee hesitant and confused in interpreting the responses of others. A buddy program is a great way to accelerate the new employees' abilities to deal with these early disconcerting issues.

By matching your new employees with a buddy—someone who has been in the organization for a while—you will not only assist in cultural integration and orientation. If done properly, your managers and supervisors will find that their interaction with new employees is much less about low-level operational issues, and much more about adding value.

What's the difference between a buddy, a coach, and a mentor?

- *A mentoring program* seeks to assist individuals with their development, both personally and professionally.
- *A coaching program* seeks to increase the individual's job-related skills.
- *A buddy program* is solely involved with providing a one-point access to operationally necessary information. In essence, *the development of the individual* is not an expected output.

What should the structure of a buddy program be?

We've designed the rest of this chapter as a briefing document that you might provide to prospective buddies. It explains how the structure of a buddy program works.

The Buddy Program—A Briefing Document

Use this text template to create an introductory letter to the new Buddies.

1. Overview

[Company] has decided to implement a Buddy Program to assist new employees in the early months of their employment with us.

This document is primarily designed to brief those who will be the new employees' Buddies, but it will also help new employees and the managers of both to understand more fully what the Buddy Program is, and what is expected of each party involved in the Buddy relationship.

2. The Orientation Program

The Buddy Program is an integral part of the company's orientation program for new employees. It is strongly recommended that you read this document in that context. Please refer to:

[List other available materials here that will give an understanding of the wider context of the orientation program.]

Buddies will be expected to occasionally attend the company's other orientation activities, including the associated classroom training, to give an overview of the program to new employees. You will be contacted by [coordinator's name] regarding this in due course.

3. Outline of the Buddy Program

The Buddy Program matches new employees with employees who have been with the company for some time (typically six to twelve months), for a period of six months, with two goals:

- To provide the new employee with a point of contact for general queries regarding day-to-day operational issues [such as the location of facilities, information processing requirements, and relevant company policies].
- To help the new employee integrate with the company by providing access to someone who is familiar with our culture, attitude, and expectations.

The program is coordinated by [name of coordinator] and supported by the line managers.

4. Goals and Objectives of the Buddy Program

By providing such a relationship, it is intended that:

- The new employee will feel more at home with the company, in a shorter period of time.
- Relatively straightforward queries regarding basic operational issues will be dealt with in a timely and non-bureaucratic manner.
- The initial confusion and uncertainty faced by all new employees will be lessened.

(continued on next page)

- Other orientation activities, such as classroom and on-the-job training, can be related to real-world activities, and the resulting basic queries can be resolved.
- Our new employees find out how best to manage us, the company, in a supportive and risk-reduced environment.
- Manager and supervisor time with new employees is freed up to deal with added-value issues.
- The new employee begins to add value more quickly, leading to increased confidence and self-esteem.
- You, the Buddy, are actively involved in making this a better place to work and making our new employees more productive.

5. Selection and Pairing of Buddies

Employees are nominated as Buddies by departmental managers on the basis of two criteria:

- The employee's interpersonal skills, and
- The employee's understanding of and commitment to the company's vision and values.

Additionally, at the end of the Buddy relationship, you will have the opportunity to nominate as a Buddy the new employee with whom you have been working, if you feel he or she fulfills these criteria.

The Program Coordinator will allocate nominated Buddies to new employees. When possible, Buddies will be matched with new employees in their own departments.

6. The Role and Responsibilities of the Buddy

The primary aspects of the Buddy's role and responsibilities are detailed in number 4. Please review that section now. Then continue on to read about the role of a Buddy versus that of a *manager, coach,* or *mentor.*

The role of a buddy must be distinguished from that of a manager, mentor, or coach:

A *mentor* is someone who is typically a more experienced employee or manager, and is involved with the all-around development of an individual.

You are *not* being asked to act as your new employee's mentor. You are not responsible for his or her growth or development as an individual, and it is not part of the role of a Buddy to take on such a responsibility. You will not be assessed on your success as a Buddy by whether or not the new employee you work with develops as an individual during the six-month period.

A *coach* is someone tasked with developing an individual's job-specific skills. You are *not* being asked to act as your new employee's coach. Although your role as Buddy may involve explaining some simple job-related issues or straightforward procedures, it is not your job to replace formal training processes. If you feel your new employee's queries are too detailed or specialized for you to answer, direct them to the supervisor or manager.

(continued on next page)

You are not the new employee's *manager* or supervisor. Your role as Buddy does not mean you will be held responsible for your new employee's performance. If queries arise regarding performance, disciplinary, or policy matters, while you are free to give your opinion and advice on how to approach the matter, you are *not* in a position to adjudicate or resolve the matter. The new employee must be directed to the manager or supervisor for resolution of the relevant issue(s).

7. Meeting with Your Buddy

After you have been notified of the name and other relevant information regarding the new employee you will be working with, it is up to you to make contact at the earliest available opportunity. This may be on the employee's first day on site; or if orientation training occurs on day one, you may wish to arrange to meet the employee for lunch or otherwise on that day.

Content of Meetings and Discussions

Your first meeting with your new employee should be introductory in nature. Show the person around your department, make introductions to their colleagues, and provide directions as to where the employee will be working. Explain the operation of any equipment or systems needed in order to commence work. Be familiar with the content of the orientation training so you do not duplicate any training being provided there.

Explain how the new employee can contact you during the day, and make it clear that you are available as needed, but that the employee should use discretion at all times. Explain that you will be meeting regularly and that non-urgent issues should be left until those times, but emphasize that anything that is materially hindering work or performance can be discussed with you immediately.

Explain the difference between a mentor, a coach, and a manager to the new employee to set clear expectations, and clear any ground rules regarding contact outside working hours. Ask if he or she has any initial queries or issues, and deal with them. Then leave the new employee to get on with the assignment! Remember, your role is to help new employees get on with the task at hand—not to prevent them from doing so!

Frequency and Timing of Meetings

You should aim to meet regularly for at least 30 minutes, once a week during their first month and at least once a month thereafter. This meeting (often best held over lunch or in an informal setting) should be used to discuss any non-urgent issues the new employee may have.

During the working day, it may be reasonable to expect as many as four or five brief queries a day from the new employee in the first few days, tapering down to one or two a day thereafter. Although all new employees are different, after two to three months, you may hear little or nothing on a daily basis. *This is a good sign*. If you are still getting a large number of urgent queries after the first month, then the Buddy program is not working, and you should speak to the Program Coordinator for advice.

(continued on next page)

Within the parameters above, it is expected that you and the new employee meet within working hours. (Your manager will let you know if you are spending too much time on this.) Some Buddies and new employees agree to meet on a social basis, outside working hours. This is an entirely discretionary matter between you and the new employee. It is up to you to indicate to the new employee how you feel about being contacted regarding work-related issues outside of working hours.

The company has no policy on this. Many Buddies have felt happy being contacted when necessary outside working hours, up to about 9 p.m. on weeknights, but not on weekends. This is entirely up to you.

8. Expectations of the Relationship

Your relationship with the new employee should be open, confidential, positive, and supportive.

Discussions between you and the new employee should be confidential. The company has no interest in knowing the details of any discussions between you and the new employee, and we are not involved in monitoring Buddy relationships. We simply ask that you be supportive of the company and your coworkers. We discourage gossip and speculation within a Buddy relationship, particularly as many new employees are not in a position to form opinions on most issues during their early months with us.

9. Available Support

If you are having any trouble with the interpretation of these guidelines, or with any aspect of the Buddy relationship, contact [name of Program Coordinator], who will be happy to give you guidance.

Making Your Buddy a Buddy—We would like to see the new employee you are working with become a Buddy in turn after being with the company for a while. If you feel he or she could fulfill such a role, find time in the last two months of the relationship to share with the employee any tips or techniques you think would help in performing such a role.

Give the name to your manager, and suggest the employee be considered as a Buddy.

10. Termination of the Relationship

The Buddy relationship between you and the new employee will be terminated if either:

- Six months pass, or
- Either party requests it.

The Buddy relationship operates under a no-fault termination mechanism. This means that if either the Buddy or the new employee so requests, the Buddy relationship immediately ends. The new employee is allocated another Buddy, and the Buddy is allocated to a different new employee.

No reasons will be sought or proffered, no discussion will ensue, no blame will be apportioned.

Contact the Program Coordinator if you wish to trigger the Buddy relationship.

(continued on next page)

Note: Many buddies form separate, social relationships with new employees that continue beyond the formal Buddy program. This is entirely a matter for the employees.

11. Review of the Relationship

At the termination of the Buddy relationship, the Program Coordinator will ask you to fill in a brief questionnaire aimed at improving the Buddy program. It does not involve the issues discussed between you and the new employee.

Other Topics You May Include in Your Buddy Introduction Document

- FAQ—containing frequently asked questions regarding the Buddy Program
- FAQ—containing questions frequently asked by new employees
- An intranet site address containing discussion group used by Buddies

Buddy Thank-You Letter and Evaluation

Dear,

Thank you so much for participating in our Buddy program. I sincerely hope you got a lot out of it personally, and that you will consider acting as a Buddy again.

This brief questionnaire is intended solely to help us in the review and redesign of the Buddy Program, to continuously improve the program to best meet everyone's needs.

Your responses and comments on the questionnaire are confidential, and are not used for any other purpose.

Please return this questionnaire to _____

by_____ (date).

Sincerely,

[Program Coordinator's Name and Personal Signature Here]

New Employee Thank-You Letter and Evaluation

Dear,

Thank you so much for participating in our Buddy program. I sincerely hope you got a lot out of it personally, and that you will consider acting as a Buddy to a new employee yourself in the future. We hope this program helped you feel welcome and comfortable in our company very quickly.

This brief questionnaire is intended solely to help us in the review and redesign of the Buddy Program, to continuously improve the program to best meet everyone's needs.

Your responses and comments on the questionnaire are confidential, and are not used for any other purpose.

Please return this questionnaire to _____

by_____(date).

Sincerely,

[Program Coordinator's Name and Personal Signature Here]

Part 4

Tools, Systems, and Checklists

INTRODUCTION

Many tasks are involved in preparing for, orienting, and training a new employee, and an organization may be faced with onboarding employees in multiple locations around a city, a country, or around the world.

Fortunately, many types of tools are available to assist with the onboarding process. In this section, we'll explore:

ONLINE TOOLS AND SYSTEMS

Today, many online tools and systems are available to deliver information, video, training, action plans, and surveys to new employees. In this section, we'll explore examples of these tools, and provide advice to help you identify the potential tools that will best meet your new employee orientation needs.

LETTER SAMPLES

This section also includes samples of letters that can be sent to new employees, new volunteers, managers of new employees, etc., to welcome the new employee and provide information about the next steps of the orientation process.

EVALUATION AND METRICS

This section includes information about the metrics you can use to measure the results of your onboarding program. Many companies also conduct surveys to ensure that new employees have received all the information, equipment, and introductions required to integrate them into the new company and to begin their new jobs at the highest level of productivity possible. This section contains examples of evaluation tools to obtain feedback for continuous improvement of the onboarding process.

CHECKLIST TOOLS

Many companies use checklists to ensure that all tasks are completed and all information is conveyed to the new employees. These checklists may be in hard-copy form, or online. This section includes checklist samples that can be used by managers and by employees to ensure all training actions are completed.

Chapter 14

Onboarding New Employees in Virtual Locations

Contributed By: Kass Larson, CEO, XEGY, Inc.

About the Author: Kass and his partner Kathy Larson founded XEGY in 1998. The vision was to create an online platform that brought together the best of what learning management systems (LMS) and business process management systems had to offer.

Kass's Contact Information:

www.XEGY.com
kassl@xegy.com
801 14th Street
Golden, CO 80401
720-259-1888

XEGY is provided as a service and is designed to be used and managed by non-technical people. It requires no internal IT support or infrastructure. As a service, XEGY can be scaled to meet the requirements of small to large organizations.

IMPLEMENTING AN EASILY REPLICATED BEST PRACTICE ORIENTATION

Your company has outlets and offices across the country and is planning on opening a number of new locations in the coming year. A new employee onboarding and training program has been created, but the challenge is . . . how do we ensure that each company location uses the same processes and completes the same training requirements within an appropriate timeframe? It is recognized that onboarding is the first touch point with each new employee and thus sets the stage for how that person views the company. Successful onboarding reaps benefits from lower employee turnover and shorter time to full productivity for each new hire.

Very few organizations are able to offer new employee onboarding workshops and training in one location—most must reach out to new employees in multiple cities and countries. Some employees work alone out of a home office, and others work in remote small group office or store locations. Yet each new employee must complete proper paperwork, decide on job options and specific training modules in each location, every time, without exception. Failure to do so can lead to gaps in compliance, safety training, and unforeseen snags in operations such as payroll issues.

Reaching all new employees in an organization and ensuring that they feel welcome and receive the information they need is an important and sometimes very challenging part of setting up an effective new employee onboarding program.

The goals of an onboarding program for virtual employees in small offices or stores include:

- Ensuring that each new employee completes all required paperwork accurately and efficiently
- Ensuring that all employees in all locations follow through with training requirements, compliance actions, certifications, etc., to achieve safety, legal, and customer satisfaction requirements
- Avoiding a situation in which each store or office begins to create its own onboarding program, resulting in wasted time and resources, and an inconsistent (and undocumented) onboarding process
- Providing the tools and resources that new employees in all locations can access easily
- Reducing the time that local managers spend with new employees presenting the same information over and over as new employees are hired
- Reducing the time that it takes to bring a new employee up to full productivity.

RECOMMENDATIONS FOR VIRTUAL NEW EMPLOYEE ONBOARDING

When designing or updating an onboarding program for a company with many virtual employees throughout the country or around the world, special considerations and tools must be employed for success. Very few medium- and large-sized corporations today do not face the issue of onboarding and training employees in multiple locations. So what special considerations and tools should be considered for a virtual onboarding program?

- *Make Use of Internet-based Access to Onboarding Forms and Information.* The Internet has become the backbone of keeping employees linked to their companies. This link should start with the hiring process. Companies can easily set up secure Web pages to guide people through the paperwork of hiring and enable them to complete most of the process online.

■ *Use an Online Tracking System of Training Actions.* With today's online tools and resource options, there is no reason not to incorporate online tools into the new employee onboarding process. Even small companies can afford to have one training computer at each location for new employees to use to access, track, and complete training programs. These types of computer training programs are also welcome and expected by the emerging workforce, who use computer and hand-held devices on a continuous basis.

■ *Use Online Videos.* Help employees to meet company executives virtually and to learn about the vision and values of the company through online videos, which can be accessed at each store or office location.

■ *Develop an Effective New Employee Web Site.* When employees are spread among many geographic locations, the company intranet becomes an even more critical tool. Centralized secure Web sites make it easy to keep information current, provide frequent updates, and create the branding and message that you want to communicate. Vibrant internal support sites keep employees' interest and build a sense of community. Creatively using internal Web sites to assist employees can reinforce and enhance the public Web site so that it attracts clients and builds company brand.

■ *Design New Employee E-Learning Modules.* In conjunction with an online tracking system for new employees, create e-learning modules for training that are factual, procedural, and process-, or company-culture oriented. Include pre- and post- testing modules to add a level-two evaluation component to ensure that each employee completes the training and has learned the content.

■ *Don't Lose Sight of the "People Connection."* Even with the importance of all of the online tools discussed in this chapter, it is important to set up methods to ensure that new employees connect well with their manager and peers in their own location, and across the organization. On-site manager visits, structured coaching sessions between new employees and managers, setting up a buddy system and/or peer shadowing training sessions, etc., all enhance learning and build relationships.

■ *Develop Multiple Onboarding Facilitators.* When a company has multiple large sites in different cities, a best-practice approach is to create standardized materials supplemented with online programs, and to also take a "train-the-trainer" approach to enlist the HR Partners in these locations to facilitate mini-orientation programs and/or larger events, such as a quarterly on-boarding welcome session.

- *Create Guides, Flip Books, and Checklists.* Use tools that are appropriate for the moment and space. Sometimes a "low-tech" tool, used in conjunction with an online training and tracking program, can provide an additional reminder to employees on the job. An example of this type of tool is a laminated, quick-reference flip book tool provided near a new employee's phone or the cash register.

- *Make Use of Today's Communication Tools.* Web phones, iPods, etc.—today's employee often is already well "trained" in the use of Web-based gaming devices, phone applications, social networking sites, etc. Rather than "fighting" this trend, embrace it! Put your training program on portable media (memory cards) that can be loaded into mobile devices such as iPods or Gameboys. Create a phone application for quick reference information. Increase relationship building and the feeling of being connected to the organization by creating a Facebook or LinkedIn group for current and new employees. The cost of development and deployment

New Hire Process—HR Steps:
The New Hire Setup Process

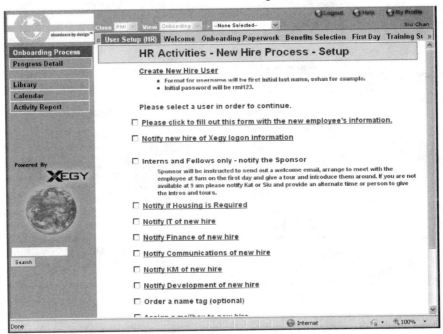

has dropped dramatically in the last several years, making this mobility technology realistic for even small companies.

- *Establish Larger, Periodic Employee Welcome Sessions.* Many companies meet the need for employees to connect in a personal way, even when they are located in multiple office or store sites, by having large welcome or orientation training sessions on a quarterly basis, at a regional location. In this situation, a local manager or HR professional is responsible for the initial new employee onboarding, the employee obtains more training online, and then the new employee is also able to meet others and make personal connections (and to learn more about the company values and culture) at the regional live event.

- *Evaluate Onboarding Success.* When the onboarding process is implemented with multiple tools, in multiple locations, and/or by multiple orientation facilitators and partners, the evaluation of the program must be thorough, and the data and feedback provided by new employees must be reviewed frequently to continuously update and enhance the program. If you are

The New Hire Welcome Screen

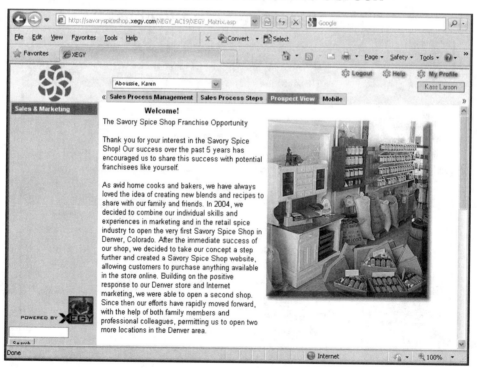

using an online orientation and tracking tool, this evaluation process can be built right into the new employee online program, and compliance reports can be accessed easily by business leaders and the HR team. Over time, the onboarding assessment data can be correlated to long-term success of employees in the organization and used as another form of feedback to improve the onboarding process.

THE ADVANTAGES OF ONLINE NEW EMPLOYEE TRACKING SYSTEMS

With the advent of online new employee training and tracking programs, a best-practice paper based onboarding program can be customized and converted into a roadmap for the new employee to follow on a self-serve online basis. An important advantage of online training delivery and tracking is that it can be integrated into more operational processes—directly connecting the learning to the work—at the point where the work is being done.

In addition to training new employees in a consistent and reliable manner that increases accountability and learning, these programs can also be used for other

The Training Progress Tracking Screen

"new" needs in the organization. The process of converting an existing manual, primarily paper- or spreadsheet-based process is similar across different departments or functions in an organization. Areas where there is a high degree of synergy in integrating training tracking into operations include

- *A New Product Launch.* Once the online new employee roadmap program structure is in place, the tool can also be used to train current employees when a new product or service is available. Companies spend the majority of their sales training dollars on product training, to ensure that the sales force fully understands the products and services they are selling; having a new employee online training program in place accelerates the training that is required for these new products and services and makes it easier to correlate training results with new product performance.

- *New Store Opening,* The same online new employee systems can be used to customize, document, and track the procedures used to open a new store in a new location. One of the primary goals in opening a new store or location is to have the employees 100 percent ready to go (trained) the minute

The Menu Training Screen

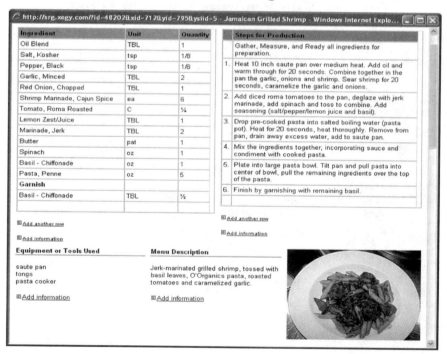

the doors open. Employee readiness should be an integrated process included in the new location development and opening process. Online systems enable a high degree of integration in managing those two departmental processes.

■ *New Compliance Training and Reporting Requirements.* Compliance is a growing concern for all organizations. HIPAA (Health Insurance Portability and Accountability Act), OSHA (Occupational Safety and Health Administration), Sarbanes-Oxley, and the emerging sustainability and environmental requirements are placing new training and reporting demands on the company. Every employee needs to understand their role in these new requirements and have the appropriate training to keep the company out of trouble. The same online new employee training site (and methods) can be used to train current employees to meet new legal requirements and

The XEGY Video Training Screen

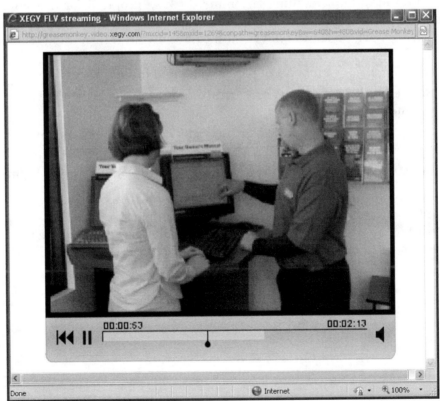

compliance training requirements. As with the New Location Opening scenarios, online compliance training opens the doors to tighter operational integration. Compliance training can be delivered and managed in the same systems that are used for compliance reporting—again bringing the training right to the point where and when it's needed on the job.

THE NEW EMPLOYEE ONLINE ROADMAP

XEGY, Inc. has created multiple online systems that provide a roadmap, training portal, and tracking and reporting systems for new employees. These systems are especially applicable for the organization with multiple stores, franchises, and locations. Examples of the screen content and tracking tools are shown on previous pages.

MEASURING THE RESULTS OF ONLINE NEW EMPLOYEE TRACKING SYSTEMS

As a result of implementing an online tracking program for new employee onboarding, new store openings, and new product launch initiatives, our clients have been able to show a direct business result and return on investment:

- 95 percent reduction of paper generated in the process
- People brought to full productivity in 50 percent of the time prior to implementing XEGY
- Employees fully trained on new medical products—meeting compliance requirements
- 30 percent reduction in time to open a new store due to tighter process controls

With today's technology, implementing an online system for new employee onboarding and training processes is easier than ever, and it can be the best possible answer to the issue of training new employees in virtual locations.

Chapter 15

Streaming Media for Encore Performances!

Contributed By: Scott Safe, Vice President of Marketing at Qumu, Inc.

About the Author: Scott Safe brings more than twenty years of experience in high-tech marketing to Qumu, Inc. Qumu is the leading producer of enterprise video solutions, with a product suite that automates and streamlines the entire video lifecycle, from capture to viewing to reporting.

Scott's Contact Information:

www.qumu.com
ssafe@qumu.com
650-396-8539
1100 GrundyLane, Suite 300
San Bruno, CA 94066

ENTERPRISE VIDEO AND NEW EMPLOYEE ONBOARDING

Human resources professionals are, by and large, experienced video users. The hoary institution of the orientation film has long brought together production professionals, IT teams, and Human Resources. However, the ongoing convergence of video technologies—the convergence of lower-cost cameras and editing tools, higher-bandwidth internal and external networks, better content management applications, new enterprise portal integration, and a proliferation of video-enabled devices from cell phones to signage—is creating a panoply of new roles for video in onboarding processes.

The vast majority of video content need not be outsourced or sent to an in-house studio, but can be handled within the Human Resources team. This may sound like an onerous new responsibility. It's not. With the right enterprise video solution, easy-to-use production and editing tools, and a little bit of know-how, making videos is as easy as meeting face-to-face—and unlike meeting face-to-face, you only have to do it once.

POTENTIAL USES FOR A HUMAN RESOURCES LIBRARY

Once you understand the video-production process, training with customized videos becomes a snap. An organization with an enterprise video solution—whether it's a software-as-a-service system, or a higher-end appliance with network administration capabilities—can create a library of video-on-demand (VOD) assets dedicated to Human Resources. Human resource professionals can then share specific videos, upload new content, and attach documentation to specific programs. The library should function as an automated and centralized extension of the Human Resources Department. Once it's up and running, video can handle a wide range of previously labor-intensive processes.

Training videos, for example, are far more effective than text-based user manuals and explanations. They're also labor savers: you just need to make one presentation, and then it's accessible as needed for infinite replays to the viewers you choose.

This training can be as specific as needed, and creation responsibilities can be left to experts within the company. The IT manager, for example, can record an explanation of how to use the company's VPN to remote employees. Hire a remote employee? Send a link to the video, and now the employee is working on the network.

You can brief field sales on how to fill out an expense report, using screen capture and a USB camera, so that they can see a talking head explaining while the process actually unfolds in front of them. Use two cameras to allow a vice president to supplement your explanation with additional insights on sales expense best practices. These presentation techniques are supported by easy-to-use programs like Qumu Create. Depending on your enterprise video solution, automated reporting can also tell you whether or not the salespeople actually viewed the video.

Certain laborious practices can be totally automated. To explain the company's benefits package, create a PowerPoint presentation laying out each aspect of the package slide-by-slide, providing audio or a talking head in another output panel. Attach necessary documentation to the stream as downloadable files, and at the end of the presentation provide your e-mail address. The entire process has become virtual.

Even compliance can be managed through a Human Resources video library. A recording of a presentation given by a certified sexual harassment or ethics instructor, combined with downloadable paperwork, can ensure compliance with corporate and government regulations.

Once a video library is up and running, the use cases will proliferate—almost any aspect of employee onboarding (including outward-facing recruitment) can be managed through video.

USING VIDEO FOR NEW EMPLOYEE ORIENTATION PROGRAMS

Enterprise video offers bold new opportunities for creating a more automated and engaging orientation and training process.

Typically, there are two options for training new employees. A member of the Human Resources team could conduct an in-person meeting, distributing hard copies of information and documentation as needed. This is a reasonable practice in a small company with a large Human Resources team, no remote offices, and copious spare time. In the age of video, face-to-face interaction is still highly effective and occasionally necessary, but it can't be routine.

Alternatively, a video can be outsourced to a professional production company. In a larger company, this can be managed by an internal studio. There are certainly advantages to this approach, and there are occasions on which professional-quality videos are the best option. A basic introduction to company culture can be professionally filmed and shown to everybody.

In a large retail company (or any organization with multiple locations), a training video made by a professional studio can be shown to a very large audience: every barista across the continent, or every short-order chef, or every forklift operator. This is the classic orientation video. It has a place in the enterprise video world: we'll get back to this.

However, videos made by professional production teams are extremely expensive. A single production can cost well into the tens of thousands of dollars and can displace studio time better used for executive broadcasts or customer-facing content. Perhaps more important, they also often fail to address any degree of specialization of labor, and are entirely inadequate as methods to distribute and explain the wide variety of necessary documentation associated with most knowledge-economy jobs. Once you move out of the domain of large-scale, generic orientation, professional production ceases to be a viable option. Video, appropriately used, becomes a day-to-day resource, and no professional studio can supply enough to match that demand.

In place of face-to-face meetings and professional films, Human Resources teams can put together training videos at their desks. With an automated enterprise video solution, this becomes an extremely simple process and provides a set of definitive advantages, even over face-to-face meetings.

PREPARING A HUMAN RESOURCES VIDEO

The vast majority of human resource videos can be made at low cost and with little labor. You need the proper technical infrastructure, and a little understanding of the production process.

As with all filmmaking, the most important stage of the creation process is pre-production. Here you have to answer a series of preparatory questions about the content.

1. What purpose will the video serve?

2. What is your video message? In other words, you need to decide whether you are creating a training video, which will be process-oriented, or an orientation video, which is intended to introduce employees to corporate culture.

3. Who is going to watch the video?

4. Where will the video be shown, and will the video need to be produced in different languages? If you're creating a video for engineers in the EMA region, you need to figure out just what languages you need to accommodate. More figuratively, HR terminology may not be intuitively comprehensible to members of the marketing or engineering teams. Be sure that you're speaking to the right audience.

Quick Tips for Good Video

- Keep it short.
- Finalize your message before starting.
- Practice. Practice again.
- Set up camera(s) and laptop. Test the sound and image before you film.
- Improve lighting and move to a more soundproofed location if necessary.
- Film it! Use multiple takes if need be.
- Publish to a common file format (.asf, for example).
- Promote the video.
- Monitor usage and read the reviews—learn and improve!

5. How long do you want the video to be? Brevity is often key; a bloated or vague video will not hold a viewer's attention.

6. Do you (or your executives or other speakers in the video) need to speak from a script, or do you plan to speak extemporaneously? A script is always a good idea: even if you know the topic inside-out, a script ensures that your final product is concise and well organized.

7. Do you need to involve an expert—an IT manager, or a certified sexual harassment workshop leader, or a team leader?

8. You also need to gauge your technical requirements and possibilities. What type of camera or cameras are you using? Are you creating a video-on-demand item for a video library, or are you planning on launching a live broadcast? Do you need involvement and support from IT? (If you're conducting a live broadcast, you likely will; with the proper enterprise video solution, a VOD presentation should be easy to upload via an employee-generated content portal.)

9. Are there downloadable documents that need to be included in the video? What level of security is needed to protect this intellectual property?

10. Do you have suitable editing software for a VOD item? For most of the videos you'll be making, simple presentation capture and editing software like Qumu Create should suffice. If you want more extensive editing capabilities, you should seek out a software suite like Adobe Premiere.

11. What will be the setting and background for the video? High-quality videos—external-facing, or those with large audiences—require special precautions in filming. You need a relatively soundproofed studio, with a proper microphone or microphones, professional three-point lighting, and a high-quality camera. However, if you're recording at your desk, you already have the studio all set up!

SHOOTING, POSTPRODUCTION, AND DISTRIBUTION

With the proper setup, the shoot should be straightforward. A simple desk-bound video shoot will succeed or fail on the strength of the content, not the quality of the camera. Nevertheless, ensure that cameras and microphones will result in comprehensible content. Make sure you've covered everything you laid out in your script. Don't delay anything to postproduction: you can do as many shoots as you need to ensure seamless execution.

Postproduction is straightforward. With the Qumu Create tool, for example, you can control multiple cameras, trim unnecessary sections, shift slide placement, and merge multiple presentations. Low-cost editing-intensive tools can offer more extensive control over one-feed video-only presentations.

Once you have a final presentation assembled, you should be able to create a VOD program. If your company has an enterprise video solution that enables an employee-generated content portal, you should be able to upload the final presentation to the HR domain on the portal. You can share the uploaded program via an automatic e-mail list, or publish it to a Web site. IT administrators can then set access privileges to ensure that the content reaches the proper viewers. In this way, you can begin to establish a complete HR video library.

THE ALL-HANDS ORIENTATION

The orientation video is a standby of many companies. However, orientation videos are often unfairly neglected and allowed to slip into irrelevance over time. An orientation video should properly be a part of a new employee's welcome to the company—and not just in large retail organizations.

Instead of a recorded video, try a live video broadcast. A live orientation broadcast, delivered quarterly, involving HR and top executives, can provide a powerful introduction to corporate culture and practices and firm up morale among new employees. Allow the executives to explain, live, what the company's history is, and what its goals are. Live is more spontaneous and easier to relate to than an old-fashioned orientation video, made offsite by a video production company that doesn't know your company at all.

Enable a live question-and-answer during the broadcast to bring viewers into a conversation with presenters. Present a poll at the end of the video to measure the effectiveness of the presentation. Create an archive so that employees who missed the orientation can review it at their convenience. A proper enterprise video solution will cover these possibilities. With this added functionality, you can make the orientation video far more engaging.

OPPORTUNITIES FOR PROFESSIONAL STUDIO INPUT

If you're working in a large company, you likely already have a professional video production studio and team. We've laid out why you don't always need a professional team to get an effective video implementation up and running. However, there are still a myriad of opportunities for a professional team in the orientation process. The live quarterly all-hands orientation, for example, could afford to have the professional touch.

However, there's one place where high-quality video could bring a concrete return: the employee handbook. Increasingly, employees don't peruse a physical handbook, but turn to a PDF or Web site for the information they need. Enliven these virtual resources with links to a fixed video collection! Since this content will be viewed by *every* new employee, you'll enjoy a return on high production values.

IF YOU DON'T HAVE AN ENTERPRISE VIDEO SOLUTION—GET ONE!

This chapter has assumed that you have an enterprise video solution currently operating inside your enterprise. If your organization lacks an enterprise video solution, talk to your IT and corporate communications departments. HR needs a solution that delivers an easy-to-use portal, a straightforward content upload process, network-friendly distribution to remote offices, and support for leading-edge players. For smaller companies, this solution may come in the form of a hosted or software-as-a-service product; for larger companies, a management appliance and various distribution and encoding appliances may also prove necessary. Video adoption may be a hard sell, but it's worth the effort. HR can reap immediate benefits by making video a routine tool in the office.

LEARN MORE

To learn more about Qumu's enterprise video offerings and to download a trial copy of Qumu Create, go to www.qumu.com.

Chapter 16

Moving Your Onboarding Program Online

Contributed By: Julie Wilson, Organizational Development Consultant and Coach

About the Author: Julie Wilson is an organization development consultant and coach at Harvard's Center for Workplace Development and a founder of Impact Consulting Partners, a consulting and coaching practice dedicated to helping managers improve the performance of their team.

Julie's Contact Information:

Impact Consulting Partners
www.juliemwilson.com
Julie@juliemwilson.com

She is a contributor to the 2001 ASTD Training and Performance Yearbook and coauthor of *The Complete Guide to Orientation and Reorientation*.

Julie graduated with honors from Queen's University, Belfast, and from the Harvard Graduate School of Education with a master's in Education, specializing in adult development and behavioral change.

GETTING OUT OF THE CLASSROOM

Everyone wants an orientation program that doesn't involve classroom time, or at the very least, reduces it as much as possible. Trying to put new hires in one place for orientation is inconvenient, time-consuming, and expensive. It makes sense to leverage technology whenever possible to complement your classroom orientation.

However, in my experience, well over 90 percent of all attempts at designing and implementing an asynchronous orientation program fail.

Why is this? The "3 Tips" noted below address the most common pitfalls and how to avoid them.

1. FOCUS ON THE PROGRAM GOALS

One of the most common pitfalls when designing an online onboarding program is not being clear about the program's goals or objectives—what do you want people to be able to do or understand as a result of having gone through the program? Too often, these basics of instructional design are ignored when it comes to designing an online onboarding program, and the program becomes a kitchen sink of miscellaneous company information. Here are a few suggested goals or objectives for an online orientation program:

Having completed the new employee online onboarding program, new employees will:

- Feel welcome and confirmed in their decision to join Company X
- Understand the company's organizational structure and how to navigate within it
- Have a greater understanding of their department's specific culture, i.e., the informal "rules of the road," behavioral expectations, and how things get done within their specific department
- Have completed a checklist of timely administrative actions
- Have articulated performance goals for their first three to six months of employment

These are just examples of what your objectives might look like; obviously, yours will be specific to the onboarding needs of your organization. Make sure these objectives form the basis of your post program evaluation to gauge whether to not the program objectives are being met and to keep your budget for the program on track.

A sample post-program evaluation form to address the objectives listed above is shown on the following page.

Online Onboarding Feedback Survey

Thank you so much for participating in our online onboarding program. We sincerely hope it was helpful in helping you make the transition to your new job here at Company X.

This brief questionnaire is intended to help us evaluate the efficacy of the program. The contents of the questionnaire are confidential and are not used for any other purpose.

Please indicate which of the following apply by circling the relevant number:

1 = Strongly disagree; 2 = Disagree; 3 = Neither agree not disagree; 4 = Agree; 5 = Strongly agree

I	feel welcome and confirmed in my decision to join Company X.	1 2 3 4 5
2.	I have a greater understanding of the complexities of the organizational structure and how to navigate within it.	1 2 3 4 5
3.	Completing the Roadmap helped me to lay the foundation of a productive working relationship with my manager.	1 2 3 4 5
4.	Completing the Roadmap helped me clarify performance expectations with my manager.	1 2 3 4 5
5.	The frequency of the meetings with my manager during the first 90 days was adequate.	1 2 3 4 5
6.	I have a greater understanding of my department's specific culture, i.e., the informal "rules of the road," and how things get done within my specific department.	1 2 3 4 5
7.	I was happy with the support provided by the program coordinator.	1 2 3 4 5

Additional comments/suggestions:

2. BEWARE OF THE TYRANNY OF CONTENT OVERLOAD

Having articulated your program goals, be ruthless when making content decisions. Many online orientation programs are designed by committee, which can mean that your program goals are held hostage to the content "specializations" of the members of your committee, for example, the health and safety person wants an entire section devoted to this topic and it does not correlate with your program objectives. Your question should always be, how does this content support the program objectives? The more your program addresses the needs of your new employees and provides them with timely tools and information, the better.

Designing your program can be a relatively quick and simple process if you stick with your objectives and try not to get too hung up on the latest technology. As an example, I designed a simple online orientation program for a client (using the objectives noted in the above section) and had a prototype up and running within ten business days. We used an internal Web site, and the headings for the online orientation were no more complex than:

- **Discussion Board.** A discussion board open to all employees (not just new hires) to make sure new employees have an online forum to ask questions and to read the discussions of others.
- **My Roadmap.** The centerpiece of the program—a downloadable one-page document that prompts new employees to have an expectation-setting conversation with their manager for the next 90 days and to clarify what success will look like at the end of the 90-day probationary period.
- **Useful Documents.** A central location from which new employees can download any necessary forms or checklists.
- **Useful Web sites.** A list of a dozen or so internal Web sites with a one-sentence explanation on each and its relevance to new hires.

An integral component of the above design is a series of e-mails that both the new employee and her manager receive via autoresponder software. Over the 90-day period, the new employee receives a series of e-mail messages, the content of which ranges from action items, reminders of goals, suggested resources and helpful tips. The dual function of these e-mails is to provide the additional structure to motivate new employees to complete the 90-day program and to remind the manager of his role in the onboarding process. We used AR plus and it has proved to be both reliable and cost effective: http://arplus3.com/.

Keep it as simple as it needs to be, but no simpler.

3. CHOOSE A DELIVERY PLATFORM THAT WORKS FOR YOUR COMPANY

Once the content has been written, it's important to deliver the message in a way that's consistent with your company culture. A company in which new employees have little access to computers using a Web-based training program is as silly as an Internet company using quill pens (though you'd be surprised to see what many companies do use).

What format are your people using? What tools are available to new hires? If your chosen platform is an intranet, do 100 percent of your employees have access to the intranet?

Similarly, if your supervisors are not fully familiar and comfortable with the platform you choose, you can assume that your orientation program has crashed too. No one will fix it, it will fall into disuse, and all that hard work will be just one more great project listed on your résumé.

Prototype early and get feedback as soon as you can—not just on the content, but also on usability.

Good luck with your world-class "asynchronous" orientation!

Chapter 17

New Employee Portals: The New Welcome Mat!

Contributed By: Karen Perron, Director of Onboarding Strategies, SilkRoad Technology, Inc.

About the Author: Karen promotes and incorporates onboarding subject matter expertise into the product development, marketing, and sales of SilkRoad's RedCarpet Onboarding and Life Events Talent Management solution. She has more than 13 years of Human Resources experience with Motorola and Freescale Semiconductor, Inc.

Karen's Contact Information:

www.SilkRoad.com
karen.perron@silkroad.com
512-992-2387
SilkRoad Technology
102 West Third Street,
Suite 250
Winston-Salem, NC 27101

In her previous position, Karen served as the Global Onboarding Program Lead at Freescale Semiconductor. In this role, Karen led the company's HR initiative to design and deliver a strategic approach to onboarding global new hire talent though utilization of technology socialization methods. Karen earned a master of science degree in Instructional Systems Design and Bachelor of Science degrees in Finance and Marketing from Florida State University.

WHAT IS A NEW EMPLOYEE PORTAL?

The initial excitement new hires and transitional employees experience over starting a new job or position can quickly develop into frustration as they run into challenges in their quest to become acclimated with the company and productive in their new jobs. They need information they can access quickly to accelerate their learning process, and a tool to track the actions they are required to complete as a new employee.

A New Employee Portal is a customized Web site created specifically to welcome new employees and to provide an online new employee learning and tracking tool. By providing a personalized online portal for every new employee, the company is able to provide information about the employee's new job, as well as information about your corporate culture and your corporate procedures early in the onboarding process.

Online portals can also be created to provide customized portals for any corporate life cycle event, such as onboarding, offboarding, transfers, and promotions, leaves of absence, and mergers and acquisitions.

Personalized new hire portals help jump-start engagement and ease transitions by providing an easy access tool to:

- Immediately connect new employees to their new company's culture and talent brand
- Deliver any dynamic, event-specific content you desire tailored to the employee's specific life cycle event, such as onboarding
- Provide new hires or transitioning employees with a myriad of information that will help them acclimate to your organization's culture, their new job, position, company, or employment situation
- Eliminate the need to manage paper-based orientation or checklists
- Complete all new-hire paperwork electronically prior to the first day on the job
- Provide the new employee handbook with details on dress code, company hours, and benefits electronically
- Provide a welcome letter or video from the CEO
- Provide new employees with access to a customized and secure new employee portal after offer acceptance and before their first day on the job
- Align your portal's look and feel with your corporate and talent brand by using your own template
- Provide support for electronic forms that can be completed and sent to the designated resource
- Provide a 90-day new employee survey to gather feedback on the process
- Allow non-technical users to easily edit and add content and images with WYSIWYG ("what you see is what you get") editors that do not require HTML knowledge

The Portal System also enables the Human Resources team to view and track the progress of new employee actions to help measure results and to identify areas of compliance and noncompliance as needed.

HOW IS A NEW EMPLOYEE PORTAL CREATED?

To create a customized New Employee Portal, Human Resource team members will identify content to be included on the site. Content may include any forms to be completed electronically, information about the company, personalized content based on location, position, department, or anything that is unique to the organization.

Content may also include (but is not limited to) verbiage, photos, videos, and links to other Web sites for the completion of required onboarding tasks. A Talent Management Software vendor, such as SilkRoad Technology, can take the customer-specified content and deliver a hosted New Employee Portal that is accessible via an Internet connection by the new hires. Other organization contacts, such as Marketing/Communications, Senior Management, and HRIS/IT may also be included in the New Employee Portal implementation process.

The set-up time for a New Employee Portal can vary based on the complexity and granularity of the content, forms, and tasks delivered. An average implementation ranges from eight to 12 weeks, which includes the design, development, testing, and deployment of the automated onboarding solution.

Quite frequently, organizations can leverage their existing new hire checklists and orientation materials as key components of the New Employee Portal. There may be opportunities for process improvements which can be incorporated, but a total re-design or start from scratch approach is typically not necessary. It is not uncommon to utilize 75 percent or more of the current process and forms, which can expedite the roll-out of the New Employee Portal.

WHAT DOES A NEW EMPLOYEE PORTAL LOOK LIKE?

Shown on the following pages are two examples of New Employee Portals that reflect the organization's talent branding and company-specific information.

These two screen examples depict the RedCarpet Administrator Dashboard view, which provides the Human Resources department with easy-to-use tools to track organizational readiness and new hire completion of tasks:

WHAT IS THE BUSINESS NEED FOR NEW EMPLOYEE PORTALS?

The following are business results achieved by a sampling of SilkRoad Technology customers who are utilizing the RedCarpet New Employee Portal as a critical ingredient in their onboarding process:

- $1,100 Return on Investment per new hire (elimination of paper, shipping, reduction in HR and Manager time, shortened classroom orientation, and improved new hire time to productivity)
- 90 percent improvement in Organization Day-One Readiness
- 37 percent increase in performance rating for Onboarding satisfaction

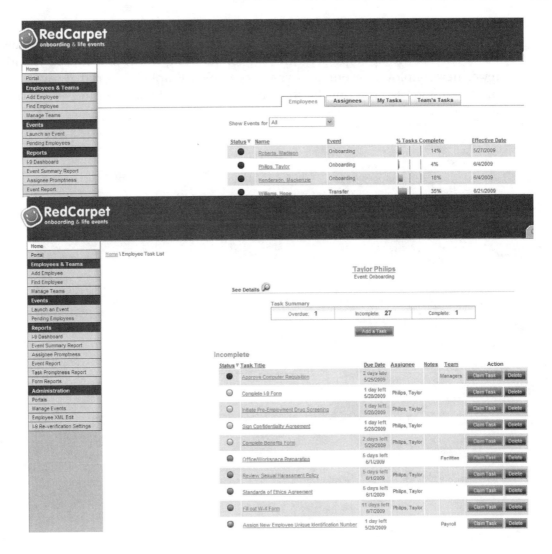

- 100 percent policy acknowledgment by all new hires
- Zero incident of manual intervention for non-acknowledgment
- 80 percent of completion of onboarding tasks by new hires before due date
- New Employee Start Date paperwork reduced from 3 hours to 10 minutes
- Processing time by Human Resource Coordinators reduced from 2 hours to 30 minutes per new employee

The New Employee Portal is especially appealing to new employees who are used to accessing information and tracking all of their daily life tasks online on a daily basis, and to virtual employees who are onboarding in remote locations with fewer new employee orientation resources. New Employee Portals provide an online solution to "roll out the welcome mat" to all of your employees in every location.

Chapter 18

Onboarding in a Social Media Workplace

Contributed By: Matt Paddock, Director of Recruiting and Management Development, Dominion Enterprises

About the Author: Matt has led talent acquisition and development programs for Dominion Enterprises since 2002, including initiatives aimed at developing management bench strength across the company and transferring organizational knowledge. Matt is an avid user of social media, both on behalf of his company and personally, including the leadership of several active online communities serving thousands of members.

Matt's Contact Information:

www.linkedin.com/in/
mattpaddock
mapdock@yahoo.com
757-255-8255
150 Granby
Norfolk, Virginia 23510

Matt earned his undergraduate degree from Oberlin Conservatory in Oberlin, Ohio, and received a master's degree from Virginia Commonwealth University in Richmond.

WHAT IS A SOCIAL MEDIA WORKPLACE?

It's fun to imagine coming to work as a new hire in what we'll call the "social mediated" workplace:

As you enter the building, you see that every employee has a name tag with lots of info about their interests and professional experience ... plus a list of friends you have in common.

Instead of bland background music, your cube or office comes supplied with a customized soundtrack that only plays the music you like.

Orientation involves creating a professional profile on the Company's intranet ... with links to your blog and your Facebook, LinkedIn, or Twitter profile.

During enrollment for company benefits, you notice many reviews written by your fellow employees about health plans and primary care physicians.

At lunchtime you are approached by a group of employees who invite you to join them ... based on your all having several favorite restaurants in common.

At the end of the day you find an email invitation to complete an online survey regarding all aspects of your first day at work ... including lunch.

If you are thinking about adding a social media component to your Onboarding program, this article provides information about the ideas and issues to discuss and to plan for success. You will not find step-by-step instructions here for setting up a new social media group or site. Why is this? At the rapid pace of change associated with online tools, these instructions would be out-of-date before this book is even published. What this article will do is provide some resources and considerations needed to form a social media strategy.

Although the list above is intended to induce a chuckle, a recent survey from Robert Half Technology found that at least half of the companies polled understand that new employees don't want to check their social networking at the door.[1] It's no surprise that this is a front-burner issue; social media have matured to become a broad space that attracts over one third of adult Internet users, across about 20 main sites.[2] Additional sites and related services seem to spring up almost daily.

The Robert Half study also shows that social networks and other social online services—usually referred to as "social media"—are still thought of by many organizations as an extracurricular activity. Some managers see browsing Facebook or chatting via AOL Instant Messenger as equivalent to making a personal phone call on company time, but others realize they need to embrace the social media and focus on managing the message. We all recognize the difference between an employee's using the phone as a business tool and making excessive personal phone calls, so why not apply this same discretion with social media?

One business consideration is that the power and potential of social media are matched by their ability to disrupt established systems for communication and workplace decorum. The other problem is how to define policies and procedures when the social media landscape is in a constant state of flux. Before tackling these issues, let's consider how to harness the power of social media for onboarding employees.

YOUR NETWORK OR THEIRS?

Social media address one concern companies have during the onboarding process, which is effective communication with new employees. When companies communicate well during the onboarding process, employees feel welcomed, informed, and in tune with corporate culture.

When companies communicate poorly, new hires feel isolated, out of sync with their coworkers, and unaware of expectations. Beyond meetings, training, and other activities, social media have unique qualities that help employers interact efficiently and effectively with new employees. The benefit for companies is that employees aligned with organizational culture will perform more quickly and more confidently in their new roles.

Social media thrive in a networked environment. Just look at LinkedIn, a site that made the drab utility of a Rolodex enticing by allowing people to share contact information in real time. LinkedIn built on that foundation to include features like messaging, embedded applications, and user groups. Grouping is fundamental to most social media tools, whether we consider new applications like LinkedIn or older media like blogging.

In the workplace we sometimes hear negative references to groups as cliques, or associate them with political factions. Try to think of groups in social media as being more like teams in the workplace. We understand the value of cooperation in the workplace, and we see that teams are generally more productive and effective in solving difficult problems.

Apply this same notion of corporate teamwork to social media and you'll get some idea of what author James Surowiecki[3] referred to as "wisdom of the crowds." Rather than try to anticipate every shred of information your new hires will need, plug them into an existing network of knowledgeable employees. Assuming that you hire people with at least average levels of curiosity and critical thinking, you should expect them to use networking to fill in knowledge and skill gaps during their early days of employment.

If this vision of new hires acting as social media detectives to ferret out important information sounds unrealistic to you, consider this: Pew Research reported[4] in 2009 that 46 percent of Americans over the age of 18 are established users of social media, and the percentage rises to 65 percent if we consider the next wave of working adults. This means your new hires will very likely come to the workplace already highly networked.

When dealing with change (such as the first few weeks in a new job!), people have an especially strong need for the support of others. Employers can either take control of social media tools by embedding new hires in a powerful company network filled with new people who are willing and able to support the onboarding process, or leave things to chance and expect new hires to rely only on their previous personal contacts.

CORPORATE CULTURE CLUB

The utility of networking in the workplace is a developing science, and many employers feel they already have reliable methods for teaching people *how* to do their jobs. When those same companies tackle the challenge of cultural transmission, the picture becomes less clear. One ancillary benefit of adding more social media to your onboarding toolkit is developing what has been referred to as "ambient intimacy." Lisa Reichelt coined the phrase[5] on her blog in 2007:

> Ambient intimacy is about being able to keep in touch with people with a level of regularity and intimacy that you wouldn't usually have access to, because time and space conspire to make it impossible.

Social media novitiates often come away from their first few hours on Facebook, Twitter, or LinkedIn unsure of what to *do* with these sites. We instantly recognize the utility of a pencil, a stapler, or a calculator but we struggle to understand why sending 140 characters of text on Twitter adds any value to the world.

Reichelt and others have proposed that the greatest value in social media may be the ease with which we can stay informed about things happening in other people's lives. This heightened sense of goings-on with fellow employees is valuable to new hires who are still trying to find their way to the restroom. Knowing more than name, rank, and serial number makes for easier interactions with colleagues, or at least provides a conversation starter.

Employees also benefit from knowing about connections they share with other people in the organization, such as having attended the same college or having worked previously at the same company. The wonderful thing about social media is that they allow for *ambient* rather than *active* intimacy. Most new hires aren't ready to jump in and participate in every workplace conversation, but they all benefit from dipping their toes into the cultural pool. Eventually, listeners find the right conversations and become active participants, which is the ultimate payoff for companies invested in converting new employees from outsiders to insiders, and for companies that truly want the ideas and opinions of their employees to "bubble up" to the surface.

WHO'S KEEPING SCORE?

Searching the World Wide Web for the phrase "social media ROI" pulls up many pages of results, but very little to instruct us on how to measure the value of a social media strategy. In the onboarding realm, we can always ask our new hires how they felt about using social media in the workplace, and we can do technical analysis on how often particular links were clicked or intranet pages were accessed by employees. These are nice metrics for HR or OD practitioners, but they might not be as compelling for senior leaders.

Considering the time required to set up and maintain a presence on even a few sites, social media strategies can be a hard sell in the corner office. Even though it is possible to show that all your new hires are members of the company's page on Facebook, you'll need to go further to demonstrate how the time these employees spend on social media sites translates to good things for your organization. Site analytics, or tools showing detailed statistics on use of a site or service, are developing at a rapid rate. Services like bit.ly[6] allow you to send out shortened links to information online and see detailed reports on how many people clicked through, including timestamps and the location of your readers.

As one example of measuring activity and the results of social media tools in the workplace, Facebook now offers a free resource[7] called Page Insights that allows you to view activity associated with any Facebook page you create. These hard numbers are good, but the best ROI you'll have for using social media during onboarding will be testimonials from new hires.

Be sure to set clear expectations with your senior leaders so they aren't expecting to read the results of a social media campaign as they would a balance sheet. Ask employees through surveys and narratives to rate their satisfaction with the company's use of social media, and load in questions about how social media helped them become more productive sooner, solve problems, sell more, or expand their corporate network to accomplish a specific task. Also ask managers to compare the productivity of their new employees with previous groups that ramped up without the benefit of an internal social media campaign, and ask these managers to particularly hone in on productivity gains.

WHAT ABOUT PRIVACY AND DECORUM?

Corporate social media certainly won't work without executive support, but you may find obstacles at a much lower level. Another survey[8] from Pew Research showed that adults using social media value their privacy. A majority of users restrict access to their profiles and limit what content is visible to their friends. Couple this with statistics from the same study that personal use of social media far outpaces professional use, and it is clear that expecting *all* employees to opt into a social media strategy at work may be unrealistic.

The concern for privacy online is understandable considering that identity theft affects millions of U.S. adults each year[9] and that online scams have been on the rise[10] in recent years. Companies with plans to formalize social media must be sensitive to perceived privacy issues, educate employees on online privacy best practices, provide policies concerning their appropriate use in the workplace, and be extremely vigilant against real scams or misuse of official sites.

A final word of caution around social media has to do with decorum. Wikipedia defines decorum as "prescribed limits of appropriate social behavior within set situations," and the real message here is that companies can only expect appropriate use of social media by employees after some rules have been clearly communicated. The benchmark for this type of communication tends to be IBM, one of the first companies to publish[11] what it refers to as its "Social Computing Guidelines." Help new employees avoid social media landmines by spelling out clearly what they can and cannot do using company sites.

Since use of social media bridges personal and professional worlds, be sure to explain what constitutes inappropriate use of social media *outside of work*, such as mentioning certain information about an employer on a public site, blog, or as a Twitter status update. Helping new employees understand social media decorum will ensure that senior managers, legal departments, and fellow employees perceive your social onboarding initiative in a positive light.

REFERENCES

1. "Whistle — But Don't Tweet While You Work," October 6, 2009, RHT Survey http://www.roberthalftechnology.com/PressRoom?id=2531

2. Andy Kazeniace, "Social Networks: Facebook Takes Over Top Spot, Twitter Climbs," February 2, 2009 by http://blog.compete.com/2009/02/09/facebook-myspace-twitter-social-network/

3. J. Surowiecki, *The Wisdom of Crowds: Why The Many Are Smarter Than the Few, and How Collective Wisdom Shapes Business, Economies, Societies, and Nations* (New York: Doubleday, 2004)

4. Senior Research Specialist Amanda Lenhart's presentation, "The Democratization of Online Social Networks: A look at the change in demographics of social network users over time," given at AoIR 10.0 in Milwaukee, Wis., on October 8, 2009.

5. L. Reichelt, "Ambient Intimacy," March 1, 2007 http://www.disambiguity.com/ambient-intimacy/

6. http://bit.ly

7. Facebook Pages FAQ: http://www.facebook.com/help.php?page=175

8. A. Lenhart, "Adults and Social Network Sites," January 14, 2009 http://www.pewinternet.org/Reports/2009/Adults-and-Social-Network-Websites

9. 8.3 million in the U.S., according to a 2005 Synovate report commissioned by the Federal Trade Commission Synovate, "Federal Trade Commission - 2006 Identity Theft Survey Report," November 2007 http://ftc.gov/os/2007/11/SynovateFinalReportIDTheft2006.pdf

10. "Gartner Survey Shows Phishing Attacks Escalated in 2007," December 17, 2007 http://www.gartner.com/it/page.jsp?id=565125

11. IBM Social Computing Guidelines http://www.ibm.com/blogs/zz/en/guidelines.html

Chapter 19

Sample New Employee Letters

This section contains sample letters to be used in the New Employee Process. These letters can be mailed to the employee's home, they can be incorporated into a new employee packet, and they can be formatted to be placed on an online new employee training program.

The following types of welcome letters can be found in this chapter:

- A sample welcome letter from the organization to a new employee
- A sample management notification letter from the recruiting department to the manager of the new employee
- A sample welcome letter from the supervisor of the new employee
- A sample welcome letter to a new volunteer member joining an organization

Date

RE: <Position Requisition>

Dear <Employee Name>,

Welcome to Children's Hospitals and Clinics of Minnesota! We are excited and proud to have you join our organization, which champions the special health needs of children and their families.

Sample Welcome Letter submitted by:

Brad Casemore
Children's Hospital of Minnesota
Brad.Casemore@childrensmn.org

Your start date for the above position is <date>.

Along with this letter you will find a copy of your orientation schedule, information on where to park during orientation, a booklet on our Service Standards, and a benefit packet (if benefit eligible).

What to Expect on Day One of New Employee Orientation:

On Day One of orientation we review the mission and vision of Children's. You will see how you can contribute to the mission and vision by making a commitment to live the Service Standards and achieve excellence in everything you do. You will learn about our commitment to provide a Welcoming Environment, quality and patient safety, employee safety, family-centered care, benefits, and more. During the afternoon you will have an opportunity to complete your W4, sign up for direct deposit, and elect your benefits (if benefit eligible). A continental breakfast and lunch will be provided on Day One of orientation.

How to prepare for orientation:

- Read the attached parking information for details on where to park during orientation.
- If your manager has not contacted you regarding when you will be starting in the unit/department, please contact your manager prior to orientation. If you need your manager's contact information, call Human Resources at (612) 813-6227.
- Review the Service Standards booklet, and bring the booklet along with you to orientation on Day One.
- If benefit eligible, review the enclosed benefit packet and bring any questions you may have along with you to orientation.

If you have any questions prior to orientation, please contact Human Resources at (612)813-6227 between the hours of 8:00 A.M.—4:30 P.M., Monday through Friday. Again, welcome. We look forward to your contributions, your accomplishments, and your professional growth as an employee of Children's.

Workforce Planning and Staffing

Children's Hospitals and Clinics of Minnesota

Dear: **(Name)**

I have been notified that you have a new hire coming to you on **(DATE)**.

As part of our onboarding process, I have attached a copy of what we call Orientation Day 2. This pamphlet contains suggestions, procedures, and practices that you as a manager can implement to ensure a comfortable and informative first day for your employee in their new department.

Sample Manager Letter submitted by:

Ron Thomas
RThomas and Associates
Ronald-Thomas@comcast.net

Here at MSLO, Orientation is broken down into two days. Orientation Day 1 is a welcoming into the Company, a day that consists of general information such as company history, benefits, compensation, and IT procedures. Orientation Day 2 (OD2) focuses on familiarizing the employee with their new department and its counterparts. Through this pamphlet we recommend tools to help this process succeed.

What is Onboarding?

Onboarding (Orientation) is the process of integrating new employees and transforming them into productive and committed members of the organization in the shortest possible time.

Everyone has started a new job. But how many of us have good memories of that experience?. Our goal is to make our program a memorable one. On the perfect first day, paperwork would be filled out, your workspace would be set up and stocked with supplies, your manger would welcome you, and a mentor would be assigned to help you navigate the new environment.

Although orientation appears to be purely a transactional activity, it can and should be a strategic process that improves your bottom line. **How?** Remember that new employees start out as liabilities while they learn how to use their skills and experiences to make a positive contribution. The quicker employees get up to speed, the sooner they can begin contributing to your bottom line—regardless of their role or department.

Once again, this document that I have attached will give you a quick overview of important points that you, as a manager, should consider prior to your new employee's starting. This pamphlet highlights practices such as:

- Prepare your staff
- Assign a peer coach
- Set clear expectations
- Prepare new employee packet (suggested)
- Logistics of the work environment
- And more importantly prepare yourself

(continued on next page)

You will be receiving a hard copy of the attached pamphlet. Please take the time to look over this quick read—the procedures will be beneficial to both you and your new employee. If you have any questions or suggestions, please feel free to give either Ron Thomas, VP Organizational Development (x8516) or myself (x8510) a call.

Thank You!

James

[date]

Dear <employee's first name>,

Welcome to <organization> and the <department/function name> team! I am sure that you will soon find that this is a great place to work and that we care about our employees.

Sample Manager Letter submitted by:

Vicki Hoevemeyer
Delta Consulting
vicki_delta@hotmail.com

You are joining an organization that has a long, proud history of leadership in the _____ industry and is widely respected for _____. Your role as a <new employee's job title> is critical in ensuring that we continue provide the kind of <descriptive words—e.g., outstanding, customer-focused, innovative . . . > services/products to our customers for which we are known.

We're excited about your potential here, and I am looking forward to your contributions to the organization. Again, welcome to <organization>!

Sincerely,

<Supervisor Name>

<Supervisor Title>

<Supervisor's Phone Number>

[Date]

Dear Communities In Schools of North Texas Volunteers,

On behalf of our Board of Directors and Staff, I want to express our profound appreciation for the time you have agreed to donate as a volunteer to help students who are at risk of dropping out of school. Time is the most precious donation you can contribute to our organization and we simply cannot say thank you enough. You are the lifeblood of our dropout prevention program.

Sample Manager Letter submitted by:

Communities in Schools of North Texas
www.cisnt.org

The relationships you will be building with students who are victims of poverty will change their lives. A recent study indicates that 80 percent of Texas prison inmates are high school dropouts. Countless other studies have shown that dropping out of school is a process, not an event.

The process of dropping out of school often begins during the elementary years as the academic gap slowly widens. As the student reaches high school, specifically the 9th grade, unless someone like you has become an important person in their life, the gap is simply too wide to close, often as great as four or even five years. It is clear to see how your help in keeping a child victimized by poverty on track academically will change his or her life forever.

I wish you the very best success in your journey as a mentor this year. This journey will offer you joy and frustration, laughter, and maybe even a few tears, but I promise you will receive far more than you give. I look forward to hearing your stories of success!

Thank you for joining the ranks of Communities In Schools of North Texas volunteers!

Sample Welcome Letter submitted by:

Linda G. Duebner
Mary Kay Inc.
Linda.Duebner@mkcorp.com

You're Invited to New Employee Orientation!

Mark your calendar!

You are scheduled to attend New Employee Orientation (NEO) on Date, Time, Location.

What is New Employee Orientation?

NEO is an exciting and inspirational three-day program designed to give you a greater understanding of what makes our company so special and how you fit in the big picture.

While the attached agenda has details about each day, you'll notice that each day has a particular focus:

Day 1 - Make me feel important | **Day 2** - Our Products
Day 3 - Go-Give® spirit

When is it?

NEO begins promptly at 8:30 a.m. and ends by 5:00 p.m. each day. Please arrive by 8:15 a.m. daily to register. If you have scheduling conflicts, discuss them with your supervisor so you can get the most from the three days.

If you do not usually work at The Mary Kay Building and you arrive before 8:00 a.m., please press the intercom button by the glass doors and explain that you are here for New Employee Orientation.

What should I wear?

Professional attire is required at The Mary Kay Building. For detailed information about dress code, please click here to read about the dress code on InsideMK.

On the afternoon of Day 2, we will tour local Mary Kay facilities, including our Manufacturing facility and ASRS, our Corporate Warehouse facility. In order to comply with regulations at these facilities, be sure to wear **closed-toe shoes that have a fully closed heel that is no higher than 1.5".** Mules and sling-backs are not appropriate. Feel free to bring an extra pair of low-heeled shoes or tennis shoes – we'll be doing a lot of walking.

Please wear your **security badge and NEO name tag** for ID purposes.

What about food?

Breakfast, lunch, and snacks will be provided each day. If you have special dietary requests, please contact Employee & Organization Development so we can accommodate your needs.

What else?

On Tuesday afternoon, we will tour Mary Kay Ash's office, so don't forget your camera!

MARY KAY

Chapter 20

Building Relationships: A Checklist

Contributed By: Vicki Hoevemeyer, Owner/Consultant, Delta Consulting

Vicki's Contact Information

vicki_delta@hotmail.com
Palatine, IL 60074

About the Author: Vicki Hoevemeyer has over 20 years of organizational development and management/leadership development experience as both an internal and external consultant, providing services to transportation, retail, healthcare, education, building materials, nonprofit, and light and heavy manufacturing organizations in California, Arizona, Colorado, Michigan, and Illinois.

Vicki has a bachelor's degree in Social Work from Western Michigan University, and a master's degree in Organizational Development from Eastern Michigan University. She is the author of *High-Impact Interview Questions: 701 Behavior-Based Questions to Find the Right Person for Every Job* (AMACOM, 2005) and coauthor of *First-Job Survival Guide: How to Thrive and Advance in Your New Career* (JIST, 2006).

BETTER ORGANIZATIONAL SAVVY THROUGH A CHECKLIST PROCESS

The "Building Relationships Checklist" provides direction to new leaders regarding critical first contacts, and it provides the structure to assist the new employee to begin establishing relationships during the first few weeks of employment. This checklist is especially helpful for new leaders and executives, whose success is contingent upon a smooth assimilation into the organization and the ability to quickly learn who to contact to get things done.

When a new leader comes on board and is one of a multitude of management people in the organization, they have no idea who it would be most advantageous for them to meet and get to know early on in their career. The Building Relationships

Checklist is designed to identify those critical must-meet individuals. There are two primary reasons organizations should use this process:

1. People need to feel connected to others at work. One of the best pieces of supporting evidence for this is from Gallup, who found that one of the 12 indicators of engagement and retention is workplace relationships. As a result, on the Gallup 12 one of the survey items is "I have a best friend at work."

2. In order for a leader to be successful, it is imperative that he or she be given an opportunity to understand key departmental connections and interdependencies as soon as possible.

We all remember coming into new organizations where there are hundreds of other managers. Trying to figure out who to talk to and start building relationships with early on is often left to happenstance. That does nothing to engage the new leader and or to help him/her develop the kind of relationships that will be critical to his/her success. The feedback I have received from new leaders who have been provided with this opportunity is that it makes them feel that the company wants them to be successful and is making sure that they meet the people they need to build relationships with to be successful and help their department and the organization be successful.

USING THE BUILDING RELATIONSHIPS CHECKLIST

Using the sample Building Relationships Checklist in this section, and the steps below, create your own custom checklist to match your organizational structure and needs:

1. Human Resources meets with the hiring manager to review the process and the checklist. The "Other" section at the end of the form is where the hiring manager/HR manager can insert the names of non-management people, vendors, customers, or others with whom it is critical for the new leader to meet during the first three weeks.

2. Identify the critical "must-meet" people in the organization. These are people that the new leader needs to meet and start building relationships with *during the first three weeks of his/her employment.*

3. Human Resources finalizes the Building Relationship Checklist and puts it in the New Leader Onboarding Packet for discussion with the new leader on his or her first day.

The Building Relationships Checklist is developed prior to the new leader's first day and is presented to the new leader as part of the packet of onboarding information he/she receives on the first day.

Tip for Success: If HR does not get the completed checklist back from the new leader in three weeks, the HR person should follow up with the new leader to find out the status of the checklist. In some situations, the HR person will need to "run interference" to set up these meetings. In addition, assuming HR or someone else in the organization is doing a 90-day check-in with the new leader, the value of this process should be discussed with the new leader.

Building Relationships Checklist

Name		Title	
Start Date		Reports To	

Welcome to [company]! While we want all of our leaders to develop strong working relationships with each other, we realize it is not always feasible to meet and spend some time with all the other leaders during your first few weeks. For your position, your manager has identified a number of other leaders for you to meet with initially. Please spend time with each of them to find out a little bit about them and their department.

Within the next three weeks, please have one-on-one meetings with the individuals who have been checked off below, indicating the date you met with the person in the "date completed" column. During these meetings, please focus on learning about that individual's area of responsibility.

When you have finished with these meetings, please sign and date the bottom of the last page and send a copy of this Checklist to [name and department]. If you have any questions, please contact [name] at [number/ext.].

Department		Name	Title	Ext. #	Date Completed
	☐				
	☐				
	☐				
	☐				
	☐				
	☐				
	☐				
	☐				
	☐				
	☐				
	☐				
	☐				
	☐				
	☐				
Other	☐				
	☐				

Employee's Signature _____   Date _____

Chapter 21

Win, Win, Win! Evaluation Tools and Metrics

Contributed By: Robert C. Bilotti, Managing Director, Novita Training and Onboarding

About the Author: Robert Bilotti is the Managing Director of Novita and an expert on the subject of new employee onboarding. He has appeared on numerous talk shows and in print discussing what makes for an

Robert's Contact Information:

www.novitaunique.com
robert.bilotti@novitaunique.com
Chicago, IL & Montclair, NJ
773-590-3636

effective new employee program—not just to the benefit of the new employee but that of the entire organization.

Robert's company, Novita, is an employee training and development firm and specializes in this topic. Robert is also an award-winning training developer and strategist, and a former Training Manager for a consumer packaged goods (CPG) company.

HOW DO I DEMONSTRATE THE VALUE OF OUR ONBOARDING PROGRAM?

If you are in charge of your organization's new employee onboarding program, chances are one or more of the following statements is probably true:

- You have more projects on your to-do list than you have budget to complete.
- You have a boss/executive board/finance department who is interested in the impact of the program on the organization and the bottom line.
- Your performance review (and perhaps your compensation) is partially based on this impact.

Don't fret. There is good news! Measuring the impact of a new employee onboarding program is easier than you might think. It's easier than the measurement of other people development initiatives. In fact, we tell our clients that if they are choosing between two or more similar initiatives on which to spend their budget dollars, choose onboarding!

When you consider that CFOs reject 90 percent of all Human Resources proposals (based on a study done by Gately Consulting) and that 50 percent of this decision is based on the financial impact of the proposal, you'll want to include solid numbers in your proposal and in your measurement of the impact. "Smile sheets" will not do. Fortunately, when it comes to onboarding, there are many other significant measures.

We also tell our clients to be a little selfish. A successful onboarding program can be great exposure for you and can positively impact your career with what we call "The Three V's":

- **Visibility**—Onboarding reaches all levels of an organization, including VP and C-level, which means everyone in the organization will have exposure to your program.
- **Validity**—Each incoming employee will have a positive first impression of you and your department. This helps you now and down the road, for when you go to employees with another program, they are eager to accept it and help since they had a good onboarding experience.
- **Value**—Onboarding has proven Return On Investment (R.O.I.), satisfying the needs of decision makers and tying back to your organization's goals.

It's like a win, win, win for new employees, the organization, and you. The caveat? Any positive impact onboarding can make is based on the program's being well developed and well executed.

THE POTENTIAL IMPACT OF ONBOARDING

How do you calculate all this wonderful R.O.I.? Before you can begin measuring, you have to understand what the potential impact is. In other words, what areas of the organization can onboarding affect? Probably more than you might first think. Based on our work with organizations, we have compiled the following list. Some are fairly obvious. Others you may not have considered.

- *Productivity*—the productivity of new employees and the counterproductivity of all employees
- *Time to productivity*—how quickly a new employee reaches full efficiency
- *Retention*—the opposite of turnover, which impacts the cost of hiring
- *Satisfaction*—how satisfied new employees are with their job and their decision to join the company
- *Employee referrals*—the likelihood that new employees will refer candidates
- *Innovation*—capturing new employees' new ideas

- *Culture*—the fabric of many companies, which can be easily disturbed
- *Safety*—can be costly in more ways than money
- *Compliance*—an informed new employee commits fewer violations
- *Loyalty*—your company's commitment to a new employee is often returned

In case you are wondering what "counterproductivity" is, think about it this way. A new employee can affect the productivity of other employees, both positively and negatively. How? Suppose a new employee is always interrupting others to ask questions (because he doesn't have all the needed information) or makes mistakes which involve others . . . that's counterproductive.

DIRECT VERSUS INDIRECT IMPACT

If you look at the above list, you can probably begin to see how you might measure such potential impacts. You might also begin to see that some of these measures have a direct impact—meaning they are directly tied to dollars and the bottom line, while others have an *indirect* impact. The impact is still there, and it can be significant, but it might be more circuitously tied to the bottom line.

Let's look at each and decide if it's direct or indirect and some sample ways to measure it.

Measuring the Impact

Impact	Direct or Indirect?	Sample Metrics

Productivity	Direct	The most direct with a wide array of measures. Caveat: some jobs (i.e., sales) are easier to measure than others. Examples:
		■ Quantitative measure of job duty or objective:
		  • Sales
		  • Customer complaints
		  • Production units
		  • Reporting errors
		■ Organizational measures, such as incremental revenue or reduction of costs
		■ Counterproductivity. Example: number of calls to the IT help desk
		■ Before and after performance ratings and evaluations

Time to productivity	Direct	A measure of productivity but about how long instead of how much. Examples: ■ Time to first sale or successful completion of other job-specific task ■ Time to full productivity as compared to "veteran" employee
Retention	Direct	The high cost of repeated hiring is well documented. Very easy to measure and huge impact. Example: ■ Turnover within first year
Satisfaction	Indirect	Similar to "buyer's remorse" and contributes indirectly to several other categories. Examples: ■ Employee satisfaction ■ Before and after "New Employee" survey
Employee referrals	Direct	Like retention, can have a huge impact and is easy to measure. Example: ■ Number of employee referrals from first-year employees

(continued on next page)

Impact	Direct or Indirect?	Sample Metrics
Innovation	Indirect	Indirect in that it can impact productivity and cost-savings. Examples: ■ Number of suggestions ■ Number of improved processes ■ Manager and leadership feedback
Culture	Indirect	Some would call it assimilation; it often affects counterproductivity. Examples: ■ Number of manager interventions ■ Number of HR interventions ■ Manager and leadership feedback
Safety	Direct	Can relate directly to bottom-line costs and is a very big concern. Examples: ■ Insurance expenses ■ Medical expenses ■ Safety fines ■ Number of accidents
Compliance	Direct	Can relate directly to bottom-line costs and is a very big concern. Examples: ■ Number of HR infractions ■ Legal expenses
Loyalty	Indirect	Encompasses elements of retention, satisfaction, and culture. Examples: ■ Before and after "New Employee" survey.

ESTABLISHING A BENCHMARK

You'll notice several comparisons of "before and after." A common mistake is measuring the effectiveness of a program once it is in place, without first measuring the situation *before the program was in place.* This is called establishing the benchmark, and just as you should do a "before" survey in order to later compare it to an "after" survey, you should measure sales, calls to the IT help desk, HR infractions, number of accidents, etc., before you implement your new or updated program. This will give you a baseline for comparing the *same* measures after implementation.

NEW EMPLOYEE SURVEYS

Particularly with indirect impacts, a survey is many times part of your measurement (but should not be the only measurement as surveys are the least-regarded metric by finance/bosses/executives). To create your survey, work backwards. In other words, think about the potential impacts we have discussed or other objectives you might have for your onboarding programs, and write survey questions that will allow you to quantify these concepts. Wherever possible, make the questions closed-ended, though allowing for additional open-ended comments is many times where you will obtain the most useful (and interesting) feedback.

A few tips about your New Employee survey:

- Choose employees who were hired no more than one year ago unless that will give you too small a sample, in which case you should then open it up.
- Aim for at least 10 to 20 people to make the results worthwhile.
- Promise anonymity or, better yet, use an outside vendor. Surveys conducted by third parties always get better (more honest) results because employees are less worried about repercussions.
- Survey all new employees, not just administrators or contributors. Executives are not too busy to participate.
- Have employees complete it online (there are several easy-to-use, inexpensive online survey tools).
- Make it easy to understand and short but not too short. Be cognizant of people's time, but don't miss asking about important details.

We have found in implementing surveys for our clients that new employees *want* to talk about their experience—whether good or bad. And get ready for some interesting reading! New employees tend not to hold back. We've done surveys where those who have been on the job a year remember very minute details.

SOME EXAMPLES OF MEASURED RESULTS

Over the years, Novita has measured the impact of the onboarding programs we have built and implemented for organizations. A few of them include:

- Over a one-year period, a retail client's employee turnover was reduced by 35 percent.
- A home-services company saw a 23 percent improvement in the "time to first sale"; what used to take 67 days was taking 52 days.
- That same organization saw a 17 percent average increase in sales in a new employee's first year, from $500,000 to $585,000.
- A financial services client reported calls to the IT help desk within a new employee's first 90 days were reduced by 52 percent. This may not sound like a big deal, but think about the fewer needed man-hours and hardware.
- Following are the results of a New Employee Survey conducted before and after our program was implemented:

Percentage of New Employees Who . . .	Before	After	Difference
Felt satisfied with his or her new job . . .	59%	84%	+ 25%
Would recommend company to other candidates . . .	61%	82%	+21%
Found their workspace properly equipped and ready . . .	53%	86%	+33%
Rated their onboarding experience 4 or 5 (out of 5) . . .	53%	88%	+35%

INTERNAL MEASURES—THE FLIP SIDE OF R.O.I.

There are two sides to R.O.I.—the "return" and the "investment." So far, we have focused on the return. But if you achieve a high return only by making an equally large investment, the R.O.I. is negated.

The trick is a *high* return from a *small* investment, thus a higher R.O.I. To determine this, you should also be measuring internally, using metrics such as:

- Onboarding costs including materials, tools, room logistics, travel, etc.
- "Live" orientation costs versus online
- Development costs, but also time spent managing and implementing the program

For example, your onboarding program may be wildly effective (return) but if it costs a bundle and takes up too much of your time and everyone else's (investment), is it producing the desired R.O.I.? Suppose you had executives speak at a monthly new employee workshop. That usually scores high with new employees because they like to get face time with such people, but think about the drain on the executives and the "cost" of having them appear each month. What if you produced a video of the executives instead? The results might not be as good, but you'd be saving on the investment in the long run, and so have a higher R.O.I.

Examples of our clients' reduction of investment:

- A consumer products company reduced the number of "live" orientation days per year from 12 to 6, decreasing faculty costs by 50 percent, saving $115,000 per year in travel expense, and reducing lost productivity
- At a university, the time Human Resources spent per month managing the onboarding program was cut from 5 days to 2, leading to greater departmental productivity, improved individual performance, work satisfaction, and compensation

MOTIVATING MANAGERS WITH METRICS

Like many employee-development initiatives, managers play a critical role in the success (or failure) of a new employee onboarding program. What's more, some managers are not always "onboard" when it comes to implementing the new program, for fear of increased responsibility, skeptical of the as-of-yet unproven results, or simply fearful of change.

One way to motivate managers to take ownership of their share of onboarding (in our view, managers should not own the entire program or process) is by measuring how well new employees who report to them perform. Metrics such as their direct-report's productivity, retention, compliance, safety, innovation, etc., within the first six months can be used as a reflection of the manager's effectiveness when it comes to new employees. We encourage clients to include such measures in all people managers' performance review and objectives. It's a simple but powerful step to make onboarding top-of-mind.

What's more, managers are motivated by their peers' results from the program (many managers don't like to be the first one in the water), so be sure as you measure to promote and communicate the R.O.I. of your program to managers and the entire organization. (Remember the Three V's? Toot your own horn!)

METRICS AS A DRIVER OF ONBOARDING

Remember, the metrics mentioned should be used to measure your onboarding program once implemented, but should also *drive* the development of your program. Only then will you account for all the major impact areas that are most important to your organization.

As a final note, it's also worth repeating that the impact of an onboarding program can be significant, but only if it is well developed *and effectively executed*. There are too many instances of well-conceived programs failing to achieve their intended results due to poor execution.

For more information, you can visit www.novitaunique.com.

Chapter 22

I'm New Here: What Should I Learn?

Contributed By: Doris Sims, SPHR, President of Succession Builders, LLC

Doris's Contact Information:

Succession Builders, LLC
www.successionbuilders.com
doris@successionbuilders.com
214-906-3155

About the Author: Doris M. Sims, SPHR is the Founder and President of Succession Builders, LLC, a talent management, succession planning, and new talent onboarding consulting firm. Her experience in organizational development spans over 20 years working in Fortune 100 and Fortune 500 companies. Doris received her master's degree in Human Resource Development from Indiana State University.

Doris is the coauthor of the talent management books *Building Tomorrow's Talent: A Practitioner's Guide to Talent Management and Succession Planning; The 30-Minute Guide to Talent and Succession Management;* and *The Talent Review Meeting Facilitation Guide.* Doris is also the author of the McGraw-Hill book *Creative New Employee Orientation Programs,* and has contributed articles to many other McGraw-Hill books and multiple periodicals, including *Training Magazine, Talent Management Magazine, Professionals in Human Resources,* and *The Consultant's Toolkit.*

DETERMINE THE NEW EMPLOYEE'S TRAINING NEEDS USING COMPETENCY CHARTS

A new employee's orientation needs don't end after the initial orientation class. After the new employee completes the general orientation, the manager and the employee should meet to discuss additional new employee training needs, based on specific competencies for the position and the employee's current competencies.

Using a competency analysis and a personalized training plan approach for new employees creates the following positive results:

- The employee becomes more productive in a shorter amount of time.

- Training needs and solutions are identified using a planned, systematic approach, rather than a haphazard, hit-or-miss approach.

- The new employees' job satisfaction and morale increase because they feel more comfortable and confident earlier in the position, and they feel valued because their development needs are being addressed.

- Once the personalized training plans are identified for new employees, the manager's time is reduced because new employees have plans to follow on their own; the manager should review the employees' progress toward completing the training plans at periodic intervals.

- Areas of training development needs are identified (rather than falling through the cracks), because the charts are developed for each position; the department will likely identify competencies for which there are currently no training materials available.

- Accuracy of the transfer of information to new employees increases; without a systematic approach to training new employees on the job, the risk that they will be trained incorrectly or that they will receive misinformation is higher.

A STEP-BY-STEP APPROACH: USING COMPETENCY CHARTS TO IDENTIFY NEEDS

Use the competency charts in this chapter to identify the job functional competencies. Compare these charts to the employee's current competency set, and then develop a personalized training plan for the employee, following the steps outlined here.

Step 1: Identify the Competencies Needed for Each Job in the Department

Before new employees arrive, the manager (working with members of the team and with the assistance of training or human resource personnel, if desired) needs to determine the Knowledge, Technical/Computer Skills, and Nontechnical Skills and Behaviors for each position in the department. This will become the "model competency chart" for each position, so it is important to include the competencies of the most highly competent employees in the department. But it is also important to include the ideas the newer, less experienced employees will have regarding "What I wish someone had taught me" when they first arrived on the job.

Ideally, a competency identification team composed of the department manager or supervisor, one or two experienced, highly competent employees, and one or two new employees should meet face-to-face to brainstorm, discuss, and finalize the competencies needed for each job function within the department.

Step 2: Complete the Competency Charts to Record the Data from Step 1

To complete the Job Functional Competency Chart provided with the information identified by the competency identification team, enter the job title, the date the competency chart was prepared, and the name or title of the person (or group) who prepared the chart. Then enter the description of each competency needed for the position, using the categories Knowledge, Technical/Computer Skills, and Nontechnical Skills and Behaviors to guide you.

Next, use the rating scale in the second column to determine the level of knowledge or skill needed in the position, referring to the scale definitions at the top of the chart. For example, retail employees need to have an awareness of the company's organizational structure (a level-1 training need), but they need to know the products they will be selling at a highly accurate level on a daily basis (a level-3 training need).

Then, identify the training resources that are currently available for each item. Training resources may be formal (instructor-led classes, online classes, a procedure guide, a job aid) or informal (for example, meet with Justin to obtain a demonstration, or sit with Carol while she answers customer calls). If no training resource is available and the item is a mid- to high-level priority, a training resource needs to be developed.

Step 3: Meet with the New Employee to Identify Individual Training Needs

Once the charts are complete for each job function in the department, copies can be made to use as worksheets during meetings between new employees and the manager. The manager should enter the new employee's name on each chart. Then, the manager and employee discuss each competency and the knowledge or skill level needed for the new employee's job function, and then compare that to the employee's current knowledge or skill level for that item. The manager then circles *Yes* or *No* on the chart to indicate if training is needed for that item.

After completing this exercise, the manager can summarize the training the employee needs to obtain on the Individual Training Plan Summary chart provided.

Then, with the employee's personalized training plan developed, the information can be entered into the form online. The employee receives a copy to use as a checklist as he or she completes the training plan, and the manager retains a copy. The employee can now use this customized training plan to schedule training courses, to determine coworkers to meet with to obtain specific information or skills, and to determine what to read on the job to learn policies and procedures.

Step 4: Meet with the Employee Periodically to Review Training Progress

The manager and the employee should meet at periodic intervals to discuss the new employee's progress in obtaining the training and competencies that have been identified for him or her on the chart.

Step 5: Update the Charts Regularly

Review and update the charts on a periodic basis, to ensure that competencies reflect the current job requirements for each position and the organization's current strategic goals.

Job Functional Competency Chart—Knowledge

Enter a description for each concept an employee in this position will need to know. Identify the knowledge level needed for each item to be successful in the position. List the training resources available for each item. Then circle the employee's current knowledge level for each item, and identify whether the employee needs training for the item. Complete this form for each job title in the department. An example follows.

Department Name/Job Title: _____ Date: _____ Prepared By: _____

Employee Name: _____ Starting Date: _____

Knowledge Level Rating Descriptions:

1 = Has/needs an awareness   2 = Has/needs to use this knowledge occasionally   3 = Has/needs to use this knowledge on a daily basis

Describe the concepts an employee will need to know to perform this job	Knowledge Level Needed	List Training Resources Available	Employee's Current Level	Is Training Needed?
	1 2 3		1 2 3	Yes No
	1 2 3		1 2 3	Yes No
	1 2 3		1 2 3	Yes No
	1 2 3		1 2 3	Yes No
	1 2 3		1 2 3	Yes No
	1 2 3		1 2 3	Yes No
	1 2 3		1 2 3	Yes No
	1 2 3		1 2 3	Yes No
	1 2 3		1 2 3	Yes No
	1 2 3		1 2 3	Yes No

Job Functional Competency Chart— Technical Skills

Enter a description for each technical skill an employee in this position will need to have. Identify the skill level needed for each item to be successful in the position. List the training resources available for each item. Then circle the employee's current skill level for each item, and identify whether the employee needs training for the item. Complete this form for each job title in the department.

Department Name/Job Title: _____   Date: _____   Prepared By: _____

Employee Name: _____   Starting Date: _____

Skill Level Rating Descriptions:

1 = Has/needs basic skill level   2 = Has/needs an intermediate skill level   3 = Has/needs an advanced skill level

Describe the concepts an employee will need to know to perform this job	Knowledge Level Needed	List Training Resources Available	Employee's Current Level	Is Training Needed?
	1 2 3		1 2 3	Yes No
	1 2 3		1 2 3	Yes No
	1 2 3		1 2 3	Yes No
	1 2 3		1 2 3	Yes No
	1 2 3		1 2 3	Yes No
	1 2 3		1 2 3	Yes No
	1 2 3		1 2 3	Yes No
	1 2 3		1 2 3	Yes No
	1 2 3		1 2 3	Yes No
	1 2 3		1 2 3	Yes No

Job Functional Competency Chart— Behavioral Skills

Enter a description for each behavior an employee in this position will need to demonstrate. Identify the behavioral skill level needed for each item to be successful in the position. List the training resources available for each item.

When you meet with a new employee, circle the employee's current behavioral skill level for each item, and identify whether the employee needs training for the item.

Department Name/Job Title: _____ Date: _____ Prepared By: _____

Employee Name: _____ Starting Date: _____

Behavioral Skill Level Rating Descriptions:

1 = Has/needs basic skill level   2 = Has/needs an intermediate skill level   3 = Has/needs an advanced skill level

Describe the concepts an employee will need to know to perform this job	Knowledge Level Needed	List Training Resources Available	Employee's Current Level	Is Training Needed?
	1 2 3		1 2 3	Yes No
	1 2 3		1 2 3	Yes No
	1 2 3		1 2 3	Yes No
	1 2 3		1 2 3	Yes No
	1 2 3		1 2 3	Yes No
	1 2 3		1 2 3	Yes No
	1 2 3		1 2 3	Yes No
	1 2 3		1 2 3	Yes No
	1 2 3		1 2 3	Yes No
	1 2 3		1 2 3	Yes No

Individual Training Plan Summary

This training plan is designed for: _____

Employee's start date: _____   Today's date _____   Prepared by _____

After the manager and employee have discussed and recorded the competency needs and the employee's current competency levels on each competency chart, this page can be used to summarize the information to create a customized training plan for the employee.

Description of the training to obtain	Who to contact for this training	Date and location	Knowledge/Skill level to attain	Complete training within…	✓
			1 2 3	First month First 90 days First Year	
			1 2 3	First month First 90 days First Year	
			1 2 3	First month First 90 days First Year	
			1 2 3	First month First 90 days First Year	
			1 2 3	First month First 90 days First Year	

If needed, make multiple copies of this form to record all applicable training needs for each employee.

189

Chapter 23

Helping Managers Onboard New Employees at Martha Stewart Living

Contributed By: Ron Thomas, Founder, RThomas and Associates.

About the Author: Ron Thomas, founder of RThomas and Associates, has over 15 years' experience in Human Resources and training and development. He was the former Vice President of Human Resources/Organizational Development at Martha Stewart Living. Prior to joining Martha Stewart he was Regional Training Manager for IBM Global Learning Services (Catapult Divisions-NY).

Ron's Contact Information:

Ronald-thomas@comcast.net
917.902.6164
26 Elk Road
Verona, NJ 07044
www.strategyfocusedhr.com
www.linkedin.com/in/
ronaldthomaslinkedin
Twitter: Ronald_thomas

Ron's work has been featured in the *Wall Street Journal, Chief Learning Officer Magazine, Workforce Management,* and *Crain's New York Business.* His blog, "Strategy Focused HR," has a national and international following. He is a guest blogger at PongoResume.com. In 2008 he was honored as "HR Person of the Year" by the New York–based HR Network. He is a sought-after speaker on the strategic impact of HR and has written numerous articles on human resources; he is a member of the Senior HR Executive Exchange program sponsored by the Society of Human Resources (SHRM).

A PRACTICAL GUIDE FOR MANAGERS TO EFFECTIVELY BRING NEW EMPLOYEES ONBOARD

Managers at Martha Stewart Living OmniMedia (MSO) and in all organizations are faced with harsh business realities in the war for talent:

- Employees no longer have loyalty to one employer.

- Employees are looking for organizations that can build their skills and experience and make them more valuable resources.

- Managers are pressured to maximize the return on talent more quickly and more efficiently than ever before.

- As a result, managers must balance leadership with management, creativity with control, and the needs of people with productivity.

What do effective managers do in this challenging environment? Effective managers focus on assimilating new employees, giving them the tools and resources they need to perform for the company and succeed in their careers. Without a proper plan for bringing new employees on board, managers run the risk of miscommunication of goals and expectations, sub-par performance, lower morale, bad decisions, and potential financial loss in the form of employee turnover.

In order to properly onboard new employees, it is important to understand the key reasons why new employees fail. Employees often:

- Are unclear or confused over key expectations, agreements, and ways of working to support others and superiors

- Fail to learn the job, the company, and the business quickly enough

- Fail to mesh with the existing culture

- Lack professional growth in skill areas where there are gaps

To avoid these pitfalls and give our managers the tools they need to properly assimilate new employees, the MSO organization created an "Orientation Day 2 Guide" that includes a step-by-step comprehensive plan for assimilating new employees into the department. Three key steps in the department orientation process include:

1. Prepare for New Employee (in advance of the employee's arrival)

2. Conduct Departmental Orientation (afternoon of first day or following morning)

3. Follow Up on Progress of New Employee (one to two weeks later)

This article includes our sample letter to the managers of new employees, as well as examples from our Leader's Guide and Orientation Day 2 Curriculum.

Sample Letter to Managers of New Employees

To help managers implement Orientation Day 2, the MSO organization has created guidelines, tools, and checklists for each step of the process. Your department is like a machine that runs with very few, but critical components. If one of those components is missing, it can make a big difference in performance. It is very important, therefore, that you replace a lost component as rapidly and effectively as possible. This guide is your tool for doing so!

All too often, a new employee's orientation is a haphazard, unplanned affair. Many managers take the sink or swim approach by abdicating responsibility and shifting the burden of orientation to the new employee. The manager, relieved that a vacant slot has finally been filled, resumes his or her duties and assumes that the newcomer will show some hustle and figure the system out. Most do, but not without a lot of fear, frustration, resentment, wasted time, and misdirected effort.

Clearly this type of manager has forgotten what it feels like to be new on a job and working in unfamiliar surroundings among strangers. From a human relations point of view, this rather callous approach does not reflect a supportive and caring environment—factors on which many employees place a high premium.

Many people would question the values of an organization that fails to meet basic employee needs at a time when they are most vulnerable. Moreover, they would also have second thoughts about the skill level of a manager who is not prepared and/or not committed to helping new employees succeed. From a business point of view, the manager has wasted valuable company resources through a lack of organization and planning, and a fundamental misunderstanding of the need for a proper orientation process.

Don't let this be you! Take this opportunity and read through the guidelines, tools, and checklists and get your new employees onboard effectively!

MSO University: Orientation Day Two

Why focus on new employee orientation?

Orientation is an opportunity to motivate your employees.

Most new employees begin the job with a high degree of motivation. They are very eager to learn and have a great desire to succeed. By taking advantage of this enthusiasm by channeling it constructively and nurturing it with positive initial experience, you ensure that new employees get off to the right start and retain a good feeling about the job and the company.

Set the Tone. As the manager, you are the person most responsible for setting the tone that greets new employees on their first day of the job. The steps you take, both before and after a new employee starts, can have short-term and long-term effects on that employee's performance and overall career with the company.

Provide Feedback. Give the new employee plenty of feedback. There's a tendency to "go easy" on the new worker those first few weeks and not say much about how his or her performance measures up. But most would prefer to know either that they are progressing normally or that they are doing something wrong so that they can correct the solution.

Express Confidence in Employees. Build up the new worker's self-confidence. Tell new hires that you expect them to succeed and that you'll do everything possible to help them. Make sure that they have the time to learn the basics of the job before you apply performance pressure.

Be Accessible. Let new hires know that you will be there to provide information and assistance when they need it. Make sure that you check in with them regularly to answer questions, to provide resource materials, and most important, to give support and reassurance when necessary. Your accessibility during the orientation period demonstrates to the new employee a high level of management support and encouragement.

Support Your Employee in Assimilating to the Culture. The new employee must assimilate a large amount of new job-related information rapidly in order to be a fully functioning team player. The list below outlines some things you can do to facilitate the process of assimilation.

Use a Systematic Approach. One factor that makes a positive impression on new employees is a high level of organization. If right from the beginning you appear to be organized and on top of things—to know the answers to any questions the new employee might have, to have all the necessary resource materials right at hand— the employee will immediately develop confidence in you and your abilities.

(*continued on next page*)

STREAMLINE THE LEARNING PROCESS

Group Information Logically. It makes sense to proceed in a logical fashion, rather than skip from services, to vacation schedule, to how the employee should get to work. By grouping related items of information together, you will increase the new hire's ability to retain what he or she has learned.

Put Important Information in Writing. An employee handbook summarizing the more important policies and procedures is a good way of reinforcing the information that has been discussed. A map of the facility showing the location of entrances and exits, rest rooms, lunchroom, offices, and similar facilities, is also a good idea.

Check Progress. To ensure steady progress, you should review what has been learned at the end of each day for a certain period of time. This can be done either by you or by the employee's mentor. It is also a good time to see if the new employee has any questions and to praise him or her for catching on quickly.

COMMON PITFALLS TO AVOID WHEN BRINGING ON A NEW EMPLOYEE:

- Make sure a work area has not been created or assigned. (Let him sit in a hall or share a cube!)
- Schedule the new employee to start work while her supervisor is on vacation.
- Leave the new employee standing in the company reception area for a half hour while the reception staff tries to figure out what to do with him.
- Leave the new employee at her workstation, to manage on her own, while coworkers pair up and head out to lunch.
- Show the new employee his office and don't introduce him to coworkers or assign him a mentor.
- Assign the new employee to a staff person who has a major career-impacting deadline in three days.
- Assign the new employee to (you fill in the blanks!) your most unhappy, negative, company-bashing, staff member.
- Assign the employee "busy work" that has nothing to do with her core job description, because you are having a busy week.

MSO University: Orientation Day Two, Step One

STEP 1: PREPARE FOR THE NEW EMPLOYEE

An employee's first day on the job can leave a lasting impression. By preparing in advance and following an orderly and systematic approach, the manager can make a positive lasting impression. In order to help the employee's first day in the department run smoothly, there are a few key activities a manager should complete in advance:

<u>Prepare your staff—</u>

To conduct an effective orientation, you will need the cooperation of your staff. In order to obtain their cooperation, you will need to brief them on the new employee and your expectations of the role they will play in helping the new employee adapt. Listed below is some information you'll want to cover with your staff.

- Employee name and brief background information
- Start date
- Roles various staff members will play in the orientation
- Impact that a new employee might have on them

By asking various members of your staff to participate in the orientation process, they will have a vested interest in creating a successful orientation. This can be done informally but it is often effective in the form of an e-mail or memo. **A sample departmental memo is included in the Tools section.** Please note: It is also important to alert your department Business Manager to the new employee's arrival, especially if the new employee will be completing expense reports for himself and/or others.

<u>Assign a peer coach to assist the new employee when he/she arrives—</u>

To help new employees move smoothly through the orientation period, many organizations assign a sponsor or peer coach to new employees. A peer coach should be someone who knows the job and the company culture and can help the new employee "learn the ropes" quickly and avoid pitfalls. Typically, the peer coach is an experienced employee with a successful track record and good attitude. In addition to these attributes, you should also consider the following when selecting a peer coach.

Relevant Knowledge and Skills: Is the individual highly skilled in the area in which the new hire will be working? Will he/she be a role model, demonstrating the type of behavior you want to reinforce?

Teaching Ability: Does the individual enjoy teaching/helping others? Is he/she patient and sympathetic? Does he/she have the experience and know-how to answer questions?

(continued on next page)

Flexibility: Will the individual adjust his/her schedule to spend time with the new employee? Can he/she relate well to others with different personalities?

Sense of Humor: Does the person have a sense of humor? Can he/she ease tension and anxiety with a little humor at the right time?

Clarify your expectations of the new employee—

Short-term: Make a list of activities that the new employee can focus on 1) the first day and 2) the first week on the job. Example activities include:

- Reviewing the INET for information
- Reading the MSO Annual Report
- Completing a mini-project
- Shadowing other team members to learn the job and get up to speed quickly
- Taking an online training course to sharpen skills

Long-term: Write out the goals you would like this employee to accomplish within six months to one year. Example goals include:

- Own and complete a substantial project within the first six months,
- Actively contribute to major department project by gathering research and contributing ideas/ input,
- Get acclimated to MSO by understanding/articulating the business strategy, goals and objectives and
- Complete two online training courses in first year.

Be prepared to discuss the goals you've identified in detail with the employee upon his/her arrival. **Have the employee write down the goals on the Goals/Expectations Template.**

Prepare New Employee Packet—

To help the employee get up to speed quickly, it is best to compile a folder with all the relevant department information. Below is a suggested list of what to include

- Agenda for the Day
- Agenda for Manager Meeting
- Department Organization/List of Members with Titles
- Department Goals and Objectives
- Job Description for New Employee
- Goal/Expectations Template

(continued on next page)

- List of Recommended Activities for the first day/week
- List of Recommended Training Courses
- Floor plan(s)
- Agenda for Peer Coach Meeting
- Agenda for Business Manager Meeting, if necessary

<u>Ensure that logistics have been taken care of for the new employee—</u>

Ensure that the new employee has a space to work with the right tools (i.e., computer) and any other necessary resources when he or she arrives.

<u>Prepare Yourself—</u>

Schedule time on your calendar to meet with the new employee on his or her first day and throughout the first week. As the manager, time you spend with the employee is most important in clearly articulating the goals of your department and what you expect of the new employee in support of those goals.

Also, create a checklist for yourself of important points you want to communicate to the new employee on his/her first day. Important points may include:

- Follow-up on items from Orientation Day 1, such as HR-related paperwork
- Key responsibilities of the new employee,
- Goals and expectations for the first 6 months to a year,
- How the department communicates (i.e., weekly status meeting day and time),
- Activities the employee should focus on during first day/week,
- Your preferred working style (i.e., collaborative or hands-off), and
- Other key departmental policies and procedures.

Ensure that the new employee's job description is up-to-date and accurately reflects the requirements and responsibilities of the job. An updated job description will be helpful to you in communicating clearly what is expected of the new employee. An updated version of the job description should be submitted to the Frank Heller, Director of Recruiting, prior to the new employee's arrival.

TOOLS

- Sample new employee announcement e-mail/memo
- Sample agenda for new employee's first day in the department
- Sample meeting agenda for Employee/Manager meeting
- Overview of Orientation Day One and sample follow-up points
- Sample department organization and/or list of department members with titles
- Sample department goals and objectives
- Sample job description for new employee
- Goals/Expectations template
- Sample first-day work assignments
- Sample meeting agenda for Employee /Peer Coach meeting
- Sample meeting agenda for Employee/Business Manager meeting
- Step one checklist

Sample Memo/E-mail Announcing New Employee's Arrival (Example One)

To: Department Members (and department Business Manager when appropriate)

From: Manager of Department

Date: (insert date)

Subject: New Team Member

I am pleased to announce that (insert new employee's name) will be joining our team as (insert job title/responsibility.) He/she comes to us with experience in the areas of. . . . (insert more detail.) He she will be working with members of our team to. . . . (insert more detail.)

(Insert new employee's name) first day will be (insert date.) I have asked (insert name of a current team-member) to be the (insert new employee's name) peer coach. Although (insert name of peer coach) will officially be responsible for supporting the transition of our newest team member in the first few weeks/months, I ask each of you to make him/her feel welcome.

Thank you for helping to make (new employee's name) orientation to our department a smooth and pleasant experience.

Sample Memo/E-mail Announcing New Employee's Arrival (Example Two)

To: All Relevant Departments

From: Manager's Name

Date: Monday, June 9, 2003

Subject: New Team Member: New Team Member Name

I am pleased to announce that today **New Team Member Name** will be joining our team as **New Member Title** reporting to me. She comes to us with financial analysis experience both at **Previous Companies**, where she performed extensive financial modeling and analysis across a wide range of transactions. **New Member Name** has also worked as a **previous title**. She graduated from the **School Name** with a Bachelor of Business Administration and a Master in Professional Accounting. In addition, **other highlights of her/his career**.

New Member Name will be working with members of our team to support **Job Responsibilities**.

I have asked **Employee Name** to be **New Member** peer coach. Although **Employee Name** and I will officially be responsible for supporting the transition of our newest team member in the first few weeks, I ask each of you to make her feel welcome. **New Member Name** phone number will be xxx. xxx.xxxx. For now she will be sitting in **Office Location** next to the large conference room on the twenty-fifth floor.

Thank you for helping to make **New Member Name** orientation to our department a smooth and pleasant experience.

Sample Agenda for Employee's First Day in the Department

AGENDA

(Insert Department Name)

(Insert Date)

Welcome and Introduction to the Team, including Assigned Peer Coach

Tour of the Facility and Department

Meeting with Manager

Meeting or Lunch with Department

Meeting with Peer Coach

Meeting with Business Manager (if appropriate)

End of Day Check-In with Manager

Additional Comments:

Sample Meeting Agenda for Employee/Manager Meeting

AGENDA

(Insert Department Name)

(Insert Date)

(Insert time for meeting, at least two hours)

Follow-up on Important Points for Orientation Day One

Benefits paperwork

Desktop support issues

Time card/vacation tracker questions

Corporate credit card/expense reporting questions (refer to Business Manager if necessary)

Online training sign-up

Background Information and Working Environment

History of company and department

Important products and services

Tour the facility

Department Information

Department goals and objectives

Department organization and interaction with other departments

Administrative details including working hours, office rules, office procedures, etc.

New Employee Roles and Responsibilities

Job description

Standards of performance

How employee fits into department organization including smaller work groups

Performance Goals

Key goals for employee in first 6 months to one year

Check-in and support

Additional Comments:

OVERVIEW OF ORIENTATION DAY ONE AND SAMPLE FOLLOW-UP POINTS

OVERVIEW OF ORIENTATION DAY ONE

Day One of Orientation is designed as an overall introduction to the company.

The session starts with a historical perspective of our journey from a start-up enterprise to a publicly traded company.

Then, presenters from various departments come before the group and discuss how important policies affect employees and answer any questions the new hires have. Content includes:

- Introductions, Company History and Overview—Presenter's Name and phone extension
- Compensation/Time Card, Vacation Tracker—Presenter's Name and phone extension
- Benefits—Presenter's Name and phone extension
- Recruiting—Presenter's Name and phone extension
- Customer Service—Presenter's Name and phone extension
- Office Services/ID Photos/Facility Tours—Presenter's Name and phone extension
- Desktop Support, INET—Presenter's Name and phone extension
- MSO University—Presenter's Name and phone extension

To assist employees in managing all of the pertinent information shared that day, each employee also receives a New Employee Handbook to serve as a reference for need-to-know information presented by the various departments.

Orientation Day One Sample Follow-Up Points

Employee benefits questions and paperwork due by week's end to the **Benefits Manager, Ext. xxx**

Any desktop support issues reported to the **Help Desk, Ext. xxx**

Complete first time card by end of first or second week as indicated by HR reminder e-mails. **Contact Payroll Department, Ext. xxx** with questions.

Sign up for corporate American Express card if necessary. Contact **Department, Ext. xxx** with questions.

Sign up for instructor-led video or online training by contacting **Training & Development, Ext. xxx**

Sample Department Organization/List of Team Members

<u>Name:</u> VP, Human Resources/Organizational Development

<u>Name:</u> Director Training & Development

<u>Name:</u> Corporate Trainer

<u>Name:</u> Training Coordinator

Sample Department Goals and Objectives

The goal of the Corporate Training & Development Department is to provide training programs to increase the knowledge and skills of MSO employees.

We will provide this service in a proactive environment, readily responding to the changing business needs of the MSO organization. This will allow employees to improve their performance and make a greater contribution towards meeting the goals and objectives of the company.

Sample Job Description for New Employee

Title	Training Coordinator
Description	Functions as an assistant to the Director, Corporate Training & Development and Sr. Trainer. Responsible for the administrative aspects of training activities. The Training Coordinator will conduct training workshops, one-on-one training, as well as assist in other assignments as directed by the Director, Corporate Training & Development and Sr. Trainer.
Responsibilities	Maintain the administrative aspect of training activities, administer the registration process, track requests for training, assure timely registration, create training course calendars, conduct training workshops and one-on-one instruction, as directed by the Director, Corporate Training & Development. Assist in developing and maintaining training materials in paper and electronic form. Assist in distributing written materials for user consumption and the translation of those materials into electronic form (e.g., Windows Help Files, intranet files). Work with the Director, Corporate Training & Development in reporting and tracking of budget expenses. Develop and maintain training vendor relations. Maintain learning library and training database and provide reports as requested.
	Assist Help Desk, as directed, in application training/solutions for MSO community. Assist in the training and development of MSO community through registration to formal courses, counseling, and recommending training curriculums. Ensure supervisor approval is received for each employee to register. Interact with users and obtain feedback. Assist in organizing in-house and external training classes. Assist in tracking MSO employee individual training hours to ensure they are attending appropriate type and amount of training. Other duties as assigned by the manager.
Skill Sets/ Qualifications	1+ years of experience in Training & Development. Candidates should also have experience in applying/implementing new strategies based on research and new technologies. Must be skilled with 2+ years of experience with the following applications: PC & Mac Systems, Windows/NT OS, MAC OS, MS Office (Excel, Word, PowerPoint, Access), Lotus Notes a plus.

Goals and Expectations Template

Use the following chart to identify goals in different work areas. After you have identified the goals and expected outcomes, assign a priority to them.

Goal*	Expected Outcome(s)	Timeframe for Completion	Priority (A,B,C)	Reviewed with Employee

*All goals should be <u>SMART</u> in order to be most motivating to the new employee:

S—Specific	*Is the goal exact?*
M—Measurable	*Can you quantify the goal?*
A—Achievable	*Is the goal challenging but not overly difficult?*
R—Realistic	*Can the goal be achieved within the current environment?*
T—Time bound	*Have you set a deadline for when the goal should be achieved?*

Sample First Day Work Assignments

- Review files and projects from predecessor
- Review organization and product information relating to the department
- Set up meeting with key people—those with whom the new employee must interact regularly
- Work on the procedures, processes and tasks related to the job
- If pertinent, observe a co-worker operating in a similar position or with similar responsibilities
- Accurately complete a time card at the end of the day
- Answer the telephone according to department or organization standards

Sample Meeting Agenda for Employee/Peer Coach Meeting

AGENDA

(Insert Department Name)

(Insert Date)

(Insert time for meeting, at least two hours)

Introductions

Peer coach to share background and experience with the company, main responsibilities and role(s) within the department

New employee to share background and understanding of new role within the department

Description of Peer Coach Role

Helping the new employee transition to the company, learn the culture, answer questions, etc.

Peer coach is available to help employee as needed in first few weeks and months on the job

Question & Answer

Peer coach to answer new employee's questions regarding the company, the department, the job, etc.

Additional Comments:

Sample Meeting Agenda for Employee/Business Manager Meeting

AGENDA

(Insert Department Name)

(Insert Date)

(Insert time for meeting, at least two hours)

Introductions

Business Manager to describe his/her main responsibilities and role(s)

New employee to share background and understanding of new role within the department

Invoice Coding/Expense Reporting, etc.

Business manager discusses invoice coding (if appropriate) and expense reporting (if appropriate) procedures

Question & Answer

Business manager to answer new employee's questions regarding the procedures

---

Additional Comments:

Step One: Quick Reference Manager Checklist

What	Who	When	Complete
Prepare your staff Call the new employee and welcome him/her to the team Send a memo to your staff informing them of the new employee's arrival (including the department Business Manager on the distribution when appropriate)	Manager	Prior to new employee's arrival	
Assign a peer coach Assign a staff member to assist the new employee when he/she arrives Meet with the assigned peer coach to discuss your expectations interactions with the new employee	Manager	Prior to new employee's arrival	
Document the goals and expectations you have of the new employee Short-term: Create a checklist of activities for the new employee's first day Long-term: Create a prioritized list of mid-year/annual goals for the new employee	Manager	Prior to new employee's arrival	
Prepare new employee packet Create a checklist of information to communicate to the new employee during his/her first day Create a checklist of activities for the new employee's first week on the job.	Manager	Prior to new employee's arrival	
Prepare the new employee's work area; ensure that workspace, computer, etc. have been arranged for the new employee	Manager	Prior to new employee's arrival	
Prepare yourself Schedule time to spend with the new employee on her first day and throughout the first week Ensure that the employee's job description is up-to-date and that an updated version has been given to Human Resource.	Manager	Prior to new employee's arrival	

MSO University: Orientation Day Two, Step Two

STEP 2: CONDUCT THE DEPARTMENT ORIENTATION

After the employee has completed the Company Orientation conducted by Corporate Training & Development, the manager can begin department orientation. It is extremely important to arrange a warm welcome for employees on their first day in the department. Below are the key steps for the manager to arrange and complete (and work with others to complete) during departmental orientation:

Welcome the new employee—

Introduce the new employee to the members of the department, briefly explaining the roles played by each team member. Review the list of the department members and titles as included in the new employee packet.

Help the employee become acclimated to the environment by conducting a tour of the facility pointing out his or her work area, other department locations, copy rooms, mailroom, lunch and rest room facilities.

Conduct an employee/manager meeting—

Follow up on important points from Orientation Day One:

- Go over benefits paperwork.
- Address desktop support issues.
- Address time card/vacation tracker questions.
- Address corporate credit card/expense reporting questions (refer to Business Manager if necessary).
- Facilitate online training sign-up.
- Provide background information.
- Briefly review the background history of the company including culture, values, philosophy, etc.
- Review the various products/services MSO provides, focusing on those the employee will be most concerned with. Step the individual through relevant products/services most applicable to his or her job.
- Provide information about the working environment.
- Review the floor plan, pointing out department locations, especially those that the employee will work with closely. Note other MSO locations and the main operations that occur in each.
- Discuss department information.

(continued on next page)

- Review department goals and objectives.

- Review the department hierarchy and how the department works with other areas of the company. This may be a simple explanation of how the work unit functions and how the unit works with other units. Even if the new employee doesn't remember details, a general understanding of the bigger picture is essential to learning where he or she fits in.

- Review the organization chart and discuss who the new employee will be working and the nature of the relationships. Discuss how the new employee's job supports the rest of the department and how it interacts with other areas of the company.

- Explain important administrative details including working hours, office rules, etc.

- Review specific roles and responsibilities of the new employee.

- Explain what the job entails and review an up-to-date job description.

- Point out the standards of performance required of the job, making sure the employee understands key performance areas.

- Set performance goals.

- Discuss your performance expectations for the employee, highlighting the key goals you would like the employee to achieve in his or her first six months to a year. Have the employee write/type up the goals using the Goals/Expectations template. Tell him or her you will allow time to learn and will provide support as needed.

- Let the employee know that you will be checking in on his or her performance periodically.

- Make the new employee aware of any formal performance reviews that take place in the department, annually for instance.

- Let the employee know that you are accessible should he/she have issues/challenges they need to discuss, especially during the first few weeks and months on the job.

- Make the employee aware of how he/she can go to other members of the department (such as the peer coach) for help as he/she acclimates to the environment.

Conduct an employee/department meeting or lunch—

Give the other members of the team/department the opportunity to discuss the way the department works together, how it works with other groups, and informal customs and standards. A "brown bag" lunch is often a good informal way for team members to introduce themselves to the new employee. The lunch also gives the employee the opportunity to see the entire group together and start to understand team dynamics and interactions.

Arrange an employee/peer coach meeting—

Introduce the new employee to his or her peer coach. (The peer coach is a team member who knows the job and the company culture and is assigned by the manager to help the new employee "learn the ropes" quickly and avoid pitfalls. The peer coach is usually an experienced employee with a successful track record and good attitude.)

(continued on next page)

The peer coach schedules a brief meeting with the new employee to explain his or her role in helping the new employee transition to the company, learn the culture, answer questions, etc. The peer coach should share any specific points/information that will help make the new employee successful at MSO.

The peer coach should support the new employee by checking in frequently and making himself/herself available should the new employee have questions in the first few weeks and months on the job.

<u>Manager check in with the employee at the end of the day</u>—

- Review activities employee should do on first day/week.
- Answer questions employee may have.
- Reinforce how happy everyone in the department is to have the new person onboard.

TOOLS

- New Employee Packet
- Training resources recommended by manager, including complete list of all online courses available
- Floor plans of MSO locations
- Step Two Checklist

Step Two: Quick Reference Manager Checklist

What	Who	When	Complete
Personally greet the employee Introduce the new employee to coworkers, including the peer coach	Manager	Day 2 of Employee Orientation	
Conduct a tour of the building and department Orient the new employee to his or her desk or workstation Pantries/cafeteria Conference rooms Location and operation of copiers and fax machine Mail room location/Mail procedures (instructions are in the New Employee Handbook from Orientation) File locations, filing scheme if applicable Storage locations Location of rest rooms	Manager or knowledgeable team member	Day 2 of Employee Orientation	
Conduct employee/manager meeting Follow-up on Important Points from Orientation Day One Provide an overview of the department and its relationship to the rest of the organization Review job description, responsibilities and work schedule Review organization and departmental policies and procedures Show the employee how to complete the time card Review activities for the day/week	Manager	Day 2 of Employee Orientation	

(continued on next page)

What	Who	When	Complete
Conduct an employee/department meeting or lunch	Manager/ Department members	Day 2 of Employee Orientation	
Conduct an employee/peer coach meeting	Peer Coach	Day 2 of Employee Orientation	
Conduct an employee/business manager meeting (if appropriate)			
End of day check-in Meet with the employee at day's end to answer questions, review important information, give encouragement, and reinforce how happy everyone is to have him or her on the team	Manager	Day 2 of Employee Orientation	

MSO University: Orientation Day Two, Step Three

STEP 3: FOLLOW UP ON PROGRESS OF NEW EMPLOYEE

Once you've completed the new employee's introduction to the department, the next and final important step is follow-up one to two weeks later. During the follow-up stage, the manager should check in on the employee's progress toward the goals discussed in the departmental orientation. At this time the manager can help the employee identify and resolve any issues/challenges, and therefore increase the potential for good performance. Below are the specific steps for the manager to complete during the follow-up stage:

Manager/Peer coach check in—

- Ensure that the relationship is working in support of the new employee.
- Identify and resolve issues/challenges.
- Revise/change peer coach relationship as necessary.

Conduct an employee/manager meeting to check progress—

- An employee may feel abandoned if you are not accessible during their initial few weeks/months. Be sure to check in with the new employee periodically to answer questions and demonstrate support. Your attention will keep the new employee motivated and will reinforce the positive feelings toward the department and the organization.
- Check in regarding the progress toward the goals you set with the employee initially.
- Discuss issues/challenges employee is facing regarding roles/responsibilities, buddy/mentor, team interactions, etc.
- Devise a plan to help employee work through and overcome challenges/issues.
- Refer to training resources and recommend courses that may help employee as he/she acclimates to MSO over time.
- Revise goals as necessary.

TOOLS

- Points to discuss with peer coach
- Sample agenda for employee follow-up meeting
- Goals/Expectations template, completed on employee's first day
- Training resources

POINTS FOR MANAGER TO DISCUSS WITH PEER COACH

- Check-in regarding peer coach relationship
- Discuss what's working well with peer coach relationship
- Discuss opportunities for improving the relationship to be more productive and helpful to the employee

Sample Meeting Agenda for Employee/Manager Follow-Up Meeting

AGENDA

(Insert Department Name)

(Insert Date)

(Insert time for meeting, approximately 30 minutes to one hour)

Check-in on Progress toward Goals

Review progress toward each goal

Discuss issues and challenges employee is facing in achieving goals

Devise a plan to help employee work through and overcome challenges/issues

Check-in regarding Peer Coach relationship

Discuss what's working well with peer coach relationship

Discuss opportunities for improving the relationship to be more productive and helpful to the employee

Question & Answer

Manager and employee to share other questions, concerns, feedback, etc.

Additional Comments:

Step Three: Quick Reference Manager Checklist

What	Who	When	Complete
Manager/Peer coach check-in	Manager	One–two weeks after dept. orientation & periodically thereafter	
Conduct Employee/ Manager check-in meeting	Manager	One–two weeks after dept. orientation & periodically thereafter	
Make training recommendations to aid in New Employee development	Manager	One–two weeks after dept. orientation & periodically thereafter	
Manager/Peer coach check-in	Manager	One–two weeks after dept. orientation & periodically thereafter	
Conduct Employee/ Manager check-in meeting	Manager	One–two weeks after dept. orientation & periodically thereafter	
Make training recommendations to aid in New Employee development	Manager	One–two weeks after dept orientation & periodically thereafter	

MSO University: Orientation Day Two, Training Resources

MSO UNIVERSITY TRAINING RESOURCES

To ensure that the new employee continues to sharpen skills and/or develop new skills, the manager may want to recommend training courses to be included in the new employee's list of goals.

Below is a sample of courses available through Corporate Training & Development. Check the INET under MSO University for an updated schedule of courses. Contact the VP, Human Resources/Organizational Development XXXX, with questions or specific course requests.

ONLINE COURSES

Online Training: Over 600 business and technical courses are available online, including:

Business Management Courses:

Basics of Effective Communication

Leading Effective Meetings

Making a Presentation

Managing Your Time

Writing For Business

Technical Courses:

Dreamweaver

Illustrator

Microsoft Office

Photoshop

PowerPoint

See complete list of courses to view all courses available and recommend specific courses to the new employee. Courses are accessible via our corporate iNet or from home via the Internet 24 hours a day, 365 days a week. All of the courses are very interactive, easy to use and easy to learn from. The self-study courses are time flexible and allow the student to start and finish the course modules as your time allows.

(continued on next page)

INSTRUCTOR-LED TRAINING

MSO University also offers instructor-led management and technical courses. Actual courses offered are subject to change. An updated schedule of courses can be found on the INET under Training & Development, MSO University, Course Schedule. Courses that have been offered include those listed below:

Management Courses (managers and above only):

Succeeding as a Manager (management refresher/core skills)

Effectively Managing People (management and communication style)

Leading Managers (AVP and above)

Managing Conflict (conflict as opportunity)

How to Coach Others for Outstanding Job Performance

Managing Your Career (tools to manage professional development)

Managing "On Demand" (applying management skills)

Exploring Strategic Elements of Leadership (AVP and above)

Technical Courses (for all employees):

Excel

Word

PowerPoint

Photoshop

Quark

Illustrator

OUR RESULTS

After a year of implementing this process, we pulled together a group of hiring managers and a separate group of new hires to access the assessment.

Our findings were right on target. The hiring managers were very appreciative that they had guidelines and that they were followed religiously by all. Some of our managers were very new or first-time managers and they were not left to wonder how to integrate the new employee into the team. They all stressed how it was basically common sense.

One manager recalled that when he joined a previous company, he started the first day and his manager was on vacation for two weeks and it was basically left for him to figure out what to do. He said the bad experience did not endear him to the company and he left within the year. Another manager spoke about reviewing the process with his team so as to make the integration flawless.

The new hires group that we spoke to had all been hired within the year. Each with the exception of one was pleased with their onboarding into their department. One attendee mentioned that after a year "the honeymoon is still on." They all felt a strong bond with their team members. Not a one has gone through this type of process with their former companies. We did receive some interesting tidbits of information. One suggested that we give an abbreviated overview of the onboarding process during orientation, which we eventually added. The new hire that did not go through the complete process was, however, pleased with the portion that he did go through. As a follow-up, we had a meeting with his manager and had some of his peers who attended the manager session follow up as well.

This process was just one of the many innovations that we added during my tenure at MSO. We were constantly looking for best practices for each of our initiatives and at the end of the year, we would assess every program to make sure that they stayed fresh and, more important, that we were making the connection and reaching the goal that we started with.

Chapter 24

Asking for Feedback from New Employees

Contributed By: Ron Thomas, Founder, RThomas and Associates

About the Author: Ron Thomas founder of RThomas and Associates, has over 15 years experience in Human Resources and training and development. He was the former Vice President of Human Resources/Organizational Development at Martha Stewart Living. Prior to joining Martha Stewart, he was Regional Training Manager for IBM Global Learning Services (Catapult Divisions-NY).

Ron's Contact Information:

Ronald-thomas@comcast.net
917.902.6164
26 Elk Road
Verona, NJ 07044
www.strategyfocusedhr.com
www.linkedin.com/in/ronaldthomaslinkedin
Twitter: Ronald_thomas

Ron's work has been featured in the *Wall Street Journal, Chief Learning Officer Magazine, Workforce Management,* and *Crain's New York Business.* His blog titled Strategy Focused HR has a national and international following. He is a guest blogger at PongoResume.com. In 2008 he was honored as "HR Person of the Year" by the New York–based HR Network. He is a sought-after speaker on the strategic impact of HR and has written numerous articles on human resources. He is a member of the Senior HR Executive Exchange program sponsored by the Society of Human Resources (SHRM).

OBTAINING DESCRIPTIVE FEEDBACK FOR CONTINUOUS IMPROVEMENT

Many times our metrics to measure the new employee onboarding process consist of a series of items to be rated by employees, along with an open-ended comments section. This type of evaluation process makes it easier to see trends and to calculate specific results, but it may not gather all of the descriptive feedback and ideas from the new employees that is needed for specific and continuous improvement. Martha Stewart Living OmniMedia (MSO) has created a descriptive evaluation tool to gather this type of information, obtaining feedback about

- The new employee's recruiting experience
- The new employee's experience working with the Human Resources department
- The new employee's feedback on their Day 1 and Day 2 Orientation Programs
- The new employee's perspective on the training and development resources available
- Overall impressions and feedback about the MSO Onboarding Program

In addition, the evaluation form also asks the new employee for their solutions and ideas to address their feedback comments about the onboarding program. The evaluation question and format is shown below.

Orientation Day 1: Give us your thoughts about your first day.	
Feedback	**Potential Solution(s) or Next Steps**
1.	
2.	
3.	

Orientation Day 2 & Beyond—Department Orientation: Tell us your thoughts on your second day experience and integrating into your department.	
Feedback	**Potential Solution(s)**
1.	
2.	
3.	

Chapter 25

The Inside Track to Improve Retention

Contributed By: Lisa Ann Edwards, Director of Global Learning and Development at Corbis, and Christina M. Lounsberry, Learning and Development Consultant

About the Authors: Lisa Ann Edwards is a talent development professional whose expertise is based on more than 20 years of experience in the media, technology, printing, and publishing industries.

Edwards has coauthored *Managing Talent Retention: An ROI Approach* (Pfeiffer, 2009) and *Measuring ROI in Coaching for New Hire Employee Retention: A Global Media Company*

Lisa and Christina's contact information:

Lisa@ManagingTalent
Retention.com
Seattle, Washington
Director, Learning &
Development
Corbis
www.corbis.com
Christie@ManagingTalent
Retention.com

published in the *ROI in Action Casebook* (Pfeiffer, 2008). In her role as head of learning and development for a global media company, Edwards is responsible for designing and implementing effective talent development solutions that ensure talent engagement, improve talent retention, and serve to feed the talent pipeline.

Christina M. Lounsberry is a Learning and Development Specialist and is an experienced facilitator, classroom instructor, and Human Resources specialist. She has both developed and facilitated numerous programs covering various topics including, leadership, sales, and new hire onboarding.

Lounsberry coauthored "Measuring ROI in Coaching for New Hire Employee Retention: A Global Media Company" published in the *ROI in Action Casebook* (Pfeiffer, 2008). Lounsberry currently works as an independent consultant specializing in the development and marketing of training programs.

COACHING TO ENHANCE THE NEW EMPLOYEE EXPERIENCE

Ruche Media Company (RMC)[1] is a global media company with 24 offices located around the world. The corporate headquarters of this $260M organization is based in a major metropolitan city located in North America. Most of the 1,100 employees are based at the corporate headquarters while the remaining workforce is located in sales offices located in major metropolitan cities throughout the world.

During an evaluation of RMC's employee turnover it was discovered that turnover was highest among employees in their first year of employment at the RMC corporate office. In fact 12 percent of all new hires departed prior to their one-year anniversary. Exit interviews and surveys showed that many individuals mentioned chaos, confusion, and disorganization as one of the reasons for departing the company within the first year.

To address these issues, RMC created a New-hire Coaching Pilot Program titled *The Inside Track*. The goal of this program is to provide additional information, resources, and support to new employees through several coaching sessions during their first six months with the company.

The Inside Track consists of two different types of coaching opportunities for participants. The first is through 60-minute group sessions held every month for four consecutive months. In addition to the group sessions, employees are also able to participate in up to eight 30-minute individual sessions with a professional internal coach.

For the initial pilot a select group of new employees who had joined RMC in the corporate office in the past four months were invited to an initial informational session to learn more about *The Inside Track*. Attendees received a brief overview of the program and were able to ask questions before deciding if they would like to commit to participate. Because this was a pilot with a limited number of spaces available the importance of remaining in the program once they had committed was communicated to the prospective participants. More than 90 percent of the participants who attended the information meeting enrolled in the program, which began the following week with 13 participants.

At the beginning of the initial pilot program, participants completed a pre-assessment survey that was designed to measure their level of engagement and commitment to the organization. Participants also completed this survey at the conclusion of the program along with several open-ended questions related to their perception of the impact study.

Results of the post-assessment survey, which was collected on a five-point scale, were positive, averaging a 5.0 composite rating for program satisfaction. In addition to participants' satisfaction with the program, RMC also compared participants' level of engagement and commitment to the organization before and after the program. Overall, there was an 11 percent improvement on all items related to engagement, showing that not only was the program something that participants felt was worthwhile, but it also impacted their overall perceptions of RMC and their role within the company.

PREPARING *THE INSIDE TRACK* COACHING PROGRAM

There were several things that needed to be developed prior to launching *The Inside Track*. The first was a one-page promotional overview to provide to managers and prospective participants. The second was the pre- and post-assessment surveys that would be used to guide the group coaching sessions and to help evaluate the effectiveness of the program.

Both surveys included questions to help assess the employee's level of engagement and commitment. Each of these questions are also believed to be correlated to specific bottom-line measurables such as retention, profitability, productivity, and customer satisfaction. The post-assessment survey also contained five reaction-level questions asking the participants to rate their satisfaction with the program.

Prior to beginning *The Inside Track*, the outline and materials for both individual and group sessions also needed to be developed. Group coaching sessions took place once a month for four months. Each one-hour session had a specific topic and included an activity and time for discussion.

The topic of Session I focuses on strengths, how participants are using their strengths in their jobs, and how their new role corresponds to the goals and aspirations they had for themselves prior to beginning work at RMC. The activity for this session involves a worksheet to help participants identify their strengths as well as a section for reflecting on their short- and long-term goals.

The topic of Session II is the concept of managing up, how to ask for what they need from their manager to further their development and success. The content for this topic is based on a specific learning model of development that RMC utilizes. Explaining this model to participants enabled them to identify their own development level within this framework and to partner with their manager to receive the additional resources that, based on the framework, they need to be successful.

Session III focuses on successful career management strategies and includes an overview of RMC's performance evaluation process. The activity for this session asks participants to consider what specific things they could do in their current role to receive an exceptional rating on their performance review, based upon their current goals and other evaluation criteria. Finally, Session IV covers career development tactics and a discussion of how to avoid common career pitfalls.

The individual coaching portion of the program consists of up to eight 30-minute sessions for each participant. Prior to beginning their first individual session, participants were required to define an issue that they would like to work on with the coach. Both the coach and the participant also signed a confidentiality agreement prior to the beginning of the sessions to assist in facilitating open, candid discussions during these meetings.

MATERIALS AND RESOURCES FOR *THE INSIDE TRACK*

Beyond the materials developed specifically for *The Inside Track*, RMC required only a few resources to conduct the program. A survey tool was needed to administer both the pre- and post-assessment surveys and to analyze the data. For this, RMC used an outside, subscription-based, Web survey tool. To conduct both the individual and group coaching sessions, RMC used the services of an internal staff member who was a certified professional coach.

While this program has not yet been fully implemented beyond the pilot at RMC, it was designed to be used on an ongoing basis as new employees were hired into the company. One proposal for continuation was to incorporate the group coaching sessions into the existing New Hire Orientation program as an extension of the initial first week event that all new hires attend. Follow- up meetings, including the content of the group coaching sessions, could be held every one to two months and include all employees hired within a specific time period. Individual coaching sessions could be offered to all new employees or to a select group in key positions, depending upon the resources available.

FOLLOW-UP ACTIONS

Once the program is in place, one of the most important follow-up steps is to ensure that results are communicated regularly with all of the key stakeholders, including managers, senior leaders, program sponsors, human resources, and participants. The results of the pre- and post-assessment should be prepared on a scheduled basis with a summary sent out to all relevant parties. Highlighting individual success stories, with the permission of the participants involved, can also be helpful.

OUR RESULTS

One area of success of *The Inside Track* was measured by asking for the participants' reaction to and satisfaction with the program. Participants were asked to provide input on their reaction to the solution, their perspective on the different elements of the program, and whether or not they accomplished the goal they set for themselves at the start of the program. Using the post-assessment survey to collect this information, data was collected on a five-point scale. As expected, the results were positive, averaging a 5.0 composite rating.

In addition to participants' reactions, RMC also measured participants' level of engagement and commitment to the organization before and after the program. Overall, there was an 11 percent improvement on all items related to engagement.

Since *The Inside Track* was being conducted as a pilot program, the Return on Investment of the program was also calculated. This was done based upon the methodology of The ROI Institute.[2] Using this method, it was determined that the program provided RMC with a Return on Investment (ROI) of 251 percent. This indicates that for every $1 RMC invested to conduct the program, $2.51 was returned after the costs of the program were captured.

An example of the survey tool used in *The Inside Track* program is shown on the next page.

New Hire 30-Day Follow-Up Survey

1. In which office do you work or are you based out of?

2. My manager has scheduled weekly 1:1 meetings with me.

3. My manager has explained my department's goals and helped me set individual goals for the year.

4. I have the equipment and resources I need to do my job.

5. I have registered for my health benefits or I have declined coverage with Human Resources (HR).

6. I know who my HR Generalist is.

7. I am comfortable approaching my HR Generalist with questions or concerns.

8. I have a clear understanding of my role in the organization's success and that of my department.

9. I have a clear understanding of my job duties, responsibilities, and expectations.

10. I have met and interacted with employees outside my department and am more familiar with the office environment.

11. I was assigned a Buddy.

12. My experience with my Buddy was positive and helpful.

13. I was satisfied with the knowledge and skills of my Buddy.

14. I have good familiarity with the Zoom Web site.

15. I have a clear understanding of the Employee Recognition Program.

16. I have worked through the "At Your Desk" guide from New Hire Orientation.

17. The "At Your Desk" exercise was helpful in learning more about the company.

18. I have good familiarity with the software and tools that are necessary for me to do my job.

19. I know how to find and register for training.

20. I am comfortable approaching my manager with questions and concerns.

21. My manager treats me with respect and helps me address concerns.

22. I am satisfied with my decision to work at [Company Name]

23. Please provide any overall comments or suggestions:

REFERENCES

1. This case was prepared to serve as a basis for discussion rather than to illustrate either effective or ineffective management practices. Names of places and organizations have been disguised.

2. www.ROIInstitute.net

Chapter 26

Checklists and Buddies for New Employees

Contributed By: By Jeanne Baer, President of Creative Training Solutions

About the Author: President of Creative Training Solutions, Jeanne designs and conducts training programs that create more effective, productive teams and individuals. A consultant and trainer for businesses, government agencies, and professional associations, she is also a frequent presenter at state and national conferences. Jeanne's education includes a B.A. from the University of Nebraska, and graduate work in accelerated learning principles from Colorado State University.

Jeanne's Contact Information:

Creative Training Solutions
www.cts-online.net
Lincoln, NE
402-475-1127
800-410-3178
jbaer@cts-online.net

A prolific author, Jeanne has written more than 190 "Managing Smart" columns for *Strictly Business* magazine and other publications, and her views have been quoted by *Investor's Business Daily* and other newspapers. Jeanne's book *You Can't Do It All: Effective Delegation for Supervisors* was published in 1999 by Media Inc., and produced as a Web-based course in 2001 by Provant, Inc. Jeanne's work has also been published in two books by Harvard Business School Press, two by Pfeiffer-Jossey Bass, two by ASTD, and many by McGraw-Hill.

A CHECKLIST TO HELP MANAGERS ORIENT AND PREPARE NEW EMPLOYEES

In my consulting practice, I have observed a common mistake made by organizations, which led to the creation of this checklist. Although organizations dedicate many resources to recruiting, interviewing, and hiring the right candidate, once the new employee is on board, they don't furnish him or her with critical information quickly.

Of course, the company's HR professionals conduct an orientation or at least guide new employees through the myriad forms that must be completed. But what new employees are really hungry for is comprehensive and realistic information about what's required to perform the job. They also need a great deal of training, coaching, and other forms of assistance that can only come from the people they report to.

Therefore, I designed a checklist for use by supervisors and managers. I often conduct public seminars, revealing innovative ways to recruit and retain great employees. Because I provide this checklist at every seminar, it has received close examination and extensive discussion. As a result, I know it's a helpful tool!

Many managers also assign a buddy, sponsor, or mentor to the employee to provide an additional resource in the department to the new employee and to build relationships. This chapter includes tips for selecting buddies and the typical responsibilities of a buddy.

Helping New Employees Succeed

For most new hires, starting a new job is exciting but also a little frightening. Employees differ, of course, in their dreams and goals and in a willingness to take risks. Your first job is to give a new employee comprehensive and realistic information about what's required to perform this job. Then you'll need to be sure s/he gets training, coaching, and other forms of help.

Think of someone you recently hired, and put a checkmark by the things you did to help your new employee succeed. Which do you think are the most important?

- Explain important procedures and how the employee's work fits in with the completed product (or service).

- Explain what training and development will be available to help him or her learn the job; then be sure s/he gets it.

- Conduct or arrange for a tour and an in-depth orientation.

- Define the job accurately and completely; check for understanding.

- Explain the role of the employee in your department and company to him or her.

- The first day, take the employee to lunch in your company cafeteria if you have one. Arrange for others to eat with him/her for the first week.

- Make sure the new employee understands emergency procedures, what to do in case of an accident, and other safety issues.

- Introduce the employee to a "model" (a coworker who has acquired the skills needed for success) to observe and learn from.

- Help the employee establish peer relationships. Ideally, assign a "buddy" to him/her— someone who can show the new hire around and answer questions.

- Help the new employee understand your unique culture: What's the dress code? When and how do people take lunch and other breaks? When/how do people get together to meet or solve problems? What time do people typically arrive at work? How strict are policies and procedures?

- Give the employee regular feedback on progress.

- Make the job as manageable as possible and conditions as predictable and controllable as you can, until the employee gets his or her feet on the ground.

- Help the employee with personal problems (within limits) that have a bearing on job performance—primarily, listening to him/her and referring the employee to professional sources of help such as an employee assistance program.

Have you done other things to help new employees succeed? If so, jot them down so you can share your ideas with others and remember to do these things again in the future.

A "Buddy" Checklist

Many organizations develop "buddy" programs for a coworker to give personal assistance to the new employee on an as-needed basis. The following checklist suggests both criteria to select a "buddy" and a list of typical "buddy" activities. Be sure to build in recognition or extra compensation for the "buddy," since being a "buddy" is an extra-added responsibility.

HOW TO SELECT A "BUDDY"

The best person to be a "buddy" . . .

- Has worked for your organization more than a year
- Has something in common with the new employee (age, education, temperament, etc.)
- Is given time to be accessible to the new employee
- Has a good performance history
- Is skilled in the new employee's job
- Is proud of your organization
- Has patience and good communication and interpersonal skills
- Wants to be a "buddy"
- Is a positive role model (other employees think well of him/her)
- Has been selected in advance and given training in "buddy" responsibilities

SOME WAYS A "BUDDY" CAN HELP

- Be an information source for the new employee on policies, procedures, work rules, customs, etc.
- Help the new employee understand his/her assignments
- Help the new employee get to know other people s/he'll be working with and for
- Help train the new employee
- Go to lunch with him/her
- Be a tour guide
- Provide feedback and encouragement to the new employee about the work s/he's doing
- Identify resources
- Help, temporarily, to sort priorities for the new employee

Chapter 27

Self-Directed Orientation Modules

Contributed By: Alan Clardy, Towson University

About the Author: Dr. Alan Clardy, Ph.D. is Professor of Human Resource Development at Towson University and Director of the masters degree program in HRD there. He has over 25 years of corporate and professional experience in Human Resources, having worked as a corporate training director, a vice president of human resources, and a private HR consultant.

Alan's Contact Information:

Towson University
Psychology/HRD Program
8000 York Road
Towson, MD 21252
410-704-3069

Dr. Clardy received his doctorate from the University of Maryland College Park. He is the author of *50 Case Studies for Management and Supervisory Training* (HRD Press) and *Studying Your Workforce* (Sage). His consulting practice specializes in the custom design and implementation of performance management and service quality systems, along with *Getting in Gear*, his new employee orientation, training, and management program.

NO COMPUTER OR TRAINER REQUIRED!

Many companies have multiple locations but not multiple computers and Internet access to orient their new employees in a consistent manner. This chapter describes a prepackaged but completely customizable, booklet-based program for new employee orientation, training, and management, called *Getting in Gear*.

The heart of the *Getting in Gear* program is a series of almost 30 self-directed learning assignments organized into five modules. The modules are designed to be completed by the new employee, with one-on-one supervisor meetings scheduled between each module for additional learning and for review of the employee's progress with the orientation program. *The program requires no computers, no human resource personnel, and no training personnel.*

The learning assignments are to be completed by the employee while on the job. They are designed to help the employee learn what is needed to become successful on the job as quickly as possible. The employee completes the learning assignments during the normal workday, and while learning and doing regular job duties.

Anchoring the completion of one module and the start of the next are six meetings between the new employee and his or her manager, supervisor, or team leader. The agenda for each meeting is provided, making each meeting a preprogrammed dialogue between the manager and the employee. The purpose of each meeting with the supervisor is to review and confirm what the employee has learned over the prior week, and to prepare the employee for the learning assignments in the next module.

TARGET AUDIENCE

Getting in Gear is a customizable, comprehensive orientation package especially designed for firms that do not have a good orientation program in place yet want to make sure their newly hired employees are effectively brought on board and made productive quickly. And while *Getting in Gear* can be used for any company in any industry, it is especially suited for:

- Branch offices or operations centers that are not located near a corporate office or training center
- Companies that have few new employees at any one time, making it difficult to have an instructor-led orientation program
- Employees who may not have easy access to a computer in the workplace, making an online orientation program unsuitable
- Companies without formal training personnel or with few human resource personnel; companies that rely on supervisors to train new employees
- Companies that want an additional, customized, on-the-job training component for employees and supervisors to use that complements their generic classroom program

PROGRAM LENGTH AND DETAILS

Getting in Gear recommends that the modules be completed in the sequence provided; each module takes about a week to complete. As recommended, the complete learning cycle would then take about five weeks to complete. However, because the manager or supervisor decides what learning assignments to use and when to schedule the meetings, the total time required is at the supervisor's discretion.

The *Getting in Gear* program comes in the form of an *Employee Handbook* and a *Leader's Manual.* The *Employee Handbook* contains all the learning assignments and becomes the employee's self-directed learning workbook. The new employee is given this in the employee's first formal meeting with the supervisor, which often occurs on the employee's first day on the job. The *Leader's Manual* contains not only the learning assignments given to the employee, but also several other sets of materials, all packaged together for easy and convenient use. The materials include:

- The plan and overview for the complete *Getting in Gear* program
- Guidelines for enlisting coworker support in orienting the new employee
- Scheduling forms and completion checklists (which can serve as an official record of the employee's completion of orientation training)
- A learning plan for each module, including the complete set of learning assignments and the learning objectives for that module
- A complete agenda for each meeting with the employee
- Instructions for how each learning assignment is to be completed, which may include training guidance for how the supervisor can prepare for certain assignments (for example, one learning assignment directs the supervisor to communicate the mission of his or her unit to the new employee; a short instructional piece in the *Leader's Manual* explains how to develop a mission statement for the unit if there is none)

The general schedule for implementing *Getting in Gear* occurs in two phases. In phase one, the supervisor completes various identified learning assignments. In addition to developing the mission statement, the supervisor should alert coworkers and others of the new employee's arrival, prepare an on-the-job structured learning plan, and complete a Leader–Follower Assessment.

Once these activities are completed, the supervisor can go through the *Getting in Gear* program repeatedly with any number of new employees without further preparation. In short, investing an hour or so of the supervisor's time in completing this material will pay off many times over.

Phase two starts when the new employee arrives at the workplace. See the program outline chart in this chapter for a more complete schedule.

One other note: *Getting in Gear* is a program that can be used to complement and supplement existing formal orientation programs that might be provided by Human Resources. In that case, the learning assignments covering topics that are dealt with in the formal orientation can simply be skipped.

Getting in Gear is a single-source program for new employee orientation, training, and management. There are nearly 30 separate learning assignments that cover virtually every conceivable item that a new employee should learn in order to be successful in his or her new job. Because the supervisor decides which assignments to use, the program can be used with employees at all levels and in all capacities. In effect, *Getting in Gear* allows each employee to receive a customized, individual learning plan that is the foundation for an effective working relationship between the new employee and his or her boss.

FREQUENCY AND AUDIENCE SIZE

Getting in Gear is designed to be offered on a just-in-time, as-needed basis. Whenever a new employee arrives, *Getting in Gear* can begin. Even though it can be used in group settings, the program is designed to be used with employees on a one-on-one basis.

TESTING

Getting in Gear includes several different forms of testing and assessment over the course of the program. However, the testing is non-evaluative and is used for diagnostic purposes only. The assessments are not intended as tools to determine whether a new employee should be retained or terminated.

By reviewing these learning assessments, the supervisor has a chance to assess how well the employee has learned the materials in the previous module during the follow-up meeting. There are several training modules throughout the program that require the employee to make correct responses.

For example, in one learning assignment there is a generic set of training instructions on proper phone etiquette. In the follow-up activity, the supervisor can provide examples of various problem phone calls the employee may receive, to which the employee must respond with the correct principles. Finally, there are other diagnostic devices such as the Leader–Follower Assessment, which provides a basis for the supervisor to indicate what behaviors are expected of the new employee in difficult situations.

DIFFERENT ORIENTATIONS FOR DIFFERENT FOLKS

New employee orientation is probably the most universal training program in the workplace, and the training program with the most variation in delivery. A self-directed program like *Getting in Gear* meets the orientation needs of large companies looking for a more personalized, one-on-one orientation component to be used with the supervisor; and it provides a resource for the small office or retail store that lacks easy access to computer online programs or to large classroom orientations.

THE CONTENTS OF MODULE THREE (FROM THE LEADER'S MANUAL)

In this module, you create the foundation for successful job performance by establishing the performance management conditions under which the new employee will work. This module covers:

WORKING SUCCESSFULLY

- The specific expectations for job performance
- The performance appraisal process
- How performance will be compensated
- The skills needed for competent job performance

RATIONALE

A "performance management system" requires three basic parts:

1. Identified expectations for job performance
2. Methods for evaluating job performance
3. Recognition and rewards based on performance

In addition, the employee should have help in learning the skills needed to perform effectively.

WHEN TO SCHEDULE THE MEETING

This meeting should be scheduled during the employee's second to fourth week on the job.

LEARNING OBJECTIVES

As a result of completing this module, the new employee should be able to

- Identify the specific expectations for job performance
- State how his or her job performance will be evaluated
- Describe how job performance will be compensated
- List the competencies needed for successful performance of the job

The following agenda is recommended for meeting with the employee about Module Three. The learning assignments from the Employee Handbook are shown beside each agenda item in parentheses.

NOTE: The first few weeks on the job are often stressful for new employees. The adjustment process can frequently create confusion, doubts, and even regrets.

Be sure to pay attention to how well the employee is adjusting at this time. It would be a good idea to spend a few moments asking how the employee is adjusting. Look for signs of frustration or dissatisfaction. Since the greatest chance of an employee's quitting is often during this initial period, look for danger signals and be ready to help the employee.

1. Begin by reviewing the prior Learning Assignments. Clear up any questions about

Organization history (2-1)

Organization structure (2-2)

Operations (2-3)

2. Review the Job Specification Worksheet in Module 1 (1-6). To Clarify Job Expectations (3-2), review any standards and/or objectives with the employee; make sure the employee knows what the specific expectations are by either recording expectations on the form or giving the employee a prepared copy.

3. For the Performance Appraisal Process (3-3), discuss how you will formally evaluate the employee's job performance. If your organization has a performance appraisal system, tell how that system operates. If not, you may want to establish your own procedures (3-3).

4. Identify the Skills of a Competent Employee (3-4) that the employee needs to perform his or her job competently.

5. Give the employee the assignments for Module Four. Set up the meeting date to review that module.

INSTRUCTIONS:

The purpose of this assignment is to make sure your new employee knows as clearly as possible what you expect from his or her job performance, and how you will evaluate and respond to his or her performance.

For learning assignment 3-1:

1. Refer to the Job Specifications worksheet, Module 1-6. Both you and the employee should have a copy.

2. Review the lists of job duties (especially any critical duties) and customers to make sure this information is accurate. If not, be sure to update and correct the information.

The Getting in Gear Outline

Module	Learning Assignments	Schedule
Module One: Working Here	• Knowing your office • Standards of conduct • Our mission • The work we do • Meeting your coworkers • Your job duties • Job update • Learning your job • Telephone skills	• Meeting on first day • Follow-up meeting 1 week later
Module Two: Working Knowledgeably	• About our organization • How our organization works • Understanding our competition • Products and services • Customer service skills	• Follow-up meeting near the end of second week on the job
Module Three: Working Successfully	• Job specifications • Clarifying job expectations • Performance appraisals • Skills of a competent employee	• Follow-up meeting near the end of the third week on the job
Module Four: Working Together	• Understanding your boss • Leaders and followers • Communication skills • Reporting and control	• Follow-up meeting near the end of fourth week on the job
Module Five: Working Smarter	• Managing time and priorities • Work planning • Improving the quality of your work • Streamlining the work you do • Asking for feedback • Competency improvement plan	• Follow-up meeting near the end of fifth week on the job

Products and Services

LEARNING ASSIGNMENT COMPLETED

It is important for you to know the products and services that we sell to our customers and clients. These products and services generate sales and revenue for our company, and they provide value to those people we serve. As an employee of our company, any function you choose to serve in will add value to these products and services, either directly or indirectly.

Your manager or leader will indicate what our primary products and services are and where to get information about it. Write those products in the spaces below.

To Do	Product or Service	Source of Information

Use the enclosed worksheets to learn more about the products or services noted. Make more copies if necessary.

Worksheet

PRODUCT OR SERVICE:_____

Description of the Product or Service	_____ _____
Distinguishing Features	_____ _____ _____
Price and Purchasing Options	_____ _____
Guarantees or Warranties	_____ _____ _____
Complementary Products and/or Services	_____
Typical Customer	_____

Part 5

New Employee Games and Activities

New employee orientation is filled with information, multiple benefit decisions, forms to complete, new people to meet—and all of this normally takes place on the employees' first day of work in a new company, when they are already feeling a bit overwhelmed.

Some material presented in an Onboarding program may be considered "dry," and it needs a little "kick" to jazz it up a little. Adding games and activities to your orientation program will:

- Make employees feel more relaxed.
- Help new employees to meet each other.
- Add energy to your program.
- Increase learning retention.
- Keep the new employees focused and paying attention.

This section contains games and activities to help employees learn the culture, to help employees meet each other, to provide energy throughout the program, to review information, to help new employees feel valued, and to make your orientation program both fun and informative.

Adding activities to an Orientation Session also helps energize the facilitator of the session, and makes the training experience more fun for everyone!

Chapter 28

The Product Matrix Activity

Contributed By: Corey Welch, Sales Training Manager, Sun Power Corporation.

About the Author: Corey Welch has more than 20 years of success leading, developing, delivering, and measuring learning at high tech companies such as Oracle, IBM, NEC Electronics, Cadence, and TIBCO.

Corey's Contact Information:

coreywelch2002@yahoo.com
408-737-2317
1343 Dunnock Way
Sunnyvale, CA 94087

Corey has developed several new unique onboarding programs specifically for audiences who must come up to speed quickly on complex products and services, such as sales and marketing team members. Corey has an MS degree in Training and Performance Improvement from Capella University.

THE CHALLENGE: FIND AN INTERESTING WAY TO TEACH COMPANY PRODUCT INFORMATION

The purpose of the Matrix activity is to integrate a wide range of product information that new hires receive in their first few days of onboarding and orientation. Rather than just "telling" new employees about the products provided by the company, the Matrix activity enables new employees to really delve into this information and to relate well to the value the company products provide to customers, and to the strategic aspect of the product and/or service as it relates to the overall mission and goals of the company.

The activity does not focus on detailed technical information, but focuses instead on the most frequent questions the participants will need to answer for *all* products, even if they will be specializing in a single product family or technology.

The activity is highly interactive, and adapts easily to participants with different roles, backgrounds, learning styles, and languages. Because each class develops its own data, all participants feel ownership of the content, rather than having it "delivered" to them, making the process of finding and applying the information easier for them. Another advantage is that the evolving wall chart serves as a group memory, so that participants, presenters, and management visitors can see what has already been discussed.

AUDIENCE AND TIMING

The primary audiences for this activity are those employees who will need to understand the basic elements of their company's products and services so they can deal effectively with customers as soon as they return to work. This can include salespeople (both outside and inside), marketing managers, product managers, support engineers, and a range of supporting roles, such as sales office managers.

The activity can take anywhere from an hour to several hours throughout an entire Onboarding Program, depending on the number of products and services discussed in the activity, and the number of different SME (subject matter expert) speakers who provide information about the products and services.

YOU'LL NEED

The Matrix that is built must be visible to all participants as it is being created, frequently over the course of several days. Thus, a good alternative is white butcher paper strips, ideally with a width of 36 inches (or more). The length will depend on the categories used, but can be 15–20 feet long. The strip(s) are taped to a blank wall, with tape or ink lines to define the Matrix. Make sure you have plenty of paper, markers, and masking tape for the activity.

PREPARATION

This activity is highly suited to a team delivery approach, where different SMEs will be discussing their own product, service, market, or technology area. Because the construction of the matrix is dependent on having the same categories for all subject areas, it is critical that the developer/facilitator review these categories with each SME in advance. Ideally, the SME will use the same categories to structure their presentation and handouts.

Each time the activity is delivered, a new Matrix is created using the participants' own words, so the facilitator can use a review of the previous matrix to identify possible problem areas before the next delivery. You will want to review the Matrix activity (and an example of the Matrix chart, shown in this section) with the SME to make sure he or she is prepared to discuss all items listed in the Matrix categories, and how the activity is facilitated.

The physical preparation for this activity involves creating a very large wall chart. Depending on the room and the Matrix, this setup may take 30 minutes or more. Separate team activities can also be linked to this integrative activity, and each activity may have its own set-up work.

Once the categories are defined, these will form the row and column headings for the matrix. One successful scheme is to have six to eight columns devoted to key aspects of products/services that you want the audience to remember, such as:

- Problems and Challenges
- Market Drivers
- Features
- Tools and Solutions
- Differentiators
- Qualifying Questions
- Target Market and Customers
- Competitor Strengths and Weaknesses
- Sales/Marketing Strategies (or Messages)

In this format, each of the rows would be a product, product family, service, or similar offering from your company.

CONDUCTING THE ACTIVITY

Step One:

When participants arrive, they will see an enormous wall chart with just the column and row headings filled in with names of the company's products (and/or services) and the problems and challenges, market drivers, tools, strategies, etc. associated with each product (see the example of a Matrix Chart that follows). When the company goals are discussed, you can mention that over the course of the workshop, the whole chart will be completed—by the participants.

Example of the Matrix

Product Name	Problems & Challenges	Market Drivers	Features	Tools & Solutions	Differentiators	Qualifying Questions	Target Market & Customers	Competitor Strengths & Weaknesses	Sales/ Marketing Strategies
Product #1									
Product #2									
Product #3									

Step Two:

For each learning module related to a product or service area (the rows of the Matrix), the SME/presenter should cover each of the key aspects (the columns) during their formal presentation. Ideally, the content covered should not require more than about two hours, so that participants are not overloaded.

Step Three:

After completing the presentation, the presenter must remain during the review activity and Matrix construction time. If the content they have presented is complex, a game-style review activity can be used, such as teams competing to develop "stumper" questions for other teams (but being ready to answer those questions themselves).

The types of review games can be rotated to avoid monotony, and if there is a competitive element, points, chips, or play money can be used. (This review period is optional, but highly recommended.)

Step Four:

For the Matrix construction activity, divide the group up into teams of three to eight participants. If there are a sufficient number of teams, each one can be assigned a different category (column); with fewer teams, they can take more than one column. (It is not optimal to assign the same column to more than one team, unless you do this as a part of a competitive team activity.)

The goal for each team is to synthesize into bullet points the best information that will fill in their assigned square of the Matrix. If possible, it is a good idea to use large post-it notes or pieces of paper with tape to allow them to make their bullets at their team table. (This also allows easier corrections in the following step.) Five to ten minutes can be used for the time, to force them to come to consensus quickly. With large groups, it may be helpful to include a small team number on each sheet to help in the debrief.

Step Five:

After all the teams have posted their answers for each box along the row, a team member is responsible for presenting the bullet points to the rest of the class. After each brief presentation, the SME/presenter provides feedback and (gentle) corrections to any errors. As they provide these corrections, the team is responsible for updating the box on the chart with a new piece of paper or fixing the previous one.

Step Six:

If you have an audience that responds to a competition, you can decide on a "winner" for best content. This can be the decision of the SME/presenter, facilitator, or a class vote (with each team voting for the best them *other* than their own team).

DEBRIEFING THE ACTIVITY

Over the course of the workshop, the entire Matrix will be completed, with a short present/debrief for each subject module. Because the Matrix stays on the wall throughout the workshop, it is an excellent review tool at the end and/or beginning of each day. One approach for the review can be a "gallery walk," where individuals or teams are asked to choose their favorite box (or row or column) and be prepared after a five-minute preparation to present a summary of that box in 60 seconds.

If you are able to schedule the workshop so that the Matrix is completed by the next-to-last day, you can transcribe the Matrix (Excel is a good tool) and hand out the printed version as people graduate. (Many new hires have found it useful to post this custom Matrix above their desk or in their briefcase.) The transcribed version can also be send out with follow-up materials or as a "reward" for those who complete their post-workshop evaluation.

If you have designed a follow-up workshop for new hires six weeks to three months after the initial workshop, you can retain the Matrix the participants created and post it again when they return.

Sometimes the team presentations at the end of each module may have prompted questions that cannot be answered at the time. If you created a "parking lot," you can include the answers to these follow-up questions along with Matrix when you send it out.

Another way to use the Matrix for class review is to cover up some or all of the answers and ask participants to "fill in the blanks" verbally, and then reveal the original answers, while discussing any differences, missing pieces, or additions.

Chapter 29

The Mission or Vision Telephone Game

Contributed By: Doris Sims, SPHR, President of Succession Builders, LLC

Doris's Contact Information:

Succession Builders, LLC
www.successionbuilders.com
doris@successionbuilders.com
214-906-3155

About the Author: Doris M. Sims, SPHR, is the Founder and President of Succession Builders, LLC, a talent management, succession planning, and new talent onboarding consulting firm. Her experience in organizational development spans over 20 years working in Fortune 100 and Fortune 500 companies. Doris received her master's degree in Human Resource Development from Indiana State University.

Doris is the coauthor of the talent management books *Building Tomorrow's Talent: A Practitioner's Guide to Talent Management and Succession Planning; The 30-Minute Guide to Talent and Succession Management;* and *The Talent Review Meeting Facilitation Guide*. Doris is also the author of the McGraw-Hill book *Creative New Employee Orientation Programs*, and has contributed articles to many other McGraw-Hill books and multiple periodicals, including *Training Magazine, Talent Management Magazine, Professionals in Human Resources,* and *The Consultant's Toolkit*.

A FUN WAY FOR NEW EMPLOYEES TO LEARN THE COMPANY'S VISION OR MISSION

All trainers would agree that it is important for new employees to learn the company's mission statement, vision, and values, but it may be difficult to motivate employees to memorize the company's mission statement and take it to heart. The Mission or Vision Telephone Game challenges employees to memorize the mission statement in an interactive way. It also increases the team-building effect that is so important to new employees who want to feel included in their new company's culture.

Best of all, the Mission or Vision Telephone Game requires only flip-chart paper and markers; and because it is based on a game almost everyone has played in their childhood, the directions are simple and the game moves quickly.

The Mission or Vision Telephone Game works especially well in new employee orientation programs. It provides an excellent opportunity to include an activity in a training session that is often packed with lecture information about company benefits and policies, which can become overwhelming to a new employee.

AUDIENCE AND TIMING

This activity works best with a minimum of 10 people and a maximum of approximately 100 people. The activity works well for either a group of employees at multiple levels in the organization, or for a management orientation program.

Approximate Length of Time: The time period depends on the number of people playing. With 10 people playing, the game will take about 15 minutes. With 100 people playing, the game will take 20 to 30 minutes.

YOU'LL NEED

- One blank piece of flip-chart paper for each team
- One marker for each team
- One printed copy of your company's mission statement for each team

PREPARATION

No preparation is required prior to conducting the game, other than gathering the materials listed.

Important: If your company's mission statement is more than one sentence, just use the first sentence, or use the vision statement if it is shorter. You can even use the company's values instead of the mission or vision statements. If the statement you use is long, it's too difficult for the participants to remember much of anything and the game doesn't work well.

CONDUCTING THE GAME

1. Divide the class into two teams and have them line up on opposite sides of the classroom.

2. Ask the class if they remember the telephone game they played as children, when each person whispers a secret to the next person to see how different and silly the secret turned out as the last person repeated it out loud.

3. Give the first person in each team's line a printed copy of the company's mission statement. Instruct them to read the mission statement to the person in line behind them. (Encourage them to speak softly enough so the other team can't hear, rather than whispering in the other person's ear.) Emphasize that this is not a race; points will be awarded based on accuracy only. After the first person in line reads the mission statement to the second person in line, he or she sits down with the paper in hand.

4. The second person in line then repeats the mission statement (without benefit of the printed copy!) to the third person in line, who turns around and repeats it to the fourth person in line, and so on until the last person in line hears the mission statement. Each person in the line can repeat the mission statement only once to the person behind him or her. Have participants sit down once they've repeated the mission statement.

5. When the last person in line hears the mission statement, he or she moves to the flip chart and writes what was heard on the paper. It is best to position the flip charts so teams can see only their own chart. This game is fairly quiet at first, but the volume increases as the employees responsible for writing the mission statement are cheered on heartily by their teammates!

6. Ask the last two people to stay with their flip charts. Then, read the mission statement one word at a time, and instruct the people at the flip charts to record one point for each correct word. The team that has the most accurate mission statement, measured by the number of correct words, is the winner.

DEBRIEFING THE ACTIVITY

Now, display and review the company's correct vision or mission statement, while everyone's attention is clearly focused on it.

If desired, this game can be played at the beginning of the new employee orientation session as a "benchmark run." Then encourage the teams to learn the mission statement more thoroughly during the training session, with the game being played again at the end of the orientation program to see how well they have learned the mission statement.

A debriefing activity after the benchmark run can include a discussion regarding the importance of the mission to the culture, and what activities, programs, and action plans the company has in place to support the mission.

Chapter 30
The Autographs Icebreaker

Contributed By: Steve Sugar, Author and Games Writer, The Game Group

About the Author: Steve Sugar is a writer and teacher of performance games. He is the co-author of five books on games, including *Games That Teach Teams* and *Training Games.* He has written game systems used throughout the world, including QUIZO, Maestro, X-O Cise, and the template board game, Boardgame Bingo.

Steve's Contact Information:

stevesugar@comcast.net
www.thegamegroup.com
1314 Quarry Lane
Lancaster, PA 17603
717-291-7211

Steve was a faculty member of the University of Maryland Baltimore County (UMBC) where he taught undergraduate management and graduate instructional design. Steve is a frequent presenter at international ASTD, NASAGA, TRAINING, ISPI, and Lilly conferences.

AN ICEBREAKER DESIGNED TO HELP NEW EMPLOYEES BECOME ACQUAINTED

The room looked desolate with its scores of chairs splayed against its outer walls. Into this barrenness entered 40 computer engineers with heads slightly bowed. One by one, they silently slid into their seats, and sat and stared. These were Leadership Potential Candidates specially selected from every division at a large corporation's two-week program. The candidates did not seem to know each other and looked vulnerable and fidgety in their chairs.

The trainer positioned herself in the center of the large room and smiled. After her brief welcoming statement, she handed out copies of one assignment sheet containing the well-known "autographs" icebreaker to each participant. The game requires players to find someone who fits each of the characteristics listed on the sheet. The object is to fill the sheet with autographs. The real objective, of course, is to get the participants to interact with each other and create a friendlier environment.

Even after the trainer started the exercise, many participants remained seated, reading the assignment sheet with curiosity and suspicion. Then, one or two of the braver ones turned to their neighbors, asking if they identified with any of the characteristics. A trickle of conversation emerged. Then, a few participants got up from their seats, boldly going to other parts of the room. Finally, all the participants left their chairs to mingle in the ongoing exercise.

In just a few minutes, the room became a raucous social gathering, with the animated chatter of 40 participants waving assignment sheets and moving through the group in search of the elusive autograph. Chatter and laughter were now the rule as pens flashed across the room. This mild pandemonium continued for 15 minutes, ending only when the trainer invited the participants to return to their chairs. It took a few joyful minutes to quiet the room as the participants reluctantly left their newfound friends and acquaintances.

While it is important to relax the environment for learning to take place in any training program, it is especially important in new employee orientation, when participants are already a little nervous about starting a new job and meeting new people. Use this highly interactive icebreaker to create enthusiasm and to "warm" the room with friendly introductions.

AUDIENCE AND TIMING

This exercise works well with groups of 8 to 100 participants. The activity will take approximately 20 to 45 minutes to complete, depending on the class size.

YOU'LL NEED

- Game sheets and pencils or pens for each participant
- One timer (optional)
- Prizes (optional)

PREPARATION

1. Develop a set of descriptive statements that are pertinent to the audience. These descriptions can come from information on preregistration forms, from required prerequisites, or from target audience data.
2. List a set of statements on a handout.
3. Make one copy of the handout for each participant.

CONDUCTING THE GAME

The objective of the game is to complete the list by obtaining the signatures of class members who fit the characteristics listed.

1. Tell participants that they will be involved in an exercise to learn something about other people in the course.

2. Distribute one worksheet and a pen or pencil to each person.

3. Explain the task: "Find another participant who fits each of the statements, and get the person's autograph on the line next to the statement that describes him or her. All signatures must be legible."

Note: No participant may sign his or her name on any one handout more than once. When your sheet is completed, have it validated by the facilitator. (The facilitator may give a prize to the first three to five participants with completed worksheets.)

Allow participants 15 minutes to complete the exercise.

DEBRIEFING THE GAME

By reviewing the statements with the entire group, this is an excellent time to "harvest" both skills and perspectives that surface during the playing of the game.

1. This will allow all participants to meet each other and reinforces the concept that we all bring something to the learning environment. As the statements are disclosed and participants are identified, players gain a greater understanding and appreciation of their fellow participants.

2. Extended debriefing time helps new participants learn about and identify with their fellow participants, allowing for better interaction during the ongoing class and increased networking possibilities.

3. Extended debriefing for in-place teams provides an excellent way to reveal new perspectives of team members.

Here are some examples of relationship building and insight that have occurred as this activity has been facilitated:

■   On one occasion, a quiet, gentle female revealed that she had been one of the students who walked through a school segregation line. Other team members gained a new, and perhaps valuable, insight into one of their team members—a perspective that was never revealed or discussed before.

■ On another occasion, we listed the statement "Rides a Harley-Davidson." The debriefing not only identified the rider—a petite, 52-year-old grand-mother—but uncovered underlying assumptions of participants, who admitted to looking for large male bikers.

OTHER VARIATIONS OF THE ACTIVITY

1. Charge a penny for each worksheet. Declare that the first participant to fill in his or her worksheet receives the pot.

2. Use comparative statements that require participants to take note of similarities, such as "Born in the same month" or "Drives the same make automobile."

3. Use a Bingo format, such as a 5-by-5 matrix. Have participants autograph the square, and award prizes for Bingos.

4. Develop one or two statements in a foreign language. This requires players to 1) translate the statement, and 2) find someone who fits the characteristic.

Participant Handout: Autograph Game

AUTOGRAPHS

1. Complete this list by obtaining the signature of a participant who matches each statement.

2. You are limited to one signature from any one participant. The signature must be legible.

3. When completed, return the list to the facilitator for validation.

IDENTIFY SOMEONE IN THE CLASS WHO:

1. Is wearing a watch. _____

2. Was born outside of the United States. _____

3. Has created his or her own Web site. _____

4. Plays golf. _____

5. Has shaken hands with a celebrity. _____

6. Is on Facebook. _____

7. Can tie a bow tie. _____

8. Can speak more than one language. _____

9. Drives an American-made car. _____

10. Owns a cat. _____

11. Wears glasses. _____

12. Sings or plays in a band, chorus, or choir. _____

13. Has ridden a bike in the last year. _____

14. Has purchased a book on the Internet. _____

15. Has more than three first cousins. _____

Participant Handout: Autograph Bingo Questions

Ask your new coworkers to sign the Bingo box that corresponds to the number of any item listed that is a true description of them. You must have two rows of signatures to win the game.

1. Has three or more brothers and sisters.

2. Owns a Jeep or 4-wheel drive vehicle.

3. Plays a musical instrument.

4. Has season tickets to the symphony or opera (or sporting event).

5. Enjoys scrapbooking.

6. Owns a pool or ping pong table.

7. Has a middle name that starts with A, B, or C.

8. Can grill an excellent steak.

9. Has ordered anything from Amazon.com.

10. Knows the 3 ingredients in a "S'more."

11. Has a bird feeder.

12. Wears contact lenses.

13. Has a birthday in December.

14. Plays racquetball or basketball.

15. Has been married five years or less.

16. Owns any music on 78-rpm records, 8-track tapes, or cassette tapes.

17. Sings or plays in any type of band, choir, or chorus.

18. Skis (water or snow) or has gone snowboarding.

19. Is wearing shoes that tie (not slip-on shoes).

20. Has visited Europe in the past five years.

21. Enjoys dancing.

22. Rides a motorcycle.

23. Has his or her own Web site.

24. Has earned a belt in karate.

25. Is wearing a watch.

Autograph Bingo Card

1	2	3	4	5
6	7	8	9	10
11	12	13	14	15
16	17	18	19	20
21	22	23	24	25

Chapter 31

The Group Résumé Icebreaker

Contributed By: Doris Sims, SPHR, President of Succession Builders, LLC.

About the Author: Doris M. Sims, SPHR is the Founder and President of Succession Builders, LLC, a talent management, succession planning, and new talent onboarding consulting firm. Her experience in organizational development spans over 20 years working in Fortune 100 and Fortune 500 companies. Doris received her master's degree in Human Resource Development from Indiana State University.

Doris's Contact Information:

Succession Builders, LLC
www.successionbuilders.com
doris@successionbuilders.com
214-906-3155

Doris is the co-author of the talent management books *Building Tomorrow's Talent: A Practitioner's Guide to Talent Management and Succession Planning, The 30-Minute Guide to Talent and Succession Management* and *The Talent Review Meeting Facilitation Guide*. Doris is also the author of the McGraw-Hill book *Creative New Employee Orientation Programs*, and has contributed articles to many other McGraw-Hill books and multiple periodicals, including *Training Magazine, Talent Management Magazine, Professionals in Human Resources* and *The Consultant's Toolkit*.

THE GROUP RÉSUMÉ—CREATING BONDS AND DEMONSTRATING VALUE

The Group Résumé activity serves to create relationship bonds as the participants discover common interests and experiences. In addition, the debrief session of the activity serves to demonstrate the vast experience the new employees bring with them into the organization, and it validates the value that each new employee brings into the organization even on the first day of employment. Specifically, the activity:

- Helps employees realize the value, knowledge, and skills they are bringing to their new organization
- Helps new employees interact with each other and begin to build relationships

- Helps new employees understand that the *combination* of skills and talents they bring to the organization is important
- Helps employees understand that even though they are starting a new job, they each bring a unique perspective and work experience with them to jump-start their new career

AUDIENCE AND TIMING

The Group Résumé (or CV) activity can be used with employees or managers at any level in the organization. The game works equally well as a networking activity or as an introductory icebreaker game in your New Employee Program. It is a great exercise for managers in a management onboarding program, both to help them remember the past skills and experience they bring to the organization, and to remind them that their own employees bring a vast wealth of past experience, skills and knowledge to their current job.

YOU'LL NEED

The materials needed for this activity include:

- Flip-chart paper for each group of participants (typically the facilitator will divide the class into small groups of 3–6 people to work on this activity together, and each team will need flip-chart paper)
- Flip-chart markers for participants at each table
- Masking tape to secure the finished flip charts to the walls for the presentation portion of the activity

PREPARATION

The only preparation required on the part of the instructor prior to facilitating the activity is to prepare either a PowerPoint slide or a flip chart with the instructions for the activity. It will be important to leave the instructions on display during the activity to enable participants to refer back to the instructions as needed.

CONDUCTING THE ACTIVITY

Remind employees about the purpose of a résumé or curriculum vitae (CV); it is designed to tell others about your talent and skills, and to showcase the value you bring to the organization.

But rather than present a résumé as an individual, the workshop participants will work in teams to create a Group Résumé, where they will "add up" their years of experience in various areas. Every group should add up their years of experience *as a total group* on a flip chart:

- In their industry
- In their entire career
- As a manager (if it is a management orientation program)

The group can also include any of the following on their group résumé:

- The number of countries in the world they have visited
- The number of states and/or countries they have lived in
- The total number of miles the group travels each day to/from work
- The total number of jobs/positions they have held in their career
- Think of at least three creative items for your flip chart! Examples of more creative items include the total number of pets in the group, the total number of countries the group has visited, the total number of traffic tickets the group has received, the total number of bosses the group has reported to throughout their careers, the total number of electronic communication devices the group owns, the total number of commuter miles the group makes each day, etc.

Allow at least 15–20 minutes for each group to discuss these items, to add up their cumulative value, and to document a "Group Résumé Flip Chart." An example of a completed "Group Résumé Flip Chart" might look like this:

Our Group Resume

Our Names: Duane, Bonnie, Diana, and Rick

Total Number of Years in the Banking Industry: 58

Total Number of Work Experience: 72

Total Number of Years of Management Experience: 22

Total Number of First Cousins: 123

Total Miles We Drive To/From Work Each Day: 170

Total Number of Sky Dives We Have Jumped: 0

Total Number of Countries We Have Visited: 12

Total Number of Web Site Domains We Own: 8

DEBRIEFING THE ACTIVITY

As the groups are finishing up their Group Résumé flip charts, ask them to choose a leader—someone to present their Group Résumé to the rest of the class. I personally like to offer a rule that whoever took on the task to "scribe" the flip chart gets to rest and does not have to also serve as the presenter of the Group Résumé.

Another good way to help the group choose a "spokesperson" is to find out who most recently went on vacation—obviously they are the most well-rested person in the group so that person should present the Group Résumé to the class.

Then ask each Group Spokesperson to present the Group Résumé to the class. As each Spokesperson delivers this presentation, add up the total number of years of industry experience, career experience, management experience, etc., for the entire class by adding up these numbers from all of the flip charts displayed in the classroom.

When all groups have finished presenting, provide the total number of years of experience for the entire class to everyone. Make your point about the vast wealth of knowledge and years of experience this entire group is now bringing into the organization to complete the activity.

Chapter 32

A Sweet Way to Meet!

Contributed By: Rebecca Harmon, Vice President of Human Resources, DeRoyal.

About the Author: Rebecca Harmon is Vice President of Human Resources at DeRoyal. Rebecca received her bachelor's degree in Psychology with an emphasis in Industrial Organizational Psychology from the University of Tennessee along with her MBA from the University of Tennessee in 2002.

Rebecca's Contact Information:

rharmon@deroyal.com
200 DeBusk Lane
Powell, TN 37849
865-362-2341

Rebecca joined DeRoyal in 1997. She is responsible for strategic integration of business practice alignment with employee relations. In addition to Human Resources, Rebecca is responsible for management of Customer Support and Training and Development for the company.

A UNIQUE (AND TASTY!) ORIENTATION ICEBREAKER

At DeRoyal, this icebreaker is conducted during the first few minutes of the orientation program, to help employees relax and have a little fun. It also provides an opportunity for everyone to get to know the other employees in the room.

At the end of the activity, each new employee will have a new "racehorse" name, which is used throughout DeRoyal's three-day orientation program (which has an "Off to the Races" theme), and everyone will have a small candy bar to eat. Sometimes the racehorse nickname sticks with employees throughout their careers at DeRoyal! (However, the candy doesn't usually last through the game!)

DeRoyal structured this game in the hope of creating lasting friendships that begin in the orientation program.

AUDIENCE AND TIMING

This activity is ideal for a small orientation group of 20 employees or fewer. However, the activity can be done with a larger group if employees work in groups of three to five during the game. The group size will affect the amount of time needed; factor approximately five to seven minutes per employee or group.

YOU'LL NEED

- An Off to the Races! Handout for each employee
- An assortment of the following candy bars: Mr. Goodbar, Hershey's Dark, Krackle Bar, and Hershey's regular chocolate bars. These are produced and sold by Hershey's in a single bag of assorted mini-bars. You will need at least one candy bar for each new employee. Employees always appreciate additional bars to enjoy after the game!

PREPARATION

No preparation is required other than obtaining the materials listed and becoming familiar with the steps to conduct the game.

CONDUCTING THE GAME

1. Give each employee a copy of the Off to the Races! Handout.

2. Instruct the new employees to mingle and ask each other the questions on the sheet. If you have a large group, it may be better for people to work in groups of 3 to 5, rather than trying to mingle among too many people in a limited period of time.

3. After about 10 minutes, ask the employees to return to their seats, and give them each one miniature candy bar, making sure all types of candy bars are fairly evenly distributed.

4. Now each participant tells a story based on the type of candy bar received:

   - Employees with a Mr. Goodbar will tell the group about the nuttiest thing they've ever done.
   - Employees with a Hershey's Dark bar will tell the group about the "darkest" thing they've ever done.
   - Employees with a Krackle bar will tell the group about the funniest thing they've ever done.
   - Employees with a regular Hershey's bar will tell the group about the sweetest thing they've ever done.

Note: If you have a larger group (more than 20 participants), have the employees go back to their groups of three to five to tell their stories, rather than having everyone in the class present to the entire class.

5. After the stories, either the entire class (for a group of 20 employees or fewer) or the small groups of three to five will confer to come up with their racehorse nicknames for the rest of the orientation period. (See examples on the next page.)

Important: The trainer or facilitator must also share stories and answer the questions along with the new employees. When you begin with your story first, the group is able to see you as a person just like them.

DEBRIEFING THE GAME

At DeRoyal, the new employees' racehorse nicknames are used with a game board in which the new employee becomes a racehorse during the program. The movement of the horses on the game board is used to keep score for the various activities in the remainder of the program.

Employees can put their nicknames on their name tents or badges. In a large group, this would be especially helpful to keep track of all the nicknames. And of course, the employees can now enjoy their candy bars (if they haven't already done so)!

SWEET STORIES HEARD AT DEROYAL . . .

It is amazing what people will tell you when they feel comfortable with you. I've heard everything. One very funny story came from an employee who was a real sports nut. He attended a Philadelphia Phillies baseball game; he was extremely excited to get the tickets. He was so excited he became very comfortable in his surroundings and he started to pick his nose. He noticed people around him were staring not just at him, but also at a cameraman who had spotted him in the crowd—he was caught on camera at the game in front of thousands of people, picking his nose! If this wasn't embarrassing enough, he made the highlight films on the local news channel. What a moment of fame. All of his friends called to tease him—of course, everyone had seen him in his moment of glory. The entire class was in hysterics laughing from this story and decided to give him the racehorse name *One Nose from Fame*.

Another story: One of our new hires told us the story of the sweetest thing he had done. His grandmother was alone and feeling lonesome, so he bought her a puppy to keep her company. His racehorse name became *Puppy Love*.

The story that I shared at the ASTD conference took place when I was a dancer at a local theme park, DollyWood. I was performing one evening, clogging to a song with a very fast tempo, and my shoe came off and hit a man seated in the front row. I had to keep going, because the song wasn't finished. I had to dance with one shoe on and one shoe off, with this poor man staring at me. After the program was over, I found the man in the audience and apologized. He thought the whole thing was funny, thank goodness. My racehorse name became *Kick a Rock* because when I kicked my shoe off, I hit a man whose head was hard as a rock!

Participant Handout: Off to the Races!

Ask your new coworkers for their answers to the questions below.

1. What is your name?

2. Where are you from?

3. What is your favorite color?

4. What is your favorite food?

5. What hobbies do you enjoy?

6. What was your most embarrassing moment?

Chapter 33

Jeopardy! The New Employee Review Game

Contributed By: Vicki Hoevemeyer, Owner/ Consultant, Delta Consulting

Vicki's Contact Information:

vicki_delta@hotmail.com
Palatine, Illinois 60074

About the Author: Vicki Hoevemeyer has over 20 years of organizational development and management/leadership development experience as both an internal and external consultant, providing services to transportation, retail, healthcare, education, building materials, nonprofit, and light and heavy manufacturing organizations in California, Arizona, Colorado, Michigan, and Illinois.

Vicki has a bachelor's degree in Social Work from Western Michigan University, and a master's degree in Organizational Development from Eastern Michigan University. She is the author of *High-Impact Interview Questions: 701 Behavior-Based Questions to Find the Right Person for Every Job* (AMACOM, 2005) and coauthor of *First-Job Survival Guide: How to Thrive and Advance in Your New Career* (JIST, 2005).

WHAT IS . . . THE JEOPARDY NEW EMPLOYEE GAME

Most organizations have a series of talking heads for orientation and then wonder why, after four to eight hours of continuous lecture, new hires don't remember critical information about the organization. Adding interactive games to your program, such as a Jeopardy!-style game show format (using multiple-choice options rather than the traditional Jeopardy! format) engages participants and creates a fun learning environment where new hires actually remember what they learned during orientation.

The questions for a Jeopardy game can help teach (and provide a review) of the factual information that new employees need in their new role, such as:

- Employee Benefits
- Company Policies

- Harassment Prevention Policies
- Safety Procedures
- Company Culture and Values
- "Who's Who" in the Company
- Company Products and Services
- Customer Information and Customer Service Procedures
- Any On-the-Job Processes or Procedures

YOU'LL NEED

- A computer with prepared game show software and prepared questions
- A projector, screen, and a remote mouse to run the game from any point in the classroom
- A handout with the questions and correct answers for each participant to provide as a reference at the end of the game
- Prizes for winning team, and prizes for all other players (optional)

AUDIENCE AND TIMING

The Jeopardy Game works well for all types and levels of audiences. The amount of time needed for the game will be determined by the size of your group and the number of questions you include in your Jeopardy game. Typically, the activity will take approximately 60 minutes, which can be broken into two or three rounds depending upon the number of categories and questions in each round.

PREPARATION

First, identify a game show software program that you will use to create the question board and to run the game during the orientation workshop. Of course, you could create your Jeopardy game using a poster board or a flip chart, but a software program will save you time, and it is transportable and easy to update. There are a wide variety of software programs available including *Game Show Presenter*, *Gameshow Pro*, *Classroom Jeopardy!*, and *AllPlay*, with a wide range of costs.

It is also highly recommended that you purchase a "Buzz-In System" if the program you purchase does not include one—the buzzer system is used by the workshop participants to indicate they would like to answer the question. If you don't have one, it is very difficult to tell which person or team was the first to "buzz-in" to provide an answer.

Next, you will need to create the game rules and make decisions on issues such as:

- How much time will be available to play the game? (A minimum of 60 minutes is recommended.)
- How many rounds of play will you have?
- How many Jeopardy question categories will the game have, and what categories of new employee information will you use?
- Will each round increase in point values, and will the difficulty level of the questions increase with each round?
- Will there be a predetermined question that you start with or will it be random?
- If you don't use a buzzer system, how will teams indicate that they know the answer and how will you know which was the first team to indicate they know they answer?
- Can anyone on the team answer the question or does the team need to select a leader from whom you will accept the answer?
- How long will you give the team to answer the question once they have buzzed in?
- Is there a specific format you want when they answer? (e.g., they have to say the letter corresponding to the answer and read the answer such as "c. The first Monday of every week.")
- Assuming that teams will be awarded points for getting the answer right, will they lose the points associated with the question if they get it wrong?
- If the team that buzzed in first gets the answer wrong, can another team buzz in to answer the question for all or partial credit (this may be determined by the limitations of the game show program you purchase)?
- What will you do if there is a tie in the score at the end of the game?
- What if someone disagrees with what you have listed as the right answer?
- What's the penalty for unsportsman-like conduct?

TIPS FOR SUCCESS

Don't assume that people know the rules of the game, even if you are exactly following a popular game show format.

Recap the scores frequently so teams know where they stand (this also enhances the competitive factor).

Keep everyone involved. This is particularly difficult when a team is far behind other teams.

Make each round more competitive. There should be no assumption at any point that the team leading is naturally going to win.

Have a prize for the winning team. The fact that they get a prize for winning is more important than the value of the prize. Generally, you want to keep it small and even have fun with the prize.

Consider making everyone a winner. Everyone likes winning something, so think about having a small prize, different from that of the winning team, for everyone else.

Do practice runs before you launch the game. Use your colleagues to test the game and make sure that you know all the answers, that you can run the game effectively, that all the answers are understandable, that all the answers are correct, and that everything (the game and the buzzers) is working correctly.

While this may sound like a lot of upfront work, it really isn't—your main job is to identify the most important factual new employee information that should be included in the game, and then write the questions in the Jeopardy software program.

CONDUCTING THE ACTIVITY

The game show software that you select will have a structured process for running the game. You may want to consider interspersing a round of Jeopardy at more than one point in the orientation workshop. For example, if you have mandatory videos to show in your orientation workshop, shown them between the rounds of the game. Here is an example of alternating the Jeopardy game rounds with other learning events in your orientation program:

Round 1 of the game

Video: Fire Safety

Round 2 of the game

Video: Bloodborne Pathogens

Round 3 of the game

DEBRIEFING THE ACTIVITY

It is important to debrief the content of each Jeopardy question as it occurs during the game if there is any confusion about the correct answer to the question, to clear up any misconceptions and to provide any additional information pertaining to each question in a "just-in-time" format. No debrief is required other than handing out the questions and answers to participants at the end of the game show so that the new hires have them for future reference.

WHAT ARE SOME EXAMPLES OF JEOPARDY QUESTIONS?

Don't feel that you always have to be serious with every question. Once in a while, throw in a little bit of humor and/or fun into your categories and questions. Here are some examples of categories and questions for the Orientation Jeopardy game:

Category: Safety and Security	An escort is provided to your car if a. You are ill or injured b. You don't feel safe walking there alone because it's dark outside c. There is bad weather d. Any or all of the above e. A or B only
Category: Infection Control: TB	TB is spread when a person with active TB ____ and sends bacteria into the air. People breathe in the germs and become infected. a. Coughs or sneezes b. Coughs, talks, or sneezes c. Coughs, talks, sings, or sneezes d. Breathes on you
Category: [Company Name] Today	During the summer, we have two swans in Heron Pond. Their names are: a. Romeo and Juliet b. Bonnie and Clyde c. Anthony and Cleopatra d. George and Gracie

Chapter 34

25 Ways to Form Pairs, Teams, or Groups

Contributed By: Doris Sims, SPHR, President of Succession Builders, LLC

Doris's Contact Information:

Succession Builders, LLC
www.successionbuilders.com
doris@successionbuilders.com
214-906-3155

About the Author: Doris M. Sims, SPHR is the Founder and President of Succession Builders, LLC, a talent management, succession planning, and new talent onboarding consulting firm. Her experience in organizational development spans over 20 years working in Fortune 100 and Fortune 500 companies. Doris received her master's degree in Human Resource Development from Indiana State University.

Doris is the coauthor of the talent management books *Building Tomorrow's Talent: A Practitioner's Guide to Talent Management and Succession Planning*; *The 30-Minute Guide to Talent and Succession Management*; and *The Talent Review Meeting Facilitation Guide*. Doris is also the author of the McGraw-Hill book *Creative New Employee Orientation Programs*, and has contributed articles to many other McGraw-Hill books and multiple periodicals, including *Training Magazine*, *Talent Management Magazine*, *Professionals in Human Resources*, and *The Consultant's Toolkit*.

FORMING SMALL GROUPS—BE CREATIVE!

Onboarding facilitators frequently need to divide a class into pairs or teams for exercises, review games, and discussions. Here are 25 ideas to make this process fun, organized, and creative. Some of them also help your participants get to know each other a little better and can be used as a "mini-icebreaker."

These grouping techniques also serve to "name" each group in a fun way, such as the Surf Group versus the Turf Group, rather than the mundane Group A versus Group B names.

AUDIENCE AND TIMING

These grouping ideas work for any type of audience, and for large or small workshop sizes.

YOU'LL NEED

No materials are needed!

PREPARATION

No preparation is needed!

CONDUCTING THE ACTIVITY

Simply keep these ideas "on hand" and instruct the group to form pairs or small groups based on the following criteria:

To Divide Participants Into Pairs:

- Find a partner who dislikes the same vegetable you dislike (or won't eat at all).
- Find a partner who has seen the same movie you've seen.
- Find a partner who has a pet peeve that matches one of your pet peeves.
- Find a partner who has read a book that you've read.
- Find a partner who uses the same brand of laundry detergent you use.
- Find a partner who shares a favorite pizza topping with you.
- Find a partner who is wearing an article of clothing that is the same color as an article of clothing you are wearing.
- Find a partner who has a car that is the same color as yours.

To Divide Participants Into Two or Three Teams:

- To form two groups, create a group who would prefer a Fourth of July picnic and a group who would prefer a New Year's Eve party.
- To form three groups, create a Cat Group, a Dog Group, and a No Pet/ Other Pet Group (those with multiple pets should move into a group that needs more participants).

- To form two groups, create a group for those who prefer a good steak or vegetables from the land (the Turf group) and those who would prefer seafood or fish from the water (the Surf group).

- To form two groups, create a group who prefer coffee and a group who prefer tea.

- To form two groups, divide the class into the "Green Thumb" group who are able to keep either house plants or an outdoor garden alive, and the "Silk Group" who are more successful keeping a silk plant looking good.

- To form two groups, create a group who would prefer to sit in front of a roaring fire with a cup of hot cocoa in the ski lodge and those who prefer racing down a ski slope.

- To form three groups, create a group who prefers to vacation in the mountains, a group who prefers to vacation at the beach, and a group who prefers visiting man-made attractions such as historical sites, major cities, Disney World, etc.

- To form two groups, create a group of individuals who have attended at least one high school reunion, and those who have not.

- To form two groups, divide the class into those who will eat sushi, and those who will not eat sushi.

- To form three groups, divide the class into those who are most active on Facebook, those who are most active on LinkedIn, and those who prefer Face-to-Face conversations.

- To form two groups, divide the class into a "Roller Coaster" group and a "Merry-Go-Round" group based on which attraction they are more likely to ride at a theme park.

- To form two groups, divide the class into those who prefer to file their taxes as soon as possible prior to the April 15th deadline, and those who are more likely to wait until the April 15th deadline to file.

To Divide Participants into Multiple Teams:

- If there are markers on the tables, ask each workshop participant to grab a marker. Then ask them to divide themselves into groups according to marker color. Note: One "Rainbow Group" can be formed with multiple marker colors, if needed.

- Instruct participants to divide themselves into four groups: Summer Birthdays, Fall Birthdays, Winter Birthdays, and Spring Birthdays.

- Instruct participants to divide themselves into groups according to their favorite ice cream flavor. (Provide the number of flavor choices that correspond to the number of groups you need for the activity.)

- Instruct participants to divide themselves into groups according to their favorite cartoon characters, choosing from characters such as Sponge Bob, Scooby Doo, Charlie Brown, Wonder Woman, etc.

- Instruct participants to divide themselves into groups according to their favorite cookies, choosing from examples such as Oreos, Chips Ahoy, Fig Newtons, Animal Crackers, etc.

An important tip: Always stay away from controversial groups such as dividing into a Democratic or Republican party, etc. It is also a good idea to stay away from groupings that could result in a gender grouping, such as a Scrapbooking Group and a Car Show Group.

Chapter 35

Learning the Values

Contributed By: Christina M. Lounsberry, Learning and Development Consultant, and Lisa Ann Edwards, Director of Global Learning and Development at Corbis

About the Authors: Christina M. Lounsberry is a Learning and Development Specialist and is an experienced facilitator, classroom instructor, and Human Resources specialist. She has both developed and facilitated numerous programs covering various topics including, leadership, sales, and new hire onboarding.

Christina and Lisa's Contact Information:

Christie@ManagingTalent
Retention.com

Lisa@ManagingTalent
Retention.com
Seattle, Washington
Director, Learning &
Development
Corbis

Lounsberry coauthored "Measuring ROI in Coaching for New Hire Employee Retention: A Global Media Company" published in the *ROI in Action Casebook* (Pfeiffer, 2008). Lounsberry currently works as an independent consultant specializing in the development and marketing of training programs.

Lisa Ann Edwards is a talent development professional whose expertise is based on more than 20 years of experience in the media, technology, printing, and publishing industries.

Edwards has coauthored *Managing Talent Retention: An ROI Approach* (Pfeiffer, 2009) and *Measuring ROI in Coaching for New Hire Employee Retention: A Global Media Company* published in the *ROI in Action Casebook* (Pfeiffer, 2008). In her role as head of learning and development for a global media company, Edwards is responsible for designing and implementing effective talent development solutions that ensure talent engagement, improve talent retention, and serve to feed the talent pipeline.

START A CULTURE TRANSFORMATION USING A VIDEO AND A MOODBOARD PROCESS

Ruche Media Company (RMC) is a global media company with twenty-four offices located around the world. The corporate headquarters of this $260M organization is based in a major metropolitan city located in North America. Most of the 1,100 employees are based at the corporate headquarters while the remaining workforce is located in sales offices located in major metropolitan cities throughout the world.

In an effort to become an Employer of Choice, RMC initiated a culture transformation that included updating the internal values of the company. The new and improved values better aligned with the goals of the organization and the focus of the senior leadership team. These values were rolled out to the current employees as part of a larger effort through a series of programs and were added as an integral part of several new company events. The challenge we faced was ensuring that all new employees coming into the company would have the same understanding of these values and their role in them.

To begin, we turned to our existing New Hire Orientation program, which each new employee attends during their first month. The program included a section that served to introduce the current company goals and initiatives, but we wanted the message around the new values to reflect the commitment of our senior leadership, as well as the importance of each individual employee's effort to consider these values in their everyday work. To do this we decided to incorporate a video from RMC's CEO outlining the four core values and explaining how the company's goals and direction aligned with those values.

After the video, participants discuss the video and identify specific areas where the CEO gave examples of each value and what the company was doing to achieve that value. This approach allowed each new employee to receive a clear, consistent message around the values, despite the fact that new hire orientation is conducted in multiple locations around the world by different facilitators.

In addition to the video introduction we created a "Values in Action" exercise that allowed participants to reflect on the values and how they could apply them to their work. Included in this section was an overview of the behaviors associated with each value that were considered as part of each employee's annual review. We wanted the exercise to be fun and interactive and to reflect the creative nature of RMC's business, so we decided to have participants use images to describe each value.

AUDIENCE AND TIMING

The values introduction video and activity are used monthly as part of RMC's overall New Hire Orientation program that is conducted in each office. New employees attend a one-day New Hire Orientation program during their first month at the company. The program is conducted on-site, generally in a conference room, by a member of the local HR team. Current copies of the presentation and other content for this program, which includes the values introduction video and activity, are available via RMC's internal Web site for both instructors and participants to reference.

The video and follow-up discussion take approximately 30 minutes to conduct while the Values in Action activity takes approximately 45 minutes. In total, the video and moodboard values activities account for about 20 percent of the total New Hire Orientation program, further emphasizing to new hires the importance that the company is placing on them.

PREPARATION

To create this portion of the New Hire Orientation program, we first had to gather all of the information available on the new values and their associated behaviors. We worked with the Human Resources Team as well as the individuals on the team who were responsible for the culture transformation initiative. Once we had all of the relevant information, we began condensing it down into a brief summary of each value and a list of the specific behaviors associated with each to be included in the handouts and presentation.

For the video portion of the program we were lucky enough to be able to use an existing recording. Because information about the values had recently been distributed to the current employees as well, we were able to leverage some of those promotional materials, including the video of RMC's CEO explaining how the updated values aligned with our current strategy and company initiatives. However, we would have suggested this format even if the video had not already existed.

YOU'LL NEED

One of the biggest advantages to the approach that we took was that beyond the initial preparation required to create this portion of the orientation program, there are few additional resources and materials needed to conduct it on an ongoing basis. It was easily incorporated into the existing one-day program that is run monthly by a Human Resources Generalist in each office.

The "Values in Action" exercise does require a small number of office supplies be available such as:

- Poster board or flip-chart paper for each team
- Glue or tape for each team to secure photos to the poster board
- Masking tape or other material to secure the finished moodboards on the walls
- Scissors for each team

- A supply of photos for each team—you can either provide a supply of magazines, catalogs, etc. with photos to be cut and pasted, or supply computers in the classroom with Internet access and color printer access.

CONDUCTING THE ACTIVITY

Working in teams of three or four people, each team has 20 minutes to create a moodboard to illustrate one of the company values. Moodboards are often used in the photography industry and are a collection of images, phrases, and cultural references that serve as inspiration and creative guidance for a project. Team members find, cut, and paste the images (and/or text) that they feel represent and illustrate the company values onto the poster board or flip-chart paper.

DEBRIEFING THE ACTIVITY

After completing their moodboards, participants present their creations to the rest of the group with a brief explanation of why they selected their specific images or phrases. By asking participants to explain the values in their own words, we ensured that they not only learned what the values were, but also understood them and could then better apply the values to their work at RMC.

The final step that is easily overlooked is ensuring that the managers of new employees are familiar with the program and the message that new employees receive regarding the values and are able to reinforce this information on the job. We accomplished this by having a section on the internal New Hire Orientation Web site specifically for managers that includes all of the materials used in the program, a 30-day, 60-day, and 90-day checklist of items to be completed by the new employee and/or manager, and a list of possible discussion questions for managers to use as a guide in their initial one-on-ones with each new employee.

These tools helped the managers to better understand what information their employees were receiving as well as outlining what their role was in the overall onboarding process, which includes discussing with their employee how department goals and individual goals align with the company values.

OUR RESULTS

To evaluate the New Hire Orientation program, RMC utilizes a satisfaction and reaction survey that participants complete at the end of the program. They are asked to rate various aspects of the program on a 1 to 5 scale, including specific portions of the program such as the "Values in Action" exercise. This activity, along with the video introduction from RMC's CEO, consistently received a 4.0 or greater score on this survey, indicating that participants felt it was a valuable and worthwhile portion of the program.

Chapter 36
New Job Butterflies

Contributed By: Mel Silberman, President of Active Training

About the Author: Mel Silberman is a psychologist who is known internationally as a pioneer in the areas of active learning, interpersonal intelligence, and team development. As Professor of Adult and Organizational Development at Temple University, Mel has won two awards for his distinguished teaching. He

Mel's Contact Information:

www.ActiveTraining.com
mel@activetraining.com
Active Training
303 Sayre Drive Princeton NJ
08540
800-924-8157

is also President of Active Training, Princeton, N.J., a provider of products, seminars and publications in his areas of expertise. He has more than 35 years' experience creating and honing techniques that inspire people to be people smart, learn faster, and collaborate effectively.

A graduate of Brandeis University, Mel received his Ph.D. in Educational Psychology from the University of Chicago. He is also a licensed psychologist in the State of New Jersey. His book *101 Ways to Make Training Active* was voted one of the five best training and development books of all time by *Training Magazine*. Mel has also authored over 15 other publications, and served as the editor the ASTD Training and Performance Sourcebooks and the ASTD OD and Leadership Sourcebook. Mel has been honored with a Lifetime Achievement Award by the North American Simulation and Gaming Association.

WE ALL EXPERIENCE THOSE BUTTERFLIES WHEN WE START SOMETHING NEW

Use this activity to open your orientation program in a unique way that will get participants' attention immediately. Your new employees will know this is not the "same old" type of orientation they've been to at every other company. This activity emphasizes the purpose and importance of orientation, especially for those who've been through orientations at other companies and may feel they don't need to attend another orientation program.

This activity also serves as an initial icebreaker between the students and the facilitator, and helps participants recognize that everyone feels a little apprehensive as they start a new job.

AUDIENCE AND TIMING

This activity works well with five people or 500 people, or any number in between. The activity only takes approximately five to ten minutes.

YOU'LL NEED

- One sheet of $8\frac{1}{2}$ by 11-inch colored paper for the instructor and for each employee

PREPARATION

Practice following the directions prior to class until you can smoothly, and without fail, make a butterfly that matches the illustration provided.

CONDUCTING THE ACTIVITY

1. Rather than walking into the room and welcoming employees to the company and so forth in the normal way of orientation programs, try this: Walk into the room without saying anything at first, but simply pass out a sheet of colored paper to each new employee.

2. Ask the employees to follow your directions exactly, and let them know that you are not allowed to answer any questions or to give any further details on each direction. Then give the directions listed below, pausing between each sentence to follow the direction yourself to make your own butterfly, and allow the students a few seconds to follow each instruction.

Fold your paper in half.

Tear off the upper right-hand corner.

Fold your paper in half again.

Tear off the upper left-hand corner.

Fold your paper in half again.

Tear off the lower right-hand corner.

Now open your paper and you will have a butterfly just like mine!

(Of course, some of the participants will have a butterfly like yours, but others will have different shapes—some will even have a hole in the center. That is actually what you want to happen—everyone laughs at the various types of "butterflies" around the room, and now you can make your points in the debriefing of the exercise.)

DEBRIEFING THE ACTIVITY

1. Have the participants all hold up their butterflies so all can see that there are several different versions of the butterfly.

2. Ask: "Why do some of you have different butterflies? I gave the same directions to everyone!" Listen to the responses, and make the point that every direction is subject to interpretation, and people listen from their own perspectives.

3. Say: "Have you ever felt like this when starting with a new company, when you were trying to figure out the company's 'butterflies'—things like the company's culture, company policies, and procedures? Every company is different, and everyone who starts employment with a new company is trying to fit into a new place. Everyone wants their 'butterfly' to come out right. Our NEO program is designed to help provide a road map to our company's vision, values, policies, procedures, and benefits, to reduce those butterflies everyone feels when they begin a new job."

4. Now, introduce yourself, welcome the employees to the company, and go into the agenda of topics for the orientation program.

Example: The Completed Butterfly

Before conducting this activity with a class, practice following the directions to produce a butterfly that looks like the shape below.

Important: The trick to making the butterfly is to tear off (initially) the upper right-hand corner and then rotate the paper so that each subsequent tear occurs in the same corner as the previous tear. Also, your first fold will be from top to bottom, not from side to side, as some participants will do. The completed butterfly has this shape:

Chapter 37

A 90-Day New Employee Reception!

Contributed By: Vicki Hoevemeyer, Owner/Consultant, Delta Consulting

Vicki's Contact Information:

vicki_delta@hotmail.com
Palatine, Illinois 60074

About the Author: Vicki Hoevemeyer has over 20 years of organizational development and management/leadership development experience as both an internal and external consultant, providing services to transportation, retail, healthcare, education, building materials, nonprofit, and light and heavy manufacturing organizations in California, Arizona, Colorado, Michigan, and Illinois.

Vicki has a bachelor's degree in Social Work from Western Michigan University, and a master's degree in Organizational Development from Eastern Michigan University. She is the author of *High-Impact Interview Questions: 701 Behavior-Based Questions to Find the Right Person for Every Job* (AMACOM, 2005) and coauthor of *First-Job Survival Guide: How to Thrive and Advance in Your New Career* (JIST, 2005).

CELEBRATE THE 90-DAY POINT

Too often the excitement of a new person being on board wanes—for the employee as well as for the manager—after the flurry of activity during the new hire's first week or month. Recognizing that new hires are still deciding if they have made a good decision to join your organization for 90–180 days after their first day on the job, it is well worth the time and effort to hold a 90-Day New Employee Reception. This is also a great time to obtain feedback from the new hires on the onboarding process in general.

AUDIENCE AND TIMING

The 90-Day Celebration is appropriate for all levels of employees. The length of the celebration will depend on the number of agenda items (i.e., will you include presentations, activities, a full lunch, or snacks?) that you decide to include in the session.

YOU'LL NEED

The materials you will need depend on your agenda, the number of attendees, etc. If your 90-Day Celebrations become large events, you may want to work with an internal or external event planner to assist with the event. You will want to have a flipchart, markers, and masking tape at the event to take notes from the feedback provided by the new employees about their employment experience.

PURPOSE

The 90-Day Celebration provides the following benefits and objectives for the new employee:

1.   To continue to reinforce the employee's decision to join the organization

2.   To recognize the new hires and send a message that the organization values them and their contributions

3.   To provide an opportunity for new hires to expand their internal network

4.   To provide an opportunity for new hires to meet the executive staff

5.   To provide Human Resources with valuable information to improve the onboarding process

PREPARATION

1.   On a monthly, bi-monthly, or quarterly basis (depending on the number of new hires and assuming that a commitment from top leadership to attend can be assured) Human Resources sends an invitation to all new hires during the designated period. Make sure you keep the size reasonable so that all new hires who want to contribute during the debrief are given the opportunity.

2.   Determine the timing of your event. You should allow 20–30 minutes for networking/meet-and-eat (e.g., coffee and cookies) and about 20 minutes for the new hire debrief. If you also plan on having executive presentations, another 10–20 minutes could be added. It is strongly recommended, though, that the event not last more than 60 minutes.

CONDUCTING THE EVENT

Your event may begin with a "meet and greet" time period, a lunch, and/or time for executives, guests, and new employees to talk and obtain some snacks. Your event may also include an executive presentation, or a welcome from the Human Resources executive, etc.

Then, at a pre-designated (and pre-communicated time), the executives and guests leave the event, and the new hires are asked to have a seat for a feedback discussion.

DEBRIEFING THE EVENT

After a brief welcome and introduction to the debrief process, the HR facilitator leads a discussion to obtain feedback from the employees about their new employee onboarding process:

1. What did you like about corporate orientation?

2. What do you wish we had covered in corporate orientation but didn't?

3. Think back to your first few days with [organization]. Is there something you weren't told—and found out the hard way? Something you wish someone had told you about upfront?

4. If you could make three changes in your onboarding process, what would those changes be?

5. On a scale of 1 to 10 with 10 being the highest, how would you rate the training you received in your department and for your job? Why do you give it that rating?

6. Is there anything I haven't asked you about your onboarding that you'd like to make sure I know about?

The facilitator ends by thanking the new hires for their feedback.

Chapter 38

And the Category Is . . . Ford History!

Contributed By: Kristopher Kumfert, Human Resources Business Partner, Ford Motor

About the Author: Kristopher has 13 years of experience with Ford Motor, with a background in Security, Health, and Safety and Lean Manufacturing.

Kristopher's Contact Information:

Ford Motor of Canada
Oakville Assembly Complex
905-845-2411, ext. 3626
kkumfert@ford.com

Kristopher has obtained a Six Sigma Black Belt. Kristopher earned his BS degree in Administrative Studies from York University. He is currently an HR Business Partner of Salaried Personnel and Organizational Development at Ford Motor.

FORD MOTOR COMPANY INTRODUCES ITS HISTORY IN A GAME FORMAT

Since Ford is about 100 years old, new employees need to understand how that legacy contributes to what the company is today, and to our industry and our competitors. But why lecture about company history when new employees can discover it in teams? With this approach, both information retention and enjoyment of the learning experience increase.

AUDIENCE AND TIMING

This activity works well with groups of any size and with employees of all levels. The length of the game depends on the number of history questions provided and the complexity of the quiz. Ford Motor Company's quiz activity is 45 minutes in length.

YOU'LL NEED

- A quiz sheet for each participant (see the sample Ford quiz sheet)
- A pen or pencil for each participant

PREPARATION

Your quiz questions need to be prepared in advance. The Ford Motor Company quiz is lengthy. It includes about ten pages of questions, including fill-in-the-blank, multiple choice, true/false, and matching. It includes product sketches, vehicle pictures, and brand logos.

The quiz can include historical questions, such as when a certain product was introduced to the public, or how many items a competitor sold during a particular year. Other questions can focus on subsidiary information and other statistical data about sales, products, and consumers. It can be as simple or complex as the designer finds appropriate.

CONDUCTING THE ACTIVITY

Participants should be seated at round tables or in teams. The new employee orientation program leader gives the participants the following instructions:

a) Please take the quiz out of your participant package.

b) For the next 45 minutes [adjust the time frame according to your quiz's length and complexity], work as a team at your table to answer the questions in the quiz. Record your answers on the quiz.

c) You will be in competition with the other tables to see who can answer the most questions correctly. After you are done, we will go through the answers with you. You can begin now!

DEBRIEFING THE ACTIVITY

Debrief the quiz by reviewing the answers and providing additional information to add to the learning. It is suggested that the answers be displayed on Power-Point or on overhead slides, and that they *not* be located elsewhere in the participant's manual.

Have participants call out answers, and congratulate the participant contributing a correct answer. This is a light and fun method to celebrate the company's legacy, to point out fierce competition in a particular product line, and to acquaint new employees with current issues and trends in the industry.

Sample Questions from the Ford Motor Quiz

1. In 1999, the automotive industry sold _____ (number) vehicles.
    a.   54,400,000 units
    b.   78,000,000 units
    c.   12,100,000 units
    d.   8,300,000 units

2. Ford has _____ (number) of plants in _____ countries on _____ continents.
Select your answers from these numbers: 460, 1000, 380, 112, 6, 5, 3, 25, 80, 72

3. What are the top five Ford Motor Company markets?

4. What were the five top-selling vehicles (all makes) in the U.S. last year?

292

Sample Matching Game Items from the Ford Motor Quiz

1. Match the automotive company name with the year it was established.

Ford Motor Company	1903
Toyota	1935
Honda	1948
General Motors	1908
Fiat	1899
Daimler Benz	1886
	1940
	1920

2. Match the number of units sold last year to the brand.

Lincoln (US)	400,834
Mercury (US)	75,312
Volvo	625 (1998)
Mazda (equity interest sales figures)	438,000
Aston Martin	176,493
Jaguar	1,005,000

Chapter 39

Stories in a Jar

Contributed By: Doris Sims, SPHR, President of Succession Builders, LLC

Doris's Contact Information:

Succession Builders, LLC
www.successionbuilders.com
doris@successionbuilders.com
214-906-3155

About the Author: Doris M. Sims, SPHR, is the Founder and President of Succession Builders, LLC, a talent management, succession planning, and new talent onboarding consulting firm. Her experience in organizational development spans over 20 years working in Fortune 100 and Fortune 500 companies. Doris received her master's degree in Human Resource Development from Indiana State University.

Doris is the coauthor of the talent management books *Building Tomorrow's Talent: A Practitioner's Guide to Talent Management and Succession Planning*, *The 30-Minute Guide to Talent and Succession Management*, and *The Talent Review Meeting Facilitation Guide*. Doris is also the author of the McGraw-Hill book *Creative New Employee Orientation Programs*, and has contributed articles to many other McGraw-Hill books and multiple periodicals, including *Training Magazine*, *Talent Management Magazine*, *Professionals in Human Resources*, and *The Consultant's Toolkit*.

A CONTINUOUS ENERGIZER FOR NEW EMPLOYEE ORIENTATION PROGRAMS

Who says all introductions of each participant in a New Employee Workshop (or any workshop) have to all be completed at the beginning of the session (when everyone is thinking about what they are going to say, rather than listening to the introductions of others)? Rather than concentrating all of the employee introductions up front and all at once (and in the ordinary way), this game spreads the introduction of orientation class participants throughout the day, or throughout the entire orientation program. Each introduction includes a unique story about the individual.

This method allows the employees and the instructor to more easily remember the names of each participant, because they are not being bombarded with names all at once, and because it's easier to remember someone's name when you can tie it to a story. It also provides multiple fun and quick breaks through-out the information-filled orientation program.

AUDIENCE AND TIMING

This energizer will work for group sizes from 3 to 100. However, if the group size is more than approximately 30 people, not everyone's story will be read, but everyone will have a *chance* for their story to be read, and therefore a chance to win a prize.

This activity works best when conducted throughout a New Employee Orienta-tion workshop—read a few stories whenever you feel the group needs a little "pick-me-up," so that all stories are read throughout the day without missing out on anyone's story by the end of the day.

YOU'LL NEED

- A glass jar that is large enough for your hand to enter (or a bowl or large glass)
- Story Strips (see the handout)
- Prizes for the best story, the funniest story, the most unusual story, etc.
- A flip chart and markers to make note of each person's name and a "title" for the story each person told

PREPARATION

Make copies of the Story Strips handout and cut each question into a separate strip of paper. Place the strips on the centers of your classroom tables so there are plenty to choose from at each table.

CONDUCTING THE ACTIVITY

1. Ask participants to find at least *ONE* Story Strip that provides an idea for a true story about themselves—stories they are willing to share with the class (and stories that are appropriate to share with the group).

2. Give the participants a chance to jot down the basic ideas of their stories on the Story Strips. They don't need to write the entire story out.

3. Gather the Story Strips and place them in the jar.

4. Start the day with a few Story Strips. Pull a strip out of the jar, announce the name of the person selected and the basic topic of the story, and ask

the person to stand up and tell the full story. Remind the class that at the end of the day, there will be prizes for the most entertaining story, the funniest story, the most unusual story, etc. As each person tells a story, write the person's name and a short title for the story on the flip chart.

5. Throughout the day, when orientation information overload starts to wear the class down, energize the class by picking a few stories from the jar, following the directions in step 4 each time.

6. At the end of the day, ask the class to applaud *every* story as you read the names and story titles from the flip chart, but ask them to clap the loudest for the story they liked best. Award prizes accordingly.

Participant Handout: Story Idea Strips

Make copies as needed of these story strips and cut them out. Place several story strips on each classroom table so participants will have plenty of story idea choices.

Tell the story behind an interesting scar that you have.

Name: _____ Story Summary: _____
_____

Describe the most eccentric teacher or professor you had in school.

Name: _____ Story Summary: _____
_____

Tell us the story of something you did as a child or as a teenager that your parents don't know about, even to this day.

Name: _____ Story Summary: _____
_____

What do you hear yourself saying that your parents used to say?

Name: _____ Story Summary: _____
_____

Tell us about your pet peeve.

Name: _____ Story Summary: _____
_____

Describe an item in your refrigerator (or freezer) that is no longer edible, and tell us why it is still in your refrigerator.

Name: _____ Story Summary: _____
_____

What was the most unusual gift you ever received?

Name: _____ Story Summary: _____
_____

Describe your "15 minutes of fame" or a "brush with the famous" moment you have experienced.

Name: _____ Story Summary: _____
_____

(continued on next page)

Describe the best or the worst customer service experience you've had.

Name: _____ Story Summary: _____

_____

Describe your earliest memory from childhood.

Name: _____ Story Summary: _____

_____

Describe the worst date you've ever had.

Name: _____ Story Summary: _____

_____

Chapter 40

Customizable Bingo Review Game

Contributed by: Steve Sugar, Author and Games Writer, The Game Group

About the Author: Steve Sugar is a writer and teacher of performance games. He is the coauthor of five books on games, including *Games That Teach Teams* and *Training Games*. He has written game systems used throughout the world, including QUIZO, Maestro, X-O Cise, and the template board game, Boardgame Bingo.

Steve's Contact Information:

stevesugar@comcast.net
www.thegamegroup.com
1314 Quarry Lane
Lancaster, PA 17603
717-291-7211

Steve was a faculty member of the University of Maryland Baltimore County (UMBC) where he taught undergraduate management and graduate instructional design. Steve is a frequent presenter at international ASTD, NASAGA, TRAINING, ISPI, and Lilly conferences.

A SPIRITED BOARD GAME TO REVIEW COMPANY BENEFITS, POLICIES, AND MORE!

This Bingo board game provides an excellent way to review information given in a new employee orientation. The dynamics of game play require new employees to recall and apply newly learned information in a timed question-and-answer sequence.

CASE SCENARIO

The two groups eyed each other suspiciously across the table. The mood was tense.

"W-e-l-l, what's your answer?" asked the Group One member who was holding a question card.

"We need more time," members of Group Two pleaded.

"You've had more than enough time," was the reply. "Now, what is your answer?"

After a quick consultation, one member of Group Two said: "It's located in the South Wing?"

There was a short pause, then a member of Team One said: "That's correct."

"Yes-s-s-!!!" chorused Group Two, followed by a refrain of cheers and high fives.

Group Two placed its chip on the game board. Now it was Group One's turn to roll the die and answer a question.

This scene was part of a three-hour new employee orientation that culminated in playing the board game Orientation Bingo. After two hours of presentation, the group of new hires was divided into two teams, each team seated at its own game board. The teams took turns rolling the dice and responding to questions about the orientation presentation. The first team to cover five spaces in a row was declared the winner. Each player received a baseball cap sporting the company logo. Many employees wore their prizes, their "badges of excellence," long into their tenure at the company.

To prepare for the game, the lead trainer teamed with a human resources specialist to develop 60 short-answer questions about the company's personnel protocol and policies. These questions were placed onto PowerPoint—first part, showing question only; second part, showing question AND correct response(s). The lead trainer noted that preparation took twice as long to set up the game for play. "But, it's so-o worth it!" beamed the lead trainer. "Feel the excitement and look how absorbed they are with our information!"

AUDIENCE AND TIMING

This activity requires four or more players. Each game board has two teams of players, with two to five players per team. Larger classes may require multiple game boards, each with two sets of teams. Because of the flexibility in team size and team number, this game works well for both small and large orientation groups. The activity takes approximately 25 to 50 minutes to play, depending on the size of the group.

YOU'LL NEED

- One game board for each set of two teams (See the sample game board.)
- One set of questions prepared on PowerPoint for the game administrator
- One stack of question cards for each set of two teams (See the sample question cards.)

- 20 chips for each team (Each team uses a different color set of chips.)
- One die for each team (Use a die that matches the color of the team's chips, or rotate one die between the two teams.)
- One timer for the game administrator

PREPARATION

1. Prepare a series of questions concerning your company's benefits, facilities, policies, and procedures. Place these questions onto a PowerPoint presentation in two stages—the first stage showing only the question; the second stage showing the question along with the correct response.

2. Make a copy of the game board provided. Laminate the game board, if possible. Prepare one game board for each set of two teams.

3. Purchase poker-style chips and 16mm dice from your local toy store. If possible, use matching sets of chips and dice for each team, such as red chips and die for one team and white chips and die for the other team. This will simplify play.

CONDUCTING THE GAME

The objective of the game is to win by covering five board spaces in a row, horizontally, vertically, or diagonally from corner to corner.

1. Form sets of two teams, with two to five new employees on each team.

2. Have each set of teams meet at its own game board.

3. Have each team select a stack of chips and matching die (optional).

4. Place a stack of cards alongside the playing board for each set of teams.

5. Instruct each team to select a team captain. The captain is responsible for stating the team's final response.

6. Select one team to go first, or have teams roll their die to select the team that will go first. (It is a competitive advantage to go first in this game.)

Game Play—Round 1
- The first team rolls the die.
- The first team places the die on the space that matches the number of the die. This temporarily marks the space.
- The Game Administrator presents the first question on the PowerPoint.
- The Administrator allows the answering team 30 seconds to respond.

- The captain of the first team delivers his/her team's response to the captain of the second team.
- The Game Administrator gives the correct response and then elaborates on the response, as necessary.
  - If the team gives the *correct* answer, they cover the space by removing the die and replacing it with a chip.
  - If the team gives the *incorrect* answer, they remove the die from the game board.
- This concludes Round 1. Play now alternates to the opposing team.

Game Play—Round 2

- The game is played the same way for all rounds.

End of Game

The first team(s) to complete five spaces in a row wins. Distribute prizes and congratulations!

DEBRIEFING THE GAME

Following the game play, take a few minutes to transform the players back into class participants. Most facilitators have their own method of debriefing, but you may wish to follow a debriefing process of "What?" "So what?" and "Now what?" after completing the game.

Orientation Bingo Game Board

1	4	5	3	2
2	5	3	1	4
3	2	4	5	1
4	3	1	2	5
5	1	2	4	3

Sample Question Cards: Orientation Bingo

What is the name of our Chief Executive Officer?	Name all of the company's holidays.	The company's stock is traded on the NYSE under what symbol?
How many countries are we located in?	Name one of our main competitors.	Name two of our company's products or services.
What is the name of our dental care provider?	The company began service in what year?	Who would you contact if you need help with benefits?
How many hours of sick time do you earn in your first year of employment?	On what date will you receive your first paycheck?	Where do you find information about the company's sexual harassment reporting procedure?
What is the name of our Chief Financial Officer?	If you select medical insurance, when does your coverage begin?	How many people work at our company?
Where is the facility's ATM machine located?	How many speakers gave presentations in this orientation program?	What is the company's Web site address?

Chapter 41

The Hunt for Company Policies!

Contributed By: Doris Sims, SPHR, President of Succession Builders, LLC

Doris's Contact Information:

Succession Builders, LLC
www.successionbuilders.com
doris@successionbuilders.com
214-906-3155

About the Author: Doris M. Sims, SPHR, is the Founder and President of Succession Builders, LLC, a talent management, succession planning, and new talent onboarding consulting firm. Her experience in organizational development spans over 20 years working in Fortune 100 and Fortune 500 companies. Doris received her master's degree in Human Resource Development from Indiana State University.

Doris is the coauthor of the talent management books *Building Tomorrow's Talent: A Practitioner's Guide to Talent Management and Succession Planning; The 30-Minute Guide to Talent and Succession Management;* and *The Talent Review Meeting Facilitation Guide.* Doris is also the author of the McGraw-Hill book *Creative New Employee Orientation Programs,* and has contributed articles to many other McGraw-Hill books and multiple periodicals, including *Training Magazine, Talent Management Magazine, Professionals in Human Resources,* and *The Consultant's Toolkit.*

TEACH BASIC COMPANY POLICIES AND BENEFITS USING A SCAVENGER HUNT METHOD

While it is important for new employees to learn basic company policies, procedures, and benefits, it can be tedious and time consuming to present all of this information in a lengthy lecture format. Some basic and easily understandable policies can be "discovered" by employees using a scavenger hunt method, in which employees receive a list of items to "find" and a time limit in which to find them. This activity will particularly appeal to the kinesthetic learner in all of us, and it can actually reduce the time needed to teach company policies, rather than lengthen it.

The activity also serves to help new employees "crack open" an Employee Hand-book (or a Manager Handbook and actually read some of it (or, you can use an online Handbook if you have computer access in the classroom). This game provides a fun way for employees to learn the information located on the hard-copy or online Handbook, and acquaints them with the organization of the information in the Handbook and where to find the answer they need.

AUDIENCE AND TIMING

This activity works best for a group ranging from 3 to 50 employees. However, the activity could work for a larger group if the employees work in teams, to keep the activity more manageable.

The length of time needed for this activity depends upon the number of policies, procedures, or benefits the employees are to find. Factor approximately one minute per item: If you have 20 items for the employees to find, plan 20 minutes for the activity.

YOU'LL NEED

One or more sources of company information for employees to "find" policies, benefits, procedures, and company products or services. There are two ways to provide this information:

1. If you want the employees to stay in the classroom, have sources in the room such as orientation workbooks, employee handbooks, brochures, pamphlets, company policy manuals, access to the company intranet, or other hard-copy materials on the classroom tables.

2. If the employees can leave the classroom, and if your company managers support this approach, the new employees can go on an actual scavenger hunt by asking questions of current employees to see how many answers they can obtain within the time limit, or by accessing the information on a computer in another room. This approach is ideal: It is more fun and energetic (and it keeps your current employees up to date!). But it could also be impractical, depending on the company's size and flexibility about distracting current employees from their jobs, and of course, you will want to plan much more time for the activity if the employees leave the room.

   - Copies of the Company Policy Scavenger Hunt! handout for each employee
   - Pens or pencils for the employees

■ A watch or clock with a second hand
■ Prizes

PREPARATION

If the employees will be walking through the facility gathering answers on their scavenger hunt, the facilitator needs to ensure that managers and employees of each department support this plan, and that they are prepared for it. Also, the instructor needs to create an answer sheet for the handout that matches your own company policies and benefits.

CONDUCTING THE GAME

1. Refresh the employees' memories on the concept of the scavenger hunt: Participants have a list of items to find, and they normally obtain these items by going from house to house to see how many items they can gather. The participants are scheduled to meet back at the starting location at a specified time to determine who gathered the most items from the list.

2. Explain to the class that they will be participating in a Company Policy Scavenger Hunt. Then pass out a copy of the handout to each employee.

3. If they are staying in the classroom, they will find the items in their orientation workbooks and employee handbooks and whatever other sources you have provided for them. If they will be leaving the classroom, they are to move through the facility (no running, of course), asking current employees to provide the "items" on the list by answering a question. Each current employee in the facility can answer only **one** question, so the new employees must move on to another current employee once they have received one answer.

4. Write the time when the game will be over on the flip chart. (Allow approximately 1 minute per item for an in-classroom scavenger hunt, and slightly more time for an out-of-the-classroom scavenger hunt, depending on the size of your facility and how much walking they will need to do.) Instruct the class that only scavenger collections that arrive at or before the time listed on the flip chart will be accepted. Explain that the employee(s) who have the most correct items within the time limit will win a prize. Then, dismiss the class (ring a bell or honk a horn if you have any sort of sound effect).

5. When the employees return, review each item on the handout to announce the correct answer. Tell the employees they are on the honor system to mark all correct answers, and that they should write in any missing information or

make corrections if needed. If you promised prizes for the winner(s), identify at that point the participants who obtained the most correct answers within the time limit.

DEBRIEFING THE GAME

Once a team shouts out that they have located all of the scavenger items (or the first team to return to the room with all of the completed scavenger items), ask everyone to "Hold" while you review each of the answers on the team's sheet to make sure everything is correct. If everything is correct, then you have a winning team, and you will want to go over all of the correct answers so the other teams can fill in the items they missed.

Participant Handout: The Hunt for Company Policies!

The object of this activity is to collect the answers to the 20 questions below, within the time limit provided by the instructor. The individual or team that obtains the most answers in the shortest time period wins!

I need to return to the room by this time: _____:_____

Item #	Item Description	Answer or Page Number of This Information
1	Name or collect three items that can be recycled in the company. (One extra point is granted if the items are actually collected.)	
2	How many vacation days would a nonexempt employee receive in the first year if employment started on May 1?	
3	What is the company's dress code policy on Fridays?	
4	In an emergency situation within the company facility, what number should an employee call to get help?	
5	What is the company's intranet (internal) Web site URL address?	
6	What number should an employee call to obtain information in the event of Inclement weather?	
7	How many floating holidays would an employee have if he or she began employment on February 1?	
8	Who should an employee contact to reserve a conference room?	
9	What is the name of the top Human Resources manager in the company?	
10	What are the names of the medical insurance carriers employees can select from?	
11	What is the company's policy on smoking?	

(continued on next page)

Item #	Item Description	Answer or Page Number of This Information
12	Give one example of an inappropriate use of the company's e-mail system.	
13	Who should an employee contact to schedule business travel?	
14	Provide one example of "gross misconduct" behavior.	
15	What are the names of the dental insurance carriers employees can select from?	
16	When will you receive your first paycheck?	
17	Give an example of an employee "conflict of interest" situation.	
18	What is the name of the corporate newsletter?	
19	In what month will you receive your first annual performance review?	
20	What is the name of the life insurance carrier for company employees?	

Chapter 42

Have Your Passport Ready!

Contributed By: Lorraine Ukens, Owner of Team-ing with Success

Lorraine's Contact Information:

Team-ing with Success
25252 Quail Croft Place
Leesburg, FL 34748
352-365-0378

About the Author: Lorraine Ukens is the owner of Team-ing with Success, specializing in team building and experiential learning. Team-ing with Success also provides performance improvement consulting, as well as training activity books and games. Lorraine received her master's degree in Human Resource Development from Towson University in Maryland, where she also taught as an adjunct faculty member for eight years.

Lorraine is the author of training and development resources, including books (*Getting Together, Working Together, All Together Now!, Energize Your Audience!, Pump Them Up, Skillbuilders: 50 Customer Service Activities, 101 Ways to Improve Customer Service*), consensus activities (such as *Adventure in the Amazon* and *Stranded in the Himalayas*) and games (*Common Currency: The Cooperative-Competition Game*, and *What Would You Do? A Game of Ethical and Moral Dilemma*). She was the editor of and a contributor to *What Smart Trainers: The Secrets of Success from the World's Foremost Experts.*

CREATING AN INTERACTIVE TOUR OF THE COMPANY

This is an interactive data-gathering activity that provides exposure to the organization's physical facilities and information on departments that will have an impact on the employees' roles and responsibilities. The information should be incorporated into every new employee orientation process on the first day of employment.

AUDIENCE AND TIMING

This activity works well for a new employee orientation event. The activity requires a minimum of 2 participants, and a maximum of 15 participants with 10 participants as the ideal size for the exercise. The activity will take 30 to 60 minutes or longer, if you have a large facility.

YOU'LL NEED

- Passport booklets (create your own using the template and directions provided in this chapter)
- Facility maps
- Department Information Sheets (optional)
- Stickers or stamps (optional)

PREPARATION

1. Using the passport template provided, duplicate one copy for each participant. Cut along the outer edges of the passport form, then cut one (or more if needed) blank sheets of paper to match the size and shape of the passport template. Fold both sheets in half, inserting the blank paper inside the printed passport form. Lay both sheets flat, and staple at the fold line. A "booklet" is formed when the stapled sheets are folded in half.

2. Prepare a map of the facility, showing the location of departments and listing the representative for each one. If time is limited or if the facility is large, designate the specific departments that the employees are to visit. Duplicate one copy of the map for each participant.

3. Notify the appropriate department representatives of the date and time frame in which employees will be visiting. Explain that each set of employees will ask the representative for a brief description of the department's function.

4. After providing this brief description of the department, the representative is to enter his or her initials and the department name into each passport booklet. Or, each department could be identified by a sticker or stamp that can be used instead of initials, to increase the realism of traveling around the company and having the passport stamped.

5. *Optional:* Make copies of the Department Information Sheet and forward one copy to each designated department for completion, indicating a return date prior to the orientation session. Make copies of the completed information sheets for each participant as a follow-up resource.

CONDUCTING THE GAME

1. Explain to participants that one of the important features of an orientation program is gaining knowledge about the organizational facility and the people who work there. To this end, they will be completing a travel tour that will take them to various departments throughout the company.

2. Distribute one passport booklet and a facility map to each employee. Instruct each person to place his or her name on the front cover of the passport.

3. Direct the employees to form pairs (or trios, as necessary). State that each set of employees will locate and visit the departments indicated on the map. They are to ask the appropriate representative for a brief description of the department's function. After the question is answered, the representative will enter his or her initials (or stamp or sticker) and the name of the department into each person's passport booklet.

4. Announce the designated time limit (20 to 45 minutes) that the participants will have to complete the tour and return. Dismiss the participants.

5. At the end of the designated time, reassemble the returning participants.

6. If the size of the group and time allow, facilitate a group discussion as the participants share aspects of the information they gained from the various departments.

7. *Optional:* Distribute copies of the completed Department Information Sheets to each participant as a follow-up resource.

DEBRIEFING THE GAME

Lead a general discussion by asking the following questions:

- What was your overall reaction to this activity?
- Which department did you find most interesting, and why?
- How will this information benefit you in doing your job?

Explain that an important part of new employee orientation is obtaining company-level information. This activity provided information about the physical facilities as well as the key functions of departments that will have an impact on the new employees' roles and responsibilities. More importantly, each employee was actively involved in gaining this knowledge. This approach sends the message that the organization expects employees to be proactive and take initiative in completing job tasks.

In addition, orientation programs provide socialization and support to new employees. Each person has been partnered with at least one other individual who will continue to be his or her "orientation buddy." These partners can be a resources for each other as employees settle in.

Department Information Sheet

Department Name:

Department Head:

Department Function:

Products/Services:

Resource Contacts:

Hours of Operation (if applicable):

Passport Template Example

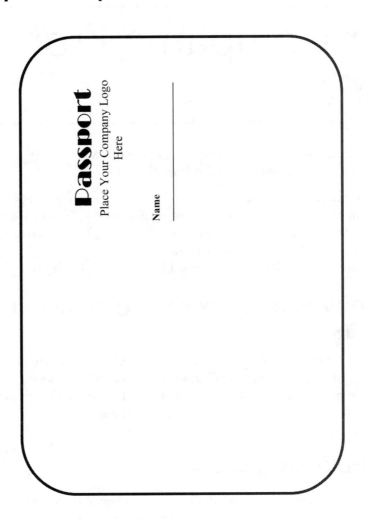

Chapter 43

Your Company: From A to Z!

Contributed By: Linda G. Duebner, Senior Employee & Organization Specialist, Mary Kay Inc.

About the Author: Linda's experience in education, training, and development spans 20 years. Her training and development background includes both technical training and employee development programs. Linda holds a BS degree in Education.

Linda's Contact Information:

Linda.duebner@mkcorp.com
P.O. Box 799045
Dallas, Texas 75379-9045

A DEEP DIVE INTO MARY KAY CULTURE AND PRODUCTS

At the end of Day 1 of the Mary Kay 3-Day Orientation Program (see the program design in the Program Development section of this book) the new employees participate in the *Mary Kay A to Z* activity. The activity is very simple to conduct, and it serves as a good reinforcement of all the culture information participants were exposed to during the day.

AUDIENCE AND TIMING

This activity works well for small or large groups; if you have a large group, you will want to divide the class into groups of 6 to 10 participants to work in small group teams. The entire activity takes a minimum of 30 minutes if you have no more than approximately 12 to 15 participants in your orientation workshop; more time will be needed for a large group of 15 or more participants.

YOU'LL NEED

- Handouts for each participant "A-Z at [Your Company Name]"—see the sample *Mary Kay A to Z* handout in this article
- Prizes for the winning group (optional)

PREPARATION

■ The only preparation needed to conduct the game is to ensure that you have enough copies of the "A-Z" Handouts for each workshop participant.

CONDUCTING THE GAME

1. Divide the class into groups of 6 to 10, depending on the size of the workshop group.

2. Distribute the "A to Z" Handout and explain that each group will come up with one word or phrase for each letter that has something to do with what they heard during the day. The goal for each group is to come up with *the most unusual word* for each letter (this is basically the board game Scattergories, just played with a Mary Kay slant).

3. Allow about 10 minutes for each group to write responses on the "A to Z" handout, and then ask each group to elect a spokesperson.

DEBRIEF THE GAME

The spokesperson for each group presents their list to the large group, with a little salesmanship. We usually use our A/V support person as the judge for which group was the most original (he's been doing this for 14 years, so he really knows unusual!) and the group who has the "most original" answers receives a group prize.

Participant Handout for the Mary Kay from A to Z Activity

MARY KAY – A TO Z!!

A	_____	N	_____
B	_____	O	_____
C	_____	P	_____
D	_____	Q	_____
E	_____	R	_____
F	_____	S	_____
G	_____	T	_____
H	_____	U	_____
I	_____	V	_____
J	_____	W	_____
K	_____	X	_____
L	_____	Y	_____
M	_____	Z	_____

Part 6
Onboarding Leaders

Some companies choose to have their new supervisors and managers attend a management orientation program in addition to the company's New Employee Orientation program, to ensure that they know applicable federal employment laws and the company policies and procedures for managers. The program may focus primarily on the initial onboarding of the new manager, or it may provide a comprehensive management development curriculum for new leaders.

In this section, you'll find the *Management Orientation Shopping List*—This is a comprehensive checklist of potential topics for a management orientation program. Simply review the list and check the topics that pertain to your company. Then use the customized list to form the basic outline for your program.

In this section you'll find:

- Ideas and tools for onboarding senior leaders and executives in the organization
- Advice and information to help you orient new leaders
- Workshop exercises and multiple pages of "management basics review questions" that can be used within any leadership onboarding program.

Chapter 44

Management Onboarding: Identifying Content

Contributed By: Doris Sims, SPHR, President of Succession Builders, LLC

Doris's Contact Information:

Succession Builders, LLC
www.successionbuilders.com
doris@successionbuilders.com
214-906-3155

About the Author: Doris M. Sims, SPHR is the Founder and President of Succession Builders, LLC, a talent management, succession planning, and new talent onboarding consulting firm. Her experience in organizational development spans over 20 years working in Fortune 100 and Fortune 500 companies. Doris received her master's degree in Human Resource Development from Indiana State University. Doris is the coauthor of the talent management books *Building Tomorrow's Talent: A Practitioner's Guide to Talent Management and Succession Planning; The 30-Minute Guide to Talent and Succession Management;* and *The Talent Review Meeting Facilitation Guide.* Doris is also the author of the McGraw-Hill book *Creative New Employee Orientation Programs,* and has contributed articles to many other McGraw-Hill books and multiple periodicals, including *Training Magazine, Talent Management Magazine, Professionals in Human Resources,* and *The Consultant's Toolkit.*

When designing or updating an management onboarding program, you will want to ensure you include all critical content. Use the lists in this section to identify topics that are appropriate to include in your management onboarding program, your management Intranet site, or in your management procedure guides.

Company Culture/Integration Topics

❏ The Company's Mission, Vision, and Values
❏ Company Strategy/Goals
❏ The Company's History
❏ Company Leaders/Executives
❏ Lunch with Company Leaders
❏ Parent Company Information

❏ The Company's Customers
❏ Company Logo(s) and Marketing Plans
❏ The Company's Competitors
❏ NYSE Symbol/Information
❏ Company Locations/Size(s)

(continued on next page)

- ❑ Company Subsidiary Information
- ❑ Recognition and Reward Systems
- ❑ The Company's Leadership Competencies
- ❑ The Company's Products Services
- ❑ Executive Presentations
- ❑ Company Growth, Past and Future
- ❑ Company Patents

Legal Topics

- ❑ Civil Rights Act
- ❑ Americans with Disabilities Act
- ❑ Equal Pay Act
- ❑ Family Leave and Medical Act
- ❑ Worker's Adjustment and Retraining Notification Act (WARN)
- ❑ Definition of a Contractor
- ❑ Sexual Harassment Definitions
- ❑ Handling a Sexual Harassment Report
- ❑ Preventing Harassment
- ❑ OSHA Requirements
- ❑ COBRA Requirements
- ❑ Age Discrimination Act
- ❑ Your Industry Regulations
- ❑ Sarbanes-Oxley Requirements
- ❑ Workers' Compensation/Safety
- ❑ Insider Trading Laws
- ❑ Affirmative Action
- ❑ Understanding Exempt versus Nonexempt
- ❑ FLSA Pay/Overtime Regulations
- ❑ Intellectual Property Policies

Management Policies and Procedures

- ❑ The Hiring and Orientation Process
- ❑ Generating/Renewing Contracts
- ❑ Performance Appraisals
- ❑ Purchasing Procedures
- ❑ Compensation/Salary Increase Policies
- ❑ Confidentiality Policies
- ❑ Vendor/Supplier Policies and/or the RFP Process
- ❑ Tuition Reimbursement Policies
- ❑ Personnel Requisition Procedure
- ❑ Stock Option Policies/Exercise Procedure
- ❑ Management Bonus Plan
- ❑ Exiting Employee Procedures
- ❑ Travel Policies and Procedures
- ❑ Budget Reports and Procedures
- ❑ Conflict of Interest Policies
- ❑ Processing an Employee's Status Change
- ❑ Proprietary Information/Property
- ❑ Progressive Discipline Procedures
- ❑ Intellectual Property Policies
- ❑ Management Training Programs
- ❑ Profit and Loss Reporting Processes

Basic Management Skills

- ❑ Interviewing and Recruiting
- ❑ Delegating
- ❑ Developing Mission/Vision
- ❑ Performance Management
- ❑ Management Procedures
- ❑ Company Policies
- ❑ Financial Acumen and Budgeting
- ❑ Effective Meetings
- ❑ Coaching, Feedback, and Appraisals
- ❑ Diversity/Communication Styles
- ❑ Setting Goals and Action Plans
- ❑ Writing a Job Description
- ❑ Talent and Succession Management
- ❑ Motivating Employees

Chapter 45

A Leadership Onboarding Program That Works!

Contributed By: Erika Lamont and Brenda Hampel, Connect the Dots Consulting

About the Authors: Brenda Hampel and Erika Lamont have consulted, coached, inspired and developed operational and human resources teams to create onboarding and leadership development experiences at TJX Companies, Cardinal Health, Audi of America, Volkswagen Group of America, Chico's FAS, Sara Lee Food and Beverage, The Ohio State University Medical Center, Coach Inc., DSW, Victoria's Secret Stores, and NCR/Teradata.

Brenda is a Human Resources professional with a degree from The Ohio State University. Erika is an Operations professional and received her degree at Miami University. They have been consulting and building solutions for Fortune 500 organizations since 1999.

Contact Information:

Connect the Dots
5995 Wilcox Place, Suite A
Dublin, OH 43016
1.877.793.8805
www.connectthedotsconsulting.com
info@connectthedotsconsulting.com

POSITIONING AND DEFINING LEADERSHIP ONBOARDING

Many organizations have put leadership onboarding programs on their lists of initiatives. The motivation for this being an area of focus can vary depending on the particular organization. Some have experienced painful turnover in a specific role or function, while others are seeking ways to speed their return on investment for the selection and recruitment processes.

Research data supports that 40 percent of leaders hired into new organizations are out after 18 months and 20 percent of internally promoted leaders are underperforming after two years on the job.[1]

After an organization has determined and articulated its business case for creating and implementing a leadership onboarding process, it may be difficult to know where and how to begin to build the process. The information in this chapter is a roadmap for a leadership onboarding process which has been tested and used successfully in organizations considered small to mid-sized, as well as Fortune 50 companies.

The Connect the Dots onboarding model starts with a definition of leadership onboarding and its role and context in the *Talent Management Cycle.*

Talent Management Cycle

Onboarding

Performance Management

Onboarding Definition:
A process that positions an organization's new leaders and associates with its vision, strategies, goals and culture. Success results from partnership of the new leaders, their managers, and their HR Business Partners.

Selection
Internal Promotions

Leadership Development

External Hires

Succession Planning

Onboarding is positioned in an organization's talent management cycle to bridge the gap between the selection process and the performance management and leadership development processes. It allows both the new leader and the organization to transition and assigns roles and responsibilities for each participant. Onboarding begins upon the job acceptance and usually ends around the four-month mark, when it is appropriate to transition to the formal performance management process. Most organizations do recognize, however, that it can take up to a full year for a new leader to be completely integrated, but best practices suggest a structured three- to six-month formal process.

The definition of leadership onboarding draws the distinction between onboarding and orientation. A typical orientation is event-based, one-way communication that is generally not tailored to a leader's needs. Its focus is to meet the basic needs of new employees and provide a setting for transactions related to starting a new job. Leadership onboarding is a longer-term program, designed specifically for a new leader but it also provides a consistent experience for all who are onboarding in the organization. Its focus is on speeding the learning process and supporting higher-level performance.

INVENTORY AND INTEGRATE

There are probably many components of a leadership onboarding process that currently exist inside organizations, and it is important to recognize them and determine the ones that are working and the ones that are not. By comparing what is being done now with a best-practice model, it is possible to build your onboarding process to fill the gaps.

Things that may already be in place you want to continue to use—

- Company information packet (or Web site or portal)
- Relocation support process
- Checklist for office set-up
- Meet and Greet schedule
- New Leader Assimilation
- Mentor or Onboarding Coach

THREE PILLARS OF SUCCESS

In our years of working with all types of organizations, we have been able to identify and articulate the three most important components of a successful leadership onboarding program. Each time we work with a client organization to build or customize their program, we focus the roles, resources and delivery around three main themes.

They are—

1.   Knowledge

2.   Relationships

3.   Feedback

The first pillar, knowledge, refers to the information that the new leaders need to acquire throughout their onboarding. It starts with a broad overview of organizational vision, mission, values, and history, and then builds to current strategies, processes, and culture. From there, new leaders need timely knowledge about their function, their teams, and their roles.

The next pillar, building relationships, is critically important to a new leader's success. This component is especially important for leaders who are brought into an organization to bring about change or lead through a crisis. But it is, of course, vital to any new leader's success as they execute their objectives through and with others.

Lastly, the providing of timely and actionable feedback is usually the missing link in most leadership onboarding programs. Organizations are typically not set up to give formal feedback, and the informal feedback on which they rely can be incomplete or missing entirely. Impressions and perceptions about the new leaders are formed very early, so it is really important to incorporate both quantitative and qualitative early feedback into the onboarding program, usually at the 45- to 60-day mark.

These three components are the foundation on which you build an onboarding program that allows you to see results that are consistent with your objectives.

BUILDING THE MODEL

Once you have identified the existing parts of the process that should be integrated into the onboarding program, it is helpful to use a time-based or phased approach to build out the process.

Below is the Connect the Dots' phased approach to leadership onboarding. It is designed to deliver the right information at the right time in the new leader's onboarding:

Too often, there is a deluge of information and meetings in the first few days and weeks on the job, and the new leader cannot retain it all because he/she does not have context or enough experience with the new culture. So, an effective program is one that delivers the information and resources "just-in-time" and provides support and accountability along the way.

In order to deliver the coaching and content that is described in this model, Connect the Dots uses *Roadmaps* for the HR partners who are facilitating the onboarding program and for the hiring managers who have direct reports who are onboarding. The *90-Day Plan* template functions as the "roadmap" for the new leaders themselves.

THE PRESTART PHASE: GET PREPARED

The *Prestart* phase is approximately the two to four weeks from the time that the new leader has accepted the new role to the start date of the new position. We like to refer to this time as a "sweet spot" because the new leader is disconnecting from her former role and is excited and energized by the new one.

This is an ideal time to get organizational information to her and establish a baseline of knowledge. Information should be mostly public and accessible on the company's Web site, in the annual report, news articles, or other non-confidential presentations. A briefing portfolio for new leaders can be created with some of these standard items, and then customized for each new leader in a particular role.

By sending pertinent information to the new leader before her start date, it sends a message that the organization is preparing for her arrival and genuinely cares about getting her up to speed. Sending a package of information also bridges that "dark period" between the offer letter and the start date. Many new leaders excitedly accept an offer, and may get some initial paperwork, but then don't hear from their new organization or get any transition support before that first day. They get the gift basket with wine and popcorn, as one of our clients did, then nothing else!

Unfortunately, many organizations miss this golden opportunity to bond with the new leader and brand themselves as a preferred employer. By introducing the new leader to onboarding process and providing some introductory information, the organization can help affirm the new leader's decision to accept the job.

Inside the organization, there are several Prestart action items that should be happening at the same time as the communication touch points with the new leader. The first and most important of this phase is the creation of the new leader's onboarding plan. Some organizations refer to this as a 90-Day Plan, or Transition Plan, but whatever the title, it should be initiated by the HR partner who is responsible for the new leader's onboarding experience and the hiring manager.

Often, the best way to begin this plan is to hold a meeting with the HR partner and the hiring manager to discuss and review the data that was collected throughout the selection process, identify specifically why this individual was chosen for this role, and note any potential barriers to a smooth transition. It is also important to mention that the objectives identified in the onboarding plan are not performance objectives, but onboarding objectives and that they should be managed and measured as such.

The Prestart phase can also be a productive one for the most senior new leaders of an organization if they have the opportunity and support to meet a few of their key stakeholders before Day One. This provides a more casual and comfortable meeting setting that will allow the new leader to meet peers, team members, or community leaders who will be instrumental in his/her success. It allows the new leader to start to understand the organization's culture and expectations before he/she is put "on the spot" in a formal meeting or presentation.

"Meet and Greets" are often a key focus for new leaders in their first weeks on the job. These are important, but they can also be somewhat frustrating and unproductive if not executed appropriately. By selecting the right people for these meetings, and by providing purpose and suggested talking points or discussion questions, these conversations can be the building blocks of key stakeholder relationships. The suggested resources for these "meet and greets" are the *Personal Network Tool* and the *Meet and Greet Suggested Agenda*.

WEEK ONE: GET SET UP

During Week One, it is important to continue to take care of all the logistical and set-up needs of a new leader. Then it is important to have a few conversations with key onboarding participants so as to lay the foundation of learning and understanding. We often joke that no organization gets credit for executing the logistics of a new leader, but it certainly suffers the wrath if these needs are not met appropriately. Also, without the basic resources, a new leader is distracted and delayed in his ability to engage in the new role and focus on the important items. If your organization does not already use a type of *Logistics Checklist*, this template will be a starting point.

Next, if a formal orientation is part of your process, it is ideal to have it fall into the first week when there are not as many other competing priorities. If there is not a formal orientation, or if the new leader does not participate, it is important that a separate meeting take place to make sure that all of the proper forms, benefit information, and any other transactional items are attended to in a timely manner. Again, these items are not always at the forefront of a leader's onboarding, but if mishandled, they can become big distractions for the new leader as well as the organization and prevent the new leader from trusting your onboarding support.

Both the HR partner and the hiring manager should take the opportunity to meet with the new leader during her first week on the job. This meeting will help to clarify onboarding objectives and introduce the *90-Day Plan* to the new leader. It also allows a dialogue that will surface any immediate questions or issues that can be resolved quickly. If distance or travel makes these meetings challenging, make every effort to conduct them by phone or video conference.

MONTH ONE: GET KNOWLEDGE AND ROLE CLARITY

The main purpose of this phase is to build on the new leader's knowledge of the organization and learn how her new role fits within the organization. It is critical for the hiring manager and HR partner to establish onboarding objectives and create opportunities for the new leader to develop key relationships.

Too often, brief introductions are made at the typical "Meet and Greet" events, and the new person often does not yet understand which people she should be connecting with to meet her onboarding objectives. With the support of a detailed 90-Day Plan, a new leader should be able to learn about the organization, meet the key people she needs to meet, and lay the groundwork for some initial "early wins," or key deliverables, that will help her garner support from her boss, her peers. and her team.

A key factor in creating an effective *90-Day Plan* is that the objectives and early wins be created and defined in a realistic timeframe. We strongly suggest that no more than five objectives be included in each of the onboarding phases and that they build on each other through the process. So, for example, the new leader needs to learn the organization's overall strategy, core processes, and "language" (acronyms and commonly used identifiers) before suggesting significant changes to her particular function's processes and team.

Next, role clarity for the new leader and the organization is extremely important and also one of the most-cited reasons for failure or derailment of a new leader.[2] By incorporating the discussion of *Role Clarity* into the onboarding conversations, the new leader will have the opportunity to test her perceptions and beliefs about the role with the hiring manager and the HR partner. This allows for open dialogue of differing ideas and surfaces potential barriers to achieving the onboarding objectives and early wins that are identified in the 90-Day Plan.

As mentioned in the Prestart phase, the commonly used "Meet and Greet" process that organizations include in their leadership onboarding programs is also part of the Month One activities. By creating and facilitating a well-designed and purposeful *Meet and Greet process*, the new leader will be able to start to build those very important relationships with her key stakeholders. Each participant should be selected strategically, according to the *Stakeholder Analysis*, and then a prepared *Meet and Greet Suggested Agenda* should be sent with each meeting invitation. These simple, yet often omitted, steps will yield highly productive first meetings and lay the foundation for productive working relationships with the participants.

These first few weeks are challenging because new leaders tend to want to make a good impression, prove that they are competent for the job, and/or bring about the change or results for which they were hired. Doing too much too fast can be a fatal error. Usually organizations want change and results, but in the context of their unique culture. By preparing a comprehensive *90-Day Plan*, including the Role Clarity discussions, and implementing a purposeful "Meet and Greet" process, the Month One phase will deliver its expected results.

MONTH TWO: GET THE CULTURE AND BUILD RELATIONSHIPS

At about the 60-day mark, a new leader should be starting to form a pretty clear picture about what it takes to be successful in her new environment. However, without the guidance of a competent HR Partner and manager, she could easily make mistakes that may cause the organization to question her "fit." Month Two is the best time to coach a new leader with information about the organization's culture and map that culture against the behaviors that the new leader has been demonstrating.

Connect the Dots has worked with organizations to create a *Culture Roadmap*. This resource clearly states the behaviors and cultural norms of the organization and can be used to coach behaviors that are missing the mark.

Timely feedback is a key part of a successful onboarding process, and is also rarely delivered. The new leader's behavior is discussed, but usually not with her! There may be undercurrents of her not being the "right fit" or "best candidate" for the job, and no actionable information is delivered to the new leader so that she can correct her mistakes. Formal and informal feedback should be integrated into the onboarding discussions as the new leader discusses progress with her manager and HR Partner. Feedback can be solicited by the manager and/or the HR Partner by using the resource *Gathering Feedback for the New Leader* with the key stakeholders who were identified as instrumental to this new leader's success.

Another opportunity for feedback that produces immediate results is a *Team Alignment*. This is a one-time event that is facilitated by an internal HR Partner, or external consultant and includes the new leader and her team. The session begins as the new leader introduces the purpose of the meeting to the whole team. The new leader then leaves the room and the team asks questions about the new leader and what her ideas are for the team. This is a highly successful model that was conceived at General Electric as the *New Leader Assimilation Process*. The session ends with a list of questions for the new leader to answer for the team and two lists of commitments: one for the new leader to the team and one for the team to the new leader.

With open, honest discussion and candid responses to their questions, the team can focus on the new leader's objectives for the team with the confidence that they each have a role. The process can also humanize the new leader and offer opportunities for the team to build stronger personal relationships that translate into at more productive working environment.

Because of the expectation to "hit the ground running" for so many new leaders, they can overlook a critical step in their onboarding: building relationships. At the highest levels in an organization, relationships are what drive most of the decision making. A new leader can seriously jeopardize her ability to be effective if she is not aligned with the right people. A top leader cannot simply depend on her title to influence her boss, her peers, or her team members. She must carefully build their trust by delivering on commitments, prove her competencies in the context of the new culture, and understand the interdependence of each relationship and her objectives and initiatives.

As a result, the new leader must focus on continuing to build relationships with those key stakeholders who were identified by her hiring manger and HR partner. Month Two is also the time for the new leader to identify additional individuals, both inside and outside the organization, with whom to build relationships.

By using the *Meet and Greet process* as a starting point, the new leader can reconnect with those people who can have the most impact on her short-term and long-term objectives. The new leader can continue to use her *Personal Network Tool* to refine and deepen these relationships. This tool assists the new leader in identifying who in her network can support each of her objectives and how to build a strategy to begin and strengthen those relationships. It provides both strategic and tactical steps in relationship building and can be useful to a new leader long after she is considered "new."

MONTH THREE: RECEIVE/ACT ON FEEDBACK AND DELIVER ON 90-DAY PLAN

By the time a new leader has reached the 90-day mark in her new role, most organizations expect results. If the new leader has delivered on commitments and objectives that were agreed upon by her manager and HR Partner at the beginning of her onboarding process, she is well positioned to build on that success in the months to follow. However, a major barrier in attaining these objectives and early wins is the absence of constructive feedback.

The new leader needs input during their early days in the position from:

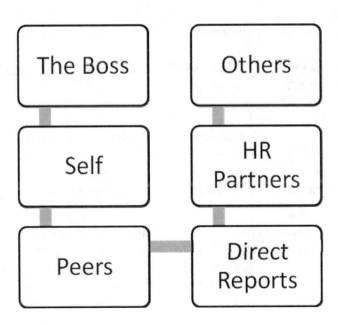

As introduced in Month Two, early feedback is a critical and often missing component of most leadership onboarding processes. There are several effective ways of collecting and delivering early feedback to a new leader during her onboarding. Building opportunities to solicit feedback as part of the onboarding conversations is one way, as is a one-time event such as the *Team Alignment* process.

Surveys that measure the actual integration of the new leader into the organization are also a critical component of the overall early feedback that a new leader needs, but often does not receive. This type of quantitative and qualitative feedback survey is one that has been created by Connect the Dots and validated by its use in Fortune 500 companies. This particular survey measures seven onboarding indicators.

At the 90-day mark it is also important to measure progress against the objectives laid out in the new leader's initial onboarding plan. How is the leader tracking on her early wins and goals? Is she displaying behaviors that map onto the organization's values and culture? What adjustments need to be made in her plan to accelerate or support her progress? What feedback can her hiring manager provide in order to help her be successful? This is usually about the time when the organization starts to expect to see the "pay-back" from its investment in the new leader. The initial assessment of the new leader's team should also be complete with recommendations as to how it moves forward to support the objectives of the organization with the addition of the leader. Appropriate decision making and risk taking are encouraged for the new leader with support in the form of constructive feedback and organizational knowledge. These can and should be provided by the hiring manager, the HR Partner and the new leader's peers.

WRAPPING UP THE PROCESS: TRANSITION TO PERFORMANCE MANAGEMENT

A best-practice onboarding process has a defined beginning and ending. Leaders cannot get away with being new forever, and organizations need to be able to transition them into their performance management or their leadership development process. Unfinished objectives are easily transferable into the leader's goals for the remainder of the year or are adjusted to address new priorities.

Debriefing is also critical at the close of the process so that the organization can refine and improve its process. A new leader who has just completed a successful onboarding experience is one who is energized and an advocate for the process. The HR Partner has also successfully begun a relationship with an influential leader and can leverage that relationship as a business partner. With a well-integrated and sustainable onboarding process, organizations are able to not only transition their new leaders smoothly for quick productivity, but create "raving fans" for their business brand. No longer is there the gap between the recruitment process and the reality of the job if the new leader, hiring manager, and HR Partner are aligned with the plan and the process.

DELIVERY METHODS

Onboarding best practice, as well as our own client experiences, suggest that there are three main delivery methods of a leadership onboarding program.

They are—

- Paper or binder
- On-line or Web-based
- Coaching

Each method has its strengths and weaknesses, which is why the CTD model creates a blend of all three so that the strengths of each may be leveraged and the weaknesses minimized. Our model creates an on-line process manager for the HR Partners who are facilitating the leadership onboarding process and one-click access to all resources and tools. They are organized by time and phase as well as by topic. There is a dashboard view for all onboarding leaders by HR Partner so that he can manage multiple leaders easily and effectively.

The delivery method to the new leader is mostly in a coaching format with printed documents provided to the new leader by the HR Partner to facilitate conversations and assignments. The HR Partner also acts as coach to the hiring manager until she is familiar enough with the process to complete her responsibilities independently.

Additionally, clearly identified roles and responsibilities for each participant in the leadership onboarding process will impact the delivery of the program significantly. These roles must be spelled out at the beginning of the design of the program and reviewed periodically so that they stay relevant. Participants include—

- New Leader
- Hiring Manager
- Human Resources
- Mentor/Coach

Lastly, every program must be structured and orderly, yet not rigid. A time-based program with specific milestones and checkpoints will provide a consistent experience for new leaders without their feeling as if they are going through a "process." It also allows the HR Partners to use their knowledge and judgment to customize the program appropriately for each of their new leaders.

MEASURING THE IMPACT

Metrics of the leadership onboarding program should always reflect the original objectives of the organization. What was the business case for leadership onboarding in our organization? Which areas did we need to address? Cultural fit? Speed to performance? Retention? Engagement? These then are the areas that are measured. Facilitated discussions, individual conversations, feedback surveys, and onboarding assignments can be included in the leadership onboarding process to collect the data.

It is critical that the measurement tools collect two kinds of data:

- Quantitative—obtained through surveys, rating systems, evaluation tools, statistical information, etc.
- Qualitative—obtained through individual interviews, focus groups, descriptive feedback forms, etc.

By asking for both, your organization will have richer information and will be able to make improvements and adjustments to your leadership onboarding program, as well as see trends in the challenges of your new leaders. The qualitative data will provide more concise and comparative measurements, while the qualitative data will provide more detailed feedback and ideas from the new managers. It is again important to include all of the participants in the onboarding process so that the data are complete.

More and more organizations are recognizing the impact of a consistent and structured leadership onboarding program.

They describe the effect that it has by—

- Creating a level playing field
- Providing each process partner with a common starting point and resources
- Giving each new leader access to the same experience and resources
- Increasing the chance that new leaders will reach their objectives

LEADERSHIP ONBOARDING IN ACTION

Organizations have experienced real success with this onboarding model. *A large, global off-priced retailer* discovered that it required a new approach to building its internal leadership "bench." It had historically relied on internal promotions; however, the changing talent pool caused them to begin to hire more leaders from outside the organization.

To meet the demands of this business change, the retail organization used the CTD model to create a consistent onboarding process that integrates the new leaders into the company culture and engages both the HR Partners and the hiring managers.

Challenges and obstacles that the new leaders experienced *without* onboarding:

- Physical environment not set up (no offices, furniture, computers, etc.).
- Didn't know how to access information.
- No structure to transition—no formal objectives.
- No one to help navigate culture—staff seemed apprehensive.
- It was assumed that they knew what to do—no real training in new position.
- For those relocating, personal transition issues overshadowed their early days.
- Not being able to contribute right away.
- Being told to put aside what they already know and just absorb information.

A formal Onboarding Impact Study identified these *results* of the program:

- Leaders said that the positions matched their expectations.
- They had a clear understanding of their roles and how it fits into the organization.
- Working with an HR Partner was very helpful—it was valuable to have someone to think things through with and act as a sounding board.
- They felt supported by their Manager and HR.
- They felt the environment was positive and welcoming.
- Transition Objectives clearly focused the first weeks on the job.
- Meet and Greets were planned and had clear intent.
- Meet and Greets were productive and led to stronger relationships.
- Early wins built confidence of new leaders and organization in the new leaders.

- Having structure the first few weeks/months was effective.
- They felt that the environment supports and encourages development on the whole.
- Having HR as a support was important.

Another example is from a *leading pediatric health and research center* that had been experiencing significant growth and change, including to its senior leadership team, during a two-year period. The organization's board encouraged this growth by recruiting nationally and internationally recognized clinical and administrative talent. The result was a significant culture shift, and the new leaders had to be integrated quickly and appropriately to be able to meet their aggressive objectives.

Using the CTD model, the hospital built their leadership onboarding process so that it allowed the new leaders to feel that they were a valued part of the organization and the community while leveraging their diverse backgrounds and experiences.

Results included:

- Better understanding by the new leaders and the hospital of the role expectations
- Smoother personal transitions by connecting relocating leaders to community resources
- Faster return on investment of the new leaders, "pay-back" to the hospital for the recruitment process
- Reinforcement of cultural elements that needed to be preserved, and a reduction in "negative" culture elements or "old ways" of doing things

The human resources team now has the tools to measure how well the new leaders are integrating (retention and engagement are up) and what parts of the hospital's selection and onboarding programs need improvement.

SUMMARY

Successful onboarding is a true partnership between a new leader and the organization. It has been a useful tool in the engagement and retention of new hires in an uncertain economy. Onboarding will continue to play a key role in the talent management process as the climate starts to shift from decline to stabilization, then to growth. It will be more important than ever to get and keep the right leaders in the right jobs.

REFERENCES

1. Valerie I. Sessa, Robert Kaiser, Jodi K. Taylor, and Richard J. Campbell, *Executive Selection: A Research Report on What Works and What Doesn't* (Center for Creative Leadership, 1998).

2. Alexcel Group. http://www.alexcelgroup.com.

Chapter 46

New Executives: Set Them Up for Success

Contributed By: George Bradt, Managing Director, PrimeGenesis

George's Contact Information:

PrimeGenesis
www.primegenesis.com
1-203-323-8501
gbradt@primegenesis.com

About the Author: George Bradt has a unique perspective on transformational leadership based on his combined senior line management and consulting experience. After Harvard and Wharton, George progressed through sales, marketing, and general management roles around the world at companies including Unilever, Procter & Gamble, Coca-Cola, and then J. D. Power and Associates' Power Information Network spin off as chief executive.

George is currently a Principal of the CEO Connection and Managing Director of PrimeGenesis, the executive onboarding and transition acceleration group he founded in 2002. George is coauthor of *The New Leader's 100-Day Action Plan* (Wiley, 2006 and 2009); *Onboarding: How to Get Your New Employees Up to Speed in Half the Time* (Wiley, 2009); and *The Total Onboarding Program: An Integrated Approach* (Wiley/Pfeiffer, 2010).

Note: The ideas presented here are adapted from *Onboarding: How to Get Your New Employees Up to Speed in Half the Time* by Bradt and Vonnegut (Wiley, 2009), which in turn draws on PrimeGenesis' work onboarding executives since 2003.

CRUCIAL EXECUTIVE ONBOARDING—THE STAKES ARE HIGH

Executive onboarding and transition acceleration for senior leaders taking on particularly complex or high-stakes situations. Since 2003, PrimeGenesis' team, tools, and perspective have reduced the rate of new leader failure from 40 percent to 10 percent by helping them and their teams deliver better results faster.

Onboarding is the process of acquiring, accommodating, assimilating, and accelerating new team members. Executive onboarding is the same process—but for executives. General onboarding and executive onboarding both aim to help new employees deliver better results faster.

However, the expectations both for the quality of the results and the value of the results to be delivered are far greater for executives, and the expectation for an executive to "ramp up" quickly into a new role is also far greater for executives, so the onboarding process becomes even more crucial to organizational success.

Ironically, although the stakes are so high, even companies with best-practice new employee onboarding programs may provide only minimal support for either new executives hired into the organization for the first time, or for new executives transitioning into new roles in their current organization.

Due to their experience level, executives are expected simply to "get to it," so they work with their previous work paradigms and move ahead quickly, knowing they must demonstrate results and make a difference quickly, with their executive-level peers watching, and often large numbers of employees watching their every move as they wonder what the new leader's approach, style, and direction will be. Working with previous paradigms, successes, and lessons learned from the past will be much more effective when paired with information about the company's culture, business needs, organizational structure, and especially the unwritten rules.

Often, new executives do not participate in the general employee population onboarding program, and they may or may not have the mentor support they need from their own executive level manager. This is a contributing factor in the high failure rate of new executives, especially within the first eighteen months in the new role. The fundamental differences between onboarding employees and onboarding executives are based on three business needs:

1. Executives must deliver *through* others in addition to working *with* others.

2. Executives generally have greater *role risks* than personal risks.

3. Executives generally have greater *relationship risks* than learning risks.[1]

WHAT IS EXECUTIVE ONBOARDING?

The overall purpose and structure of an executive onboarding approach is shown below.

Purpose: Get new executives up to speed faster

Uses: Accelerate progress of executives moving into new roles either from outside or inside the organization

Target: Supervisors of new executives

Advantages: Deploying these techniques helps executives get up to speed faster and reduces their risk of failure

Results: PrimeGenesis has used these techniques to reduce the failure rate of new executives they've helped from 40 percent to 10 percent[2]

Alignment: Include accountability and business alignment elements to avoid issues such as lack of participation and follow-through.

One organization hired a new global head of customer service. Unfortunately the division managers thought they were in charge of customer service for their divisions and did everything they could to undermine the new global head—successfully. The issue was a lack of alignment of key stakeholders, particularly peers, around the responsibilities and the inter-dependencies of the new role.

A TOTAL ONBOARDING PROGRAM

If I could wave my magic wand, no one would give approval to start recruiting anyone until they had crafted and gotten key stakeholders aligned around a Total Onboarding Program (TOP). This involves thinking through the whole plan in advance, documenting it, and getting alignment around it—a significant step in reducing new executives' role risk. A sample Total Onboarding Program Timeline[3] is shown below.

Activity	Timing	Responsibility
TOP plan alignment	_____	_____
Recruiter briefed	_____	_____
Interviews complete	_____	_____
Offer accepted	_____	_____
Personal Onboarding Plan established	_____	_____
Day one	_____	_____
100-day plan implemented	_____	_____

THE RECRUITING BRIEF

One critical element of a Total Onboarding Program is the recruiting brief. While the elements of the brief apply to all recruiting (title, department, compensation grade, start date, mission/responsibilities, vision of success, strengths, motivation, and fit), with executives it is particularly important to think through their expected impact on the rest of the organization and their organizational relationships and interdependencies. A sample brief is shown below.[4]

Sample Recruiting Brief Format

Title:_____ Department: _____

Compensation grade:_____ Start date: _____

Mission/Responsibilities:_____

_____

Vision (Picture of success):_____

_____

Strengths:_____

_____

Motivation:_____

_____

Fit:_____

_____

THE PERSONAL ONBOARDING PLAN

Co-creating a Personal Onboarding Plan (POP)[5] can be a great way for hiring managers and new executives to begin their working relationships. Ideally, they would work together to think through the job and its deliverables, stakeholders, message, pre-start, and day-one plans as well as personal and office set-up needs. Ideally, they would clarify who is doing what next. Doing this empowers the new executives to take charge of their own onboarding, knowing that their managers support them.

In particular, pre-start conversations are a good way to jump-start relationships, helping to mitigate relationship risks. The sample POP form below can be used for this purpose:

Personal Onboarding Plan (POP)

Stakeholders (up, across, down):_____

_____

Message:_____

_____

Fuzzy Front End set-up:_____

_____

Pre-start stakeholder conversations:_____

_____

Announcement cascade:_____

_____

Day one:_____

_____

First week:_____

_____

Key events:_____

_____

PLANNING THE EXECUTIVE ONBOARDING PROGRAM

The Total Onboarding Program timeline lays out the onboarding steps. For many of these steps, the hiring manager will be overseeing or leading the steps. There are a couple of pivotal points in the process that are worth going into a little more.

One organization had everyone follow the same orientation, day-one, and week-one plans with an endless parade of people wandering around their offices for meet and greets. Unfortunately, key managers lost interest in saying the same thing over and over again. The real issue is that giving a new employee an onboarding plan for them to follow produces compliance at best, with no real sense of ownership.

When planning an executive onboarding program, make sure "Three A's of Executive Onboarding" are integrated into your approach.

Accommodation

Accommodation is about doing what it takes to make your new executive ready, eager, and able to do real work on day one. Generally, this involves accommodating their work needs like office, desk, phone, ID, payroll, etc. and their personal needs like the family move, housing, schools, etc.

Assimilation

New executives need more than basic orientations. Hiring managers can help new executives assimilate by setting up onboarding conversations for them with members of their formal and informal/shadow networks.

Acceleration

Executives need different support depending upon their relative strengths as they manage three processes: strategic, operational, and organizational in pursuit of delivering results through others. An executive may also be able to accelerate faster when paired with someone in the organization with strengths that complement the new executive's strengths, as shown in the examples below:

Relative Support Needs		
Relative strengths	**versus**	**Can benefit from a strong**
Strategy/Operations	Organization	Chief Human Resource Officer
Operations/Organization	Strategy	Chief Strategy Officer
Organization/Strategy	Operations	Chief Operating Officer
—Balanced strengths across the board—		Chief of Staff

SUMMARY

Quite literally, the success of your executive onboarding program can be seen in the results of the new executives. Their roles are so visible and their contributions are so critical to the organization that their successful transition into the organization will quickly become apparent.

Onboarding executives is similar to onboarding any new employee. In all cases, get key stakeholders aligned around a Total Onboarding Program and then manage new employee acquisition, accommodation, assimilation, and acceleration. But pay particular attention to managing role and relationship risks and getting executives the resources they need to deliver results through others.

REFERENCES

1. The seven risks are: organization, role, personal, learning, relationships, delivery, and adjustment. See *The New Leader's 100-Day Action Plan* — (Bradt, et al.) for full descriptions.

2. The 40 percent failure rate comes from an internal study of 20,000 searches conducted by Heidrick and Struggles per their CEO, Kevin Kelley, as quoted by Brooke Masters in "Rise of a Headhunter," *Financial Times,* March 30, 2009.

3. This is a simplified, but usable version of this tool. See the *Onboarding* book for a more complete downloadable Total Onboarding Program tool.

4. This is a simplified, but usable version of this tool. See the *Onboarding* book for a more complete downloadable Recruiting Brief tool.

5. This is a simplified, but usable version of this tool. See the *Onboarding* book for a more complete downloadable Personal Onboarding Plan tool.

Chapter 47

The Impact of Early Feedback for New Leaders

Contributed By: Erika Lamont and Brenda Hampel, Connect the Dots Consulting

About the Authors: Brenda Hampel and Erika Lamont have consulted, coached, inspired, and developed operational and human resources teams to create onboarding and leadership development experiences at TJX Companies, Cardinal Health, Audi of America, Volkswagen Group of America, Chico's FAS, Sara Lee Food and Beverage, The Ohio State University Medical Center, Coach Inc., DSW, Victoria's Secret Stores, and NCR/Teradata.

Brenda is a Human Resources professional with a degree from The Ohio State University. Erika is an Operations professional and received her degree at Miami University. They have been consulting and building solutions for Fortune 500 organizations since 1999.

Contact Information:

Connect the Dots
5995 Wilcox Place, Suite A
Dublin, OH 43016
1.877.793.8805
www.connectthedotsconsulting.com
info@connectthedotsconsulting.com

ADD AN EARLY FEEDBACK COMPONENT TO YOUR LEADERSHIP ONBOARDING PROGRAM

No doubt you have heard the scary statistics about new leaders and their failure rates. The Center for Creative Leadership reported back in 1998 that 40 percent to 50 percent of new leaders fail during the first 18 months in their new roles.[1] The numbers being reported continue to hover around the 40 percent mark according to studies by the Alexcel Group and Monster.com.[2]

The impact, of course, is cost to the organizations that lose these new leaders. Brad Smart, author of *Topgrading*, conducted a study that found failed leaders cost each organization 24 times their base salaries.[3] For a conservative example, this would mean that a leader with a $120,000.00 annual salary costs her organization $2.8 million if she leaves and must be replaced!

The business case is clear. New leaders are at risk, and their failure costs organizations millions of dollars each year. But what is being done to address this issue?

More and more organizations are implementing formal leadership onboarding processes to smooth these transitions for new leaders and increase their chances of success. Not only are they able to integrate into their roles and culture of the organization, but they can usually do so more quickly than their counterparts who are without such support. They are able to "pay back" their organizations more quickly and help them realize a more substantial ROI.

So, the answer is easy, right? Create and deliver a leadership onboarding process that supports all the new and transitioning leaders, so that they can access critical *knowledge* about the organization, their functions and their roles, are able to build key stakeholder *relationships*, and get timely *feedback* on how they are integrating in order to be successful. The missing component in many leadership onboarding programs is the third one—*timely feedback*.

TYPICAL FEEDBACK

When leaders are transitioning, it is common for them to receive typical feedback from their managers, peers, or direct reports.

This typical feedback is usually one of the following:

- None
- "Drive-by"
- Second-hand
- Humorous

It is most common for leaders to get the "sink or swim" approach, or the "she's a smart person, she'll figure it out" approach to transition. In this case, no news is not good news. Unfortunately, this approach is not very successful because impressions and perceptions are formed very early and sometimes are difficult to change if left unchecked. The new leader who is not aware of his missteps will continue to make mistakes that no one is pointing out to him. The result can be lost time, bad decisions, damaged relationships, and even derailment.

"Drive-by" feedback is also prevalent and is found mostly in hallway conversations or other informal settings. This may be a short comment by the new leader's manager, or a peer without context or further explanation as to why a particular behavior or action didn't fit. The new leader is left with more questions than before she received the feedback and may be unsure as to what to correct or how.

Second-hand and humorous feedback are just as ineffective as "drive-by" because they also lack context or examples to help the new leader understand why something he did may have been out of line. One example might take the form of "I heard you really let them have it in that budget meeting!" Is that a good thing or a bad thing? The leader is left to decide for himself and doesn't always come to the right conclusion. The most common results of these typical kinds of feedback for new leaders are confusion, frustration, disillusionment, misperceptions, and performance issues. All can contribute to the alarming failure rate of new leaders.

WHAT'S DIFFERENT ABOUT EARLY FEEDBACK?

Early feedback as part of a formal leadership onboarding process is different. It allows the new leader to see specifically how he is or is not integrating into the culture of the organization. It is data-driven and delivered by a qualified coach so that there is context and discussion around each point. The key difference is also that this type of feedback is not performance related but onboarding specific.

THE MODEL FOR EARLY FEEDBACK

This model represents a best-practice early feedback process for new or transitioning leaders. It shows when to collect the data, who to include in the process, and what will be measured. It allows both the new leader and the organization to get an accurate snapshot of what the new leader needs to stop doing, start doing, and continue doing to be successful in her new role.

PROCESS VERSUS INTEGRATION

Many organizations use surveys to measure their leadership onboarding programs. However, these are typically "process related" and not indicators of the actual integration of their new leaders. They will ask questions such as "Was your office set up?" and "Did you receive your ID badge and parking pass?" and "Was the comp and benefit paperwork completed on time?"

Although these are important logistical details of a new leader's transition, they do not indicate whether or not that new leader is actually integrating and behaving in a way that is consistent with successful transition into the new organization. The following figure shows the seven indicators that Connect the Dots has identified as the key areas of focus when measuring if the new leader is truly integrating into her new role, function, and organization.

THE SEVEN ONBOARDING INDICATORS

At Connect the Dots, we have identified seven onboarding indicators that when measured can predict the success of a new or transitioning leader. New leaders who receive positive and constructive feedback, both quantitative and qualitative, from key stakeholders in these core areas are more likely to succeed.

HOW TO COLLECT AND DELIVER FEEDBACK

It is important to collect feedback via both formal and informal channels. What we have seen work best is to include both formal and informal collections tools in your onboarding process. The formal tools are usually surveys that ask specific questions about each of the seven indicators. The surveys are distributed to key stakeholders such as the boss, peers, direct reports, human resources partner, and any other relevant participants.

A self-assessment is critical in order to be able to measure perceptions against what the new leader is thinking. It is also important to collect data through conversations and observations. The boss, the human resources partner, and the new leader himself can solicit feedback from several sources to get a good picture of what that new leader needs to start doing, stop doing, and/or continue doing in his onboarding.

Once the feedback data have been collected, it is important to have them reviewed by an experienced and qualified participant in the process. This could be the boss, the human resources partner, or an external coach. It is important to extrapolate themes and help the leader understand both how to leverage strengths and how to bridge gaps and make adjustments. Timing is also critical in the delivery of the feedback. There should be no big gaps in time between the collection of the feedback its delivery. If there is a gap, the feedback loses its relevance and the new leader may disregard it.

KEY STEPS IN IMPLEMENTING EARLY FEEDBACK

1. Match metrics to objectives.

2. Collect quantitative and qualitative data.

3. Include all participants.

4. Report results both for individuals and organization.

We created our multi-rater survey tool *Are You Connected?*® with 27 questions that measure these seven indicators and report both quantitative and qualitative data for the individual leaders and their organizations. The survey process is designed to work like a 360, multi-rater tool. It has proved to be an invaluable source of information that allows new leaders to understand how their behaviors are being perceived and to make adjustments accordingly.

The survey is sent to key stakeholders including the new leader, her manager, peers, direct reports, and HR partner. The questions require a numeric score and also allow for comments. The results are compiled into an easy-to-read report with supporting resources and an action planning guide. A qualified facilitator guides the discussion and reviews the data with the new leader and sometimes includes the manager.

THE RESULTS

When early feedback is collected and delivered properly, the entire organization benefits.

New leaders get—

■ Timely feedback against the *seven onboarding indicators* and an action plan to address gaps

■ Opportunity to make adjustments before derailment

Hiring Managers and HR Partners get—

- A "snapshot" view of how that new leader is doing
- Specific quantitative and qualitative data to facilitate conversation

Organizations get—

- Data that show any common onboarding challenges/themes
- Data that reflect needs in the selection and/or the onboarding processes

HR ADDS VALUE

Another by-product of this powerful early feedback model when implemented with new leaders in an organization is the perceived value that HR delivers.

HR partners act as internal consultants or experts who can help the new leaders by—

- Identifying opportunities and addressing issues
- Coaching new leaders to make timely adjustments
- Speeding the "pay-back" of the new leader to the organization

ORGANIZATIONAL IMPACT

The real measurement of success is the overall impact on the new leader, her team, the department, and the organization. We have found four consistent themes in the results of our clients who use this type of feedback model.

Organizations have new leaders with

- Increased speed to performance
- Alignment with culture and objectives
- Stronger and better relationships with key stakeholders
- Higher rates of achieving performance and onboarding objectives

CASE STUDY EXAMPLES

A foreign-based luxury brand automotive manufacturer with a large U.S. presence fills its leadership roles from both its global locations and its U.S. offices. This multicultural leadership team presents a unique challenge for leaders joining the company. The U.S. Human Resources leadership team was struggling to retain new leaders who were being hired into one specific, high-profile role. The hard and soft costs of turnover were becoming obvious and painful. The culture of the organization is very strong and expects new leaders to "hit the ground running" and produce very quickly—without support or feedback. The HR team knew the turnover would continue if something was not done to support these new leaders.

Connect the Dots worked with them to implement our onboarding coaching and early feedback models. To accommodate the organizational culture, we coached the organizational development partner, as he coached the new COO. In addition, the *Are You Connected?*® The Early Feedback Survey was used to provide the COO with critical data regarding how his stakeholders experienced him during his first 90 days.

The leader onboarding coaching model and early feedback survey provided both the new leader and OD partner with the tools and resources at the right time throughout the onboarding time period. Connect the Dots advised the OD partner on which resources to use, how to deliver messages and tools and when and how to include the hiring manager. The Are *You Connected?*® Survey provided the COO with valuable feedback about how successful his stakeholders perceived him to be. Connect the Dots Consulting coached the OD partner on delivering the feedback and coaching.

Another one of our large retail clients had a similar issue with failing to provide any feedback to their new leaders. Their culture was to "be nice" and they were very uncomfortable giving any kind of constructive feedback. However, the HR leaders knew that the new leaders needed feedback in order to be successful in their complex culture. Additionally, the HR team did not have the expertise to determine the appropriate behaviors to measure.

Connect the Dots implemented the *Are You Connected?*® Early Feedback Survey with this organization's new leaders as an extension of their leadership onboarding process. We used the seven onboarding indicators and customized the survey tool to match the organization's culture and communication style. Training for the HR partners was conducted to certify them to use the tool and deliver feedback. The new leaders now have a clear view of where they are hitting and where they are missing the mark. One VP said, "The early feedback survey has literally saved some of our newest top leaders."

CONCLUSION

With the sustained failure rates of new and transitioning leaders, it is fair to say that most are probably not receiving and/or acting on early, relevant feedback during their onboarding periods. Organizations are missing the mark by not providing a structured and formal process for collecting and delivering this critical feedback. Even if your organization lacks a full-blown leadership onboarding process, your leaders can still benefit tremendously from participating in an early feedback process. The feedback process as a stand-alone has both payback and impact, and it can also be a way to gain some traction and success if you have not been able to engage your leaders in any type of onboarding activities. Feedback is powerful and, when done correctly, can speed success or prevent failure.

REFERENCES

1. Valerie I. Sessa, Robert Kaiser, Jodi K. Taylor, and Richard J. Campbell, *Executive Selection: A Research Report on What Works and What Doesn't* (Center for Creative Leadership,1998).

2. The Alexcel Group, Monster.com survey, 2007.

3. Brad Smart, *Topgrading: How Leading Companies Win by Hiring, Coaching and Keeping the Best People.* (Portfolio Hardcover, 2005).

Chapter 48

Management Onboarding Quiz Questions

Contributed By: Doris Sims, SPHR, President of Succession Builders, LLC

Doris's Contact Information:

Succession Builders, LLC
www.successionbuilders.com
doris@successionbuilders.com
214-906-3155

About the Author: Doris M. Sims, SPHR, is the Founder and President of Succession Builders, LLC, a talent management, succession planning, and new talent onboarding consulting firm. Her experience in organizational development spans over 20 years working in Fortune 100 and Fortune 500 companies. Doris received her master's degree in Human Resource Development from Indiana State University.

Doris is the coauthor of the talent management books *Building Tomorrow's Talent: A Practitioner's Guide to Talent Management and Succession Planning; The 30-Minute Guide to Talent and Succession Management;* and *The Talent Review Meeting Facilitation Guide.* Doris is also the author of the McGraw-Hill book *Creative New Employee Orientation Programs,* and has contributed articles to many other McGraw-Hill books and multiple periodicals, including *Training Magazine, Talent Management Magazine, Professionals in Human* Resources and *The Consultant's Toolkit.*

A REPOSITORY OF QUIZ QUESTIONS

Do you need questions, answers, and facilitator debrief recommendations for a Jeopardy, Bingo, or other Review Game for your Management Orientation program? This chapter provides a volume and variety of quiz content to plug into any type of review activity.

Note: This text is designed to be used for training purposes only and is not intended to be used as legal advice. Federal regulations are updated regularly, and interpretations of these regulations change based on court cases. This could change the information presented here at any time. Instructors and human resource professionals are advised to continuously obtain information and train-ing to stay current on employment law and federal regulations affecting the workplace.

Management Orientation Discussion Questions

1. Should an interviewer ask applicants if they are authorized to work in the United States?

    ■ Yes!

    ☞ Discussion Point: The interviewer should always determine if the applicant is authorized to work in the United States, because it is against the law to hire an illegal immigrant.

    However, the interviewer should not ask if the applicant is a U.S. citizen (unless the employee will be working on government contracts or government activities that require U.S. citizenship). Asking about an applicant's citizenship implies possible discrimination based on national origin, which is prohibited by the Civil Rights Act. A person does not have to be a U.S. citizen to be authorized to work in the United States.

2. If a jury awards the plaintiff in an employment law discrimination case payment for wages lost after the employee was wrongfully terminated, would that be an example of compensatory relief or punitive damages?

    ■ This is an example of compensatory relief.

    ☞ Discussion Point: The Civil Rights Act of 1991 added a provision to allow punitive damages, which are designed to punish a defendant who acted intentionally and/or with malice. The punitive damage option is not available against state or local governments. Normally, when you hear about a very large jury award provided for a plaintiff, you are hearing about punitive damages.

3. Is it legally advisable to have weight and height requirements for jobs that require good physical condition, such as police officers, emergency personnel, etc.?

    ☜ No!

    ☞ Discussion Point: It is better to require physical tests that pertain to *the essential job functions*. Weight and height requirements can imply discrimination under the Americans with Disabilities Act, and although physical appearance is not covered under the Civil Rights Act, many lawsuits have been filed (and these cost the employer money, time, and embarrassment) on the basis of weight discrimination.

    Physical tests that can be proved to pertain to the essential job functions virtually eliminate this problem, and they will help you hire better candidates. It is very possible for a person who might be perceived as overweight to be in better physical condition than a person who is considered to be of normal weight. What you are really looking for is the best candidate who can perform on the job, so that is what you should test for.

4. If an employee reports a sexual harassment complaint to you, but asks you not to do anything about it, should you still report it to your human resource representative?

    ■ Yes!

    ☞ Discussion Point: You are obligated to report the complaint, and/or go with the employee to report the alleged incident to the human resources representative for the company. Explain

(continued on next page)

to the employee that the report will be confidential, on a need-to-know basis. Only those who are required to be involved in the complaint investigation and resulting actions will know about the complaint.

Important: If a company is aware of a potential or actual sexual harassment situation and does nothing, punitive damages may be awarded if a lawsuit ensues.

5. A male supervisor sends his male workers out of town for seminars but does not send his female workers, citing their need to care for their children. What law does this violate?

    ■ The Civil Rights Act.

    ☞ Discussion Point: The Civil Rights Act of 1964 prohibits discrimination on the basis of race, sex, national origin, color, and religion. This can pertain to employment, promotions, training opportunities, and benefits.

    In this situation, the employer is out of compliance with the Civil Rights Act because he is denying the female workers a training opportunity (which can lead to advancement in position and pay). Also, the supervisor is setting himself up for a sexual harassment–hostile work environment complaint as a result of his stereotypical statements.

6. A supervisor asks an applicant if she owns a car to get to her job as a bank teller. Why was this question inappropriate?

    ■ It does not pertain to the essential job functions.

    ☞ Discussion Point: It is only appropriate to ask an applicant if he or she owns a car if the position requires employees to have a car to fulfill their responsibilities. Examples might be pizza delivery personnel or courier service personnel. However, as a bank teller, an employee will not need a car to fulfill his or her job functions.

    When interviewing candidates, make sure you stick to questions that pertain to the responsibilities of the job. In the bank teller's situation, it may be appropriate to ask candidates if they have transportation to work (avoiding the issue of *owning* a car, which is not required for employment for most jobs), *but only if the interviewer asks each candidate the same question.*

7. An employer of 50 people fails to send continuation of benefits information to a worker who was laid off. What law does this violate?

    ■ COBRA.

    ☞ Discussion Point: The Consolidated Omnibus Reconciliation Act requires employers with 20 or more employees to provide information regarding continuation of insurance to former employees and retirees and their dependents. This is one of the many reasons it is important for managers to notify their human resources personnel immediately when an employee terminates employment with the company.

    Note: If an employee is terminated for gross misconduct, COBRA benefits may not be required; however, a human resources professional should review the situation and make this determination.

(*continued on next page*)

8. The I-9 form must be obtained from an employee within how many days of employment?

   ■ Three.

   ☞ Discussion Point: The I-9 form and the appropriate identification documents (appropriate documents are listed on the I-9 form) must be obtained from the employee within three days of employment. For this reason, many employers require these forms to be completed in their new employee orientation programs.

   If the employee does not fulfill this obligation within three days of employment, the employer must terminate the employee to avoid being in noncompliance with the Immigration Reform and Control Act of 1986 (IRCA). Special circumstances may exist that would require an employee to provide proof of situations such as an extended work authorization in lieu of these normal requirements.

9. An employer pays below the current minimum wage amount. Which law does this violate?

   ■ The Fair Labor Standards Act.

   ☞ Discussion Point: The Fair Labor Standards Act includes the Equal Pay Act, minimum wage compliance, child labor laws, and regulations pertaining to overtime and the classification of employees into either exempt or nonexempt status.

10. An employee who has been with the company for three years goes on medical leave. The employee demands paid time off during her leave under the Family Medical and Leave Act of 1993. Is she correct?

    ☜ No!

    ☞ Discussion Point: The Family Medical and Leave Act provides for protected job leave to care for a newly born or adopted child, a family member with a serious illness, for placement of a child for adoption or foster care, or for the employee's own serious illness.

    The law states specific eligibility requirements for the employee to be covered under the act. This law provides for up to 12 weeks of unpaid time within a 12-month period of time. It does not provide for any paid leave time, which is what the question included. Employees may have benefits from their employer that will provide a full or partial paid leave period, such as disability benefits, vacation time, or sick time, but the Family Medical and Leave Act does not require paid leave benefits—only job protection.

11. A 20-year-old woman is turned down for a job as a model for a senior citizen vitamin supplement. The company cited a need for an older model for the job. Is the company in violation of the Age Discrimination Act?

    ☜ No!

    ☞ Discussion Point: First, the Age Discrimination Act of 1967 (ADEA) prohibits employment discrimination against individuals over the age of 40. This woman is not over the age of 40; therefore, the company has not violated this law. In addition, the company would have a very

(*continued on next page*)

valid argument that it is an essential job function to have a model for a senior citizen vitamin supplement that has the appearance of a senior citizen, and virtually all jury members would likely see the validity of this job requirement.

12. A job applicant is asked, "You have an unusual accent. Where are you from?" Is this a legally advisable interview question? Why or why not?

☞ No, this is not a legal question. It suggests potential discrimination based on national origin.

☞ Discussion Point: It is a common mistake for interviewers to ask this question, usually out of curiosity or simply to make conversation. But it can imply that the interviewer is seeking information to determine the candidate's national origin, and discrimination based on national origin is prohibited by the Civil Rights Act.

Even if the interviewer is asking to determine the *part* of a country or nation a person is from (e.g., a New York accent versus a Texas accent), this is not a legally advisable question to ask during an interview. Of course, it also has nothing to do with the essential job functions.

13. A company of 500 employees has to lay off 250 full-time employees at one work site immediately. They provide one week of severance pay for each year each employee has worked. Is this legal?

☞ No!

☞ Discussion Point: In this situation, the employer would need to provide either 60 days advance notice of employment termination, or 60 days severance pay. This is covered under the Worker Adjustment and Retraining Notification Act (WARN) of 1989. This law pertains to employers with 100 or more full-time employees (employees who work 20 or more hours per week) who have worked for the company for at least six months, when layoffs of specified numbers or percentages as defined within this law occur.

14. True or False: The Equal Pay Act of 1963 requires that the same compensation be paid for men and women who are working in the same position with the same job title.

☞ False!

☞ Discussion Point: This law provides for differences in compensation between employees of any gender when the difference is based on valid criteria such as differences in productivity or performance levels, differences in experience or background, and differences in educational levels. The law is intended to prohibit differences in compensation between men and women that are not based on any valid and accepted criteria.

15. An employee complains that other workers are using racial slurs and jokes in the workplace. What law is being violated?

■ The Civil Rights Act.

☞ Discussion Point: Using racial jokes or slurs in the workplace is a form of harassment on the basis of race, which is covered under the Civil Rights Act. The law prohibits a hostile work environment on the basis of race, sex, national origin, color, or religion.

(*continued on next page*)

16. A security guard is fired because he has a religious practice of wearing a cap at all times. What law is violated?

■ The Civil Rights Act.

☞ Discussion Point: This question is based on an actual Equal Employment Opportunity Commission (EEOC) lawsuit in 1999. The jury found in favor of the plaintiff and determined that the employer violated the Civil Rights Act on the basis of religion.

Managers need to take care not to design or try to enforce a dress code that does not respect clothing or attire requirements on the basis of religion, national origin, color, sex, or race. Employers are required to respect religious practices of employees, providing they do not create an undue hardship on the employer or violate the rights of other employees.

17. Due to financial difficulties, an employer requires all employees over 60 to retire. Is this legal? Why or why not?

♥ This is not legal. This falls under the Age Discrimination in Employment Act of 1967.

☞ Discussion Point: This question was also based on an actual EEOC lawsuit in 1999. The Age Discrimination Act protects employees over the age of 40. In this case, the employees were terminated solely on the basis of age, not on the basis of performance or any other criteria.

18. An employer decides not to hire a candidate who cannot leave a wheelchair for the flight attendant position the candidate applied for. Did this violate the Americans with Disabilities Act (ADA)?

♥ No!

☞ Discussion Point: The ADA requires employers to make reasonable accommodations for persons with disabilities that will allow the employee to complete the essential job functions. In this case, two of the essential job functions of a flight attendant are to be able to direct and assist passengers in the event of an emergency on the plane; a person who could not rise from a wheelchair would not be able to accomplish this effectively.

Also, airplane aisles currently would not allow a flight attendant in a wheelchair to serve beverages and food to passengers, and no accommodation could be made without undue hardship on the employer.

However, most often an employer is able to make an accommodation for an employee with a disability without undue hardship. Examples include installing equipment or ramps needed for wheelchair access or providing Braille computer keypads.

19. A company defines all of its assembly-line employees as exempt so they can take compensatory time instead of being paid overtime, per their own request. Is this legal? Why or why not?

♥ No. This is a Fair Labor Standards Act violation.

(continued on next page)

☞ Discussion Point: The Fair Labor Standards Act (FSLA) contains specific definitions of exempt employees (who would not receive overtime pay) and nonexempt employees. Nonexempt employees must be provided overtime pay according to the laws of their state.

It would be virtually impossible for assembly-line workers (who are not supervisors or managers) to qualify for exempt status as defined in the FSLA. Therefore, even if the employees prefer and request "comp time" rather than overtime pay for extra hours worked, the law requires that they be paid the overtime amount.

20. Name any two federal laws that prohibit employment discrimination.

   ■ Possible answers include:

   — The Civil Rights Act of 1964 and the amended CRA of 1991

   — The Equal Pay Act

   — The Age Discrimination Act

   — The Americans with Disabilities Act

   — Section 501 of the Rehabilitation Act of 1973

   ☞ Discussion Point: The Equal Employment Opportunity Commission (EEOC) oversees all of these laws. Supervisors and managers may think that knowledge of these laws is important only for human resource professionals. It's true that the supervisor and manager should partner with and rely on the HR professional to handle the situations that require expertise. But supervisors and managers need to have a basic understanding of what is covered in the laws to avoid making compliance errors during the normal course of business, and to work more effectively with the HR professional.

Multiple Choice Management Onboarding Questions

1. Which federal law defines and prohibits sexual harassment?

   A. The Equal Rights Act

   B. The Sexual Protection Act

   C. The Civil Rights Act

   D. The Work Environment Protection Act

   Answer: C—The Civil Rights Act

2. Which of the following is not an example of intellectual property owned by a company?

   A. Patents

   B. Trademarks

   C. Copyrighted Documents

   D. Company Facilities

   Answer: D—Company Facilities

3. Quid pro quo sexual harassment refers to:

   A. A corporation that consistently fails to promote females into leadership positions.

   B. A supervisor who requests sexual favors in exchange for employment or promotional opportunities.

   C. A work environment that allows slander of other employees based on their gender.

   D. Both A and C

   E. All of the above

   Answer: B—The supervisor who requests sexual favors in exchange for an employment or promotion. A quid pro quo sexual harassment situation exists when sex is requested, required, or implied to keep a job, to obtain a job, or to obtain a promotion.

4. Which of the following are correct ethical behaviors to follow if you possess inside information that could potentially affect the company's stock price?

   A. Refrain from trading any company stock you own yourself until the information is made public.

   B. Refrain from advising anyone else to trade in the company stock until the information is made public.

   C. Refrain from discussing the information with anyone else (including your spouse, family, and friends.) until it is made public.

(continued on next page)

D.   Both A and B

E.   All of the above

Answer: E—All of the above

5.   Sexual harassment can take place between:

A.   Men and women

B.   Women and women

C.   Men and men

D.   All of the above

Answer: D—All of the above

6.   Which of the following is an example of a potential conflict of interest?

A.   A bank employee also sells quilts at craft shows on the weekends.

B.   A sales employee owns company stock and she feels this motivates her to work harder to sell the company's products to customers.

C.   An employee works in a mortgage company as a loan officer and also has his own small mortgage brokerage company on the side.

D.   An employee works for a large retail grocery chain but buys her own groceries at the corner grocery store on a regular basis.

Answer: C—A potential conflict of interest exists if an employee engages in a business that competes directly with that of his or her employer.

7.   Which of the following evidence is required to prove a hostile work environment in a sexual harassment case being reviewed in a court of law?

A.   The plaintiff's attorney must show evidence that the defendant(s) deliberately intended to offend and harass the plaintiff.

B.   The plaintiff's attorney must show evidence that the defendant's words, behaviors, or possessions offended the plaintiff.

C.   The plaintiff's attorney must show evidence that the plaintiff lost his or her job or was denied another type of employment opportunity.

D.   All of the above

E.   None of the above

Answer: B—It does not matter whether the harasser intends to harass; all that matters is that the other person or persons are offended by the behavior, words, or graphic item. The court is concerned with the impact of the behavior, not with the intent of the behavior. Also, a person's job or position doesn't have to be threatened for a hostile work environment to exist.

(continued on next page)

8. When working with suppliers and vendors, which of the following could potentially be considered unethical behavior?

   A. The employee receives a rebate on a home computer system if she engages that supplier for the purpose of supplying the company's computer needs.

   B. The employee receives a free cruise vacation if he signs a contract with a relocation services vendor.

   C. The employee engages his brother-in-law as a company consultant without comparing pricing or services of comparable consultants.

   D. Both A and B

   E. All of the above

   Answer: E—All of the above. Employees should refrain from accepting substantial gifts from vendors. They should also refrain from retaining relatives as vendors or suppliers, or at least disclose the relationship to senior management or to the company's legal department.

9. Which of the following statements is true?

   A. If an employee submits to a sexual situation, then harassment definitely has not taken place.

   B. If an employer is not aware of a sexual harassment situation, then the employer is not liable for it.

   C. If the sexual harassment situation takes place at a location away from the work facility, the employer is not liable for it.

   D. None of the above

   Answer: D— None of the above A) An employee may feel pressured and then submit to a sexual situation to keep his or her job, but sexual harassment has still taken place. B) The court holds an employer liable for a sexual harassment situation even if the employer was not aware of the situation. C) As one example, if the sexual harassment behavior occurs during a business trip between two employees, the employer still retains liability.

10. Which of the following behaviors is ethical?

    A. Making copies of a vendor's copyrighted material as long as it will be used only for internal training purposes.

    B. Making copies of a software package for coworkers if they need the software to do their job.

    C. Offering customers a discount if they order a package of products rather than purchasing products singularly.

    D. Discussing aspects of your own compensation package with another employee.

(*continued on next page*)

Answer: C—It is an ethical and normal business practice to offer a discount for products that are packaged together or purchased in bulk. A) It is never ethical or legal to make copies of copyrighted materials for use within the organization; this is equal to stealing the vendor's intellectual property. B) The company must purchase either a software package for each employee or a license agreement that specifies (and charges a fee for) a number of users for the software. D) It is never appropriate to discuss any aspect of your compensation package with another employee.

11. Which of the following behaviors is ethical?

   A. Taking your company laptop home to work on your e-mail messages.

   B. Using the company's e-mail system to sell your Avon products.

   C. Accessing Internet Web sites with content that might be offensive to others or sexual in nature.

   D. Discussing the company's pending acquisition with a coworker during a business flight on an airplane.

   Answer: A—It is appropriate to use your company laptop to work on company business at a variety of locations, within the workplace and outside of the workplace. B) Employees should not use the workplace to sell products that are not associated with the employer. C) Accessing inappropriate Web sites in the workplace is cause for disciplinary action. D) A conversation concerning a company's pending acquisition can be overheard on an airplane, which could affect the stock price or the acquisition itself.

12. Which of the following is an unethical question that could portray potential discrimination during an interview with a job candidate?

   A. Do you have your own car to drive to and from our work facility?

   B. Will you ever need to take time off from work to care for your children?

   C. Would you describe yourself as having a physical handicap?

   D. Both B and C

   E. All of the above

   Answer: E—All of the above. A) It is not appropriate to determine whether the employee owns a car to get to work; however, it may be appropriate to discuss the work hours and whether the employee would be able to work during those hours. B) It is inappropriate to refer to child care needs during an interview. C) This statement may be perceived as a violation of the Americans with Disabilities Act (ADA). It is appropriate to discuss the essential job functions and ask all candidates for the position if they would be willing and able to perform these job functions.

(continued on next page)

13. Which of the following behaviors would be considered gross misconduct?

   A.   Carrying a firearm onto the company property.

   B.   Threatening to assault another employee.

   C.   Illegal drug usage.

   D.   All of the above

   Answer: D—All of the above

14. Which of the following is not a legal and ethical interview question?

   A.   The position you are applying for is a second shift position. Would you be able to work the hours of 3 p.m. to 10 p.m.?

   B.   Where are you from originally?

   C.   Are you legally authorized to work in the United States?

   D.   What other companies are you interviewing with?

   Answer: B—Asking this question can be perceived as fishing for information about the candidate's national origin. The Civil Rights Act makes it unlawful to discriminate based on national origin.

15. Which of the following is an unethical or potentially illegal use of the company's computer systems?

   A.   Intentionally forwarding an e-mail message with an attachment containing a computer virus.

   B.   Forwarding chain e-mail letters to other employees using the company's e-mail system.

   C.   Intentionally deleting company documents or programs on individual computers, on servers, or on networks.

   D.   All of the above

   Answer: D—All of the above are definitely unethical or are violations of federal, state, or local law.

16. If an employee reports a sexual harassment situation but asks you not to do anything about it, what should you do?

   A.   Tell the employee that you will not report the situation but that he or she should come back to you immediately if the problem is not resolved.

   B.   Tell the employee that the situation will not be reported, but instead a sexual harassment policy will be reissued companywide and sexual harassment training will take place.

(continued on next page)

C. Explain that you are obligated to report the situation so an investigation can take place, but that the investigation and information about the situation will be confidential, on a need-to-know basis.

D. Conduct the investigation yourself to prevent rumors from starting in the company and to alleviate the concerns of the employee.

Answer: C—As a manager, you are obligated to report the situation to your human resource representative to allow an investigation of the claim.

17. Which of the following is unethical behavior with a vendor or supplier?

A. Asking the vendor or supplier for tickets to an upcoming concert because you know they are the audiovisual crew for the event.

B. Accepting money from a vendor or supplier.

C. Asking a vendor to come into the company to demonstrate their product, even though you aren't sure if you want to purchase the product.

D. Both A and B

E. All of the above

Answer: D—Both A and B are inappropriate behaviors. An employee should never solicit a vendor gift, and accepting money from a vendor is never ethical. Answer C is a perfectly appropriate request because a demonstration can help the company decide whether they want to purchase a vendor's product.

18. Which of the following factors should be considered before accepting a gift from a vendor to ensure that acceptance of the gift would be ethical?

A. Does the cost of the gift exceed my company's limit for unsolicited gifts from vendors?

B. Could my acceptance of this gift cause me to feel obligated to purchase products or services from this vendor?

C. Would I enjoy using this gift?

D. Both A and B

E. All of the above

Answer: D—Both A and B are ethical issues to be considered before accepting a gift from a vendor. Answer C does not factor into the ethical issue.

19. Which of the following people might be considered to have inside information that should not be used to influence stock purchase decisions?

A. A sales employee who is involved in obtaining a new, significant client with the business potential to double the company's revenue in the next two years.

(continued on next page)

B.   A cocktail server who overhears a conversation between two business executives about a multi-billion-dollar company merger that has not been made public yet.

C.   The CEO's spouse who is aware that the company's financial results, which are about to be released, are not as high as the company projected to shareholders.

D.   All of the above

Answer: D—All of the above. Anyone who gains access to significant information about the organization that has not yet been announced to the public is a potential insider. Insiders do not have to be employees of the company.

If the information you learn (that has not been made public yet) causes you to want to either buy or sell stock in the company, then the potential for violating insider trading laws exists.

20.   Which of the following behaviors has (have) the potential to create a hostile work environment?

A.   One manager in the company requests sexual favors of an employee in exchange for a promotion.

B.   Racial slurs are heard frequently in the company.

C.   Many of the employees in the company have screen savers depicting sexual situations or scantily clothed models.

D.   Both A and B

E.   Both B and C

Answer: E—Both B and C. A) This is an example of quid pro quo sexual harassment, but it is not an example of a hostile work environment. A hostile work environment is characterized by "frequent and pervasive" harassment. B) A hostile work environment does not pertain only to sexual harassment; it can also pertain to racial harassment, age harassment, or national origin harassment. C) Harassment can occur in the form of visual items that are degrading or sexual in nature.

Fill-in-the Blank Interview Category Questions

Use the following codes to identify each interview question type (you may use more than one code per question):

O = Open-Ended Question

I = Integrity-Based Question

C = Case Interview Question

K/S = Knowledge- and Skill-Based Question

B = Behavioral Interview Question

(These questions can be also used to build your own interview question lists when you return to your job.)

1. _____ In your current or last position, what did you enjoy most about your job?

2. _____ How did you help increase revenue at your current or previous position?

3. _____ What do you know about our company?

4. _____ Why are you interested in this position?

5. _____ Imagine that you have just started as a new supervisor of a group of employees who were also all just hired within the last six weeks. How would you begin working with these employees?

6. _____ What important trends do you see in our industry?

7. _____ A coworker confides in you that she is being sexually harassed. How do you handle this situation?

8. _____ Describe a time in your career when you had to respond quickly to changes in your job priorities. How did you handle the situation, and what impact did the change have on you?

9. _____ Describe your most challenging experience in convincing management to accept a new idea. How did you do it, and what was the outcome?

10. _____ You overhear a conversation between two of your coworkers. One of the employees is asking the other employee to clock his time card out for him at a later time, because he has to leave work early. What are your thoughts and actions regarding this conversation?

11. _____ Describe three accomplishments you are the most proud of.

12. _____ Describe the tasks you were fully responsible for in your last position.

13. _____ What will you be looking for in this job that you didn't find in your last job?

(continued on next page)

14. _____ If you could have changed things at your last company, what would you have changed?

15. _____ Describe the one most important and the one least important course you took in high school or college. Explain why you chose these two courses in your answer.

16. _____ Describe a situation when you had to help people with differing viewpoints reach a constructive solution. What did you do, and what were the results?

17. _____ You have just been assigned to teach new employees coming into your department to learn to use the computer system they will need to use daily on the job. How will you approach this assignment? How will you know if your teaching is successful?

18. _____ What are your long-range goals?

19. _____ On your résumé, you note that you have extensive customer service experience. What are the most important things a customer service representative can do during a phone conversation with a customer to meet the customer's service and satisfaction needs?

20. _____ Your résumé indicates you have five years of experience as a data entry operator. What do you estimate your typing speed to be?

21. _____ Describe a time when you needed to work extensively with employees in other departments to solve a problem for a customer. How did you approach your coworkers to meet the customer's needs, and what were the results?

22. _____ What prompted you to apply for this position?

23. _____ The person who will fill this position will need to have an extensive and thorough understanding of our company's services. What steps will you take to learn about our company's services?

24. _____ Are you better with figures or with words? Explain your answer.

Answer Key: Fill-in-the-Blank Interview Question Categories Exercise

Note to the facilitator: All the questions are open-ended questions, so that response is always correct. For many of the questions, participants should also be able to identify the type of open-ended question, using the choices listed.

O = Open-Ended Question

I = Integrity-Based Question

C = Case Interview Question

K/S = Knowledge- and Skill-Based Question

B = Behavioral Interview Question

1. In your current or last position, what did you enjoy most about your job?—O

2. How did you help increase revenue at your current or previous position?—B, K/S

3. What do you know about our company?—K

4. Why are you interested in this position?—O

5. Imagine that you have just started as a new supervisor of a group of employees who were also all just hired within the last six weeks. How would you begin working with these employees?—C

6. What important trends do you see in our industry?—K or O

7. A coworker confides in you that she is being sexually harassed. How do you handle this situation?—I, K

8. Describe a time in your career when you had to respond quickly to changes in your job priorities. How did you handle the situation, and what impact did the change have on you?—B

9. Describe your most challenging experience in convincing management to accept a new idea. How did you do it, and what was the outcome?—B

10. You overhear a conversation between two of your coworkers. One of the employees is asking the other employee to clock his time card out for him at a later time, because he has to leave work early. What are your thoughts and actions regarding this conversation?—I

11. Describe three accomplishments you are the most proud of.—O

12. Describe the tasks you were fully responsible for in your last position.—O, K

13. What will you be looking for in this job that you didn't find in your last job?—O

14. If you could have changed things at your last company, what would you have changed?—O

(continued on next page)

15. Describe the one most important and the one least important course you took in high school or college. Explain why you chose these two courses in your answer.—O, K

16. Describe a situation when you had to help people with differing viewpoints reach a constructive solution. What did you do, and what were the results?—B

17. You have just been assigned to teach new employees coming into your department to learn to use the computer system they will need to use daily on the job. How will you approach this assignment? How will you know if your teaching is successful?—C

18. What are your long-range goals?—O

19. On your résumé, you note that you have extensive customer service experience. What are the most important things a customer service representative can do during a phone conversation with a customer to meet the customer's service and satisfaction needs?—K/S

20. Your résumé indicates you have five years of experience as a data entry operator. What do you estimate your typing speed to be?—K/S

21. Describe a time when you needed to work extensively with employees in other departments to solve a problem for a customer. How did you approach your coworkers to meet the customer's needs, and what were the results?—B

22. What prompted you to apply for this position?—O

23. The person who will fill this position will need to have an extensive and thorough understanding of our company's services. What steps will you take to learn about our company's services?—C

24. Are you better with figures or with words? Explain your answer.—O

Chapter 49

Small Group Activity: Preventing Harassment

Contributed By: Doris Sims, SPHR, President of Succession Builders, LLC

About the Author: Doris M. Sims, SPHR, is the Founder and President of Succession Builders, LLC, a talent management, succession planning, and new talent onboarding consulting firm. Her experience in organizational development spans over 20 years working in Fortune 100 and Fortune 500 companies. Doris received her master's degree in Human Resource Development from Indiana State University.

Doris's Contact Information:

Succession Builders, LLC
www.successionbuilders.com
doris@successionbuilders.com
214-906-3155

Doris is the coauthor of the talent management books: *Building Tomorrow's Talent: A Practitioner's Guide to Talent Management and Succession Planning*; *The 30-Minute Guide to Talent and Succession Management*; and *The Talent Review Meeting Facilitation Guide*. Doris is also the author of the McGraw-Hill book *Creative New Employee Orientation Programs*, and has contributed articles to many other McGraw-Hill books and multiple periodicals, including *Training Magazine*, *Talent Management Magazine*, *Professionals in Human Resources*, and *The Consultant's Toolkit*.

TALKING ABOUT SEXUAL HARASSMENT ISSUES INCREASES UNDERSTANDING

Many companies post their sexual harassment reporting procedure, give presentations on sexual harassment, and show videos on sexual harassment. These are all valid activities in the prevention of sexual harassment, but for true understanding, employees need to discuss the gray areas of potential sexual harassment behaviors and situations that pose a question in people's minds—is it or isn't it sexual harassment?

The purpose of this activity is to pose these questionable situations to stimulate discussion about when the line is crossed from acceptable behavior to sexual harassment.

AUDIENCE AND TIMING

The ideal group size for this activity is between 8 and 50 participants. The activity and discussion will take approximately 20 to 30 minutes.

YOU'LL NEED:

- Copies of the handout found in this chapter, one per participant
- Pens or pencils for the participants
- Two flip charts and markers

PREPARATION

To prepare for the activity, make copies of the handout prior to the class. Also, become familiar with the information in the handout and discuss responses and potential issues that could arise during the activity with the organization's human resource personnel and/or corporate attorney, to obtain a complete understanding of sexual harassment law (covered under the Civil Rights Act) and the organization's policies.

CONDUCTING THE ACTIVITY

1. Use this activity as part of a larger presentation on sexual harassment. This activity works well after the factual information concerning sexual harassment has already been presented.

2. Break the class up into groups of three to six (depending on the total size of the group). The participants should rearrange their seating as needed so each group can hold a discussion.

3. Pass out copies of the Sexual Harassment Table Discussions handout.

4. Instruct the groups to discuss each question and determine if the action listed is or is not sexual harassment. Participants should write down the discussion points and positions in the spaces provided.

5. After the groups have completed their responses to each question, bring the class back together as a total group.

DEBRIEFING THE ACTIVITY

Bring up one question at a time, and ask the groups if they answered yes or no. The following points can be made during this discussion (*Check with your human resource personnel or corporate attorney for additional discussion points and appropriate responses to customize the session to your company's policies and procedures.*):

The best answer to each of these questions is yes—each situation *could* be a sexual harassment behavior leading to a hostile work environment (some more immediately than others), and a hostile work environment is one form of harassment. Much depends on how something is said, the body language and facial expressions used, and how often the behavior occurs in the workplace. Frequency, severity, and pervasiveness are all factors the courts review when determining if a hostile work environment exists.

When discussing each situation, describe a scenario when it would normally not be considered sexual harassment (e.g., a coworker simply compliments someone on a new outfit), and when the line is crossed and sexual harassment might exist (e.g., "Hey, baby, that new skirt really shows off your great legs"). Some of the situations are inappropriate in any scenario (e.g., making a racial joke in the workplace).

Sexual harassment can take many forms—physical, verbal, graphics or photos, roaming or "elevator" eyes.

It doesn't matter whether the sexual harasser *intended* to offend or harm the harassed person. If someone is offended, a potential harassment situation exists.

Harassment is covered under the Civil Rights Act and includes all types of harassment, including racial harassment and gender harassment.

The reason some of these issues are gray areas is that a potential sexual harassment situation may depend on *how* a person says something, rather than *what* was said. Also, it is not possible to list every potential sexual harassment situation in the law, so the law is subject to interpretation by juries and courts.

Harassment can take place between a male and a female, a female and a male, a female and a female, and a male and a male.

Final Parting Thoughts...

Within your organization, you are the leader and the champion for the New Employee Onboarding strategy. You are responsible for the critical first impression that all new employees have as they start their career path in your organization. Your role is critical to the success of this process, and your business leaders look to you for direction, resources, and support.

There will be days where you become tired of delivering the same message and weary of handling all of the details of the orientation process. There are things you can do to help keep yourself energized as you continue to welcome and train new employees:

- Remember, if you are bored, the new employees will be bored. So change it up! Try a new activity or game in the onboarding program. Try a new way of presenting the information. (And by the way, please don't ever say, "I know this is boring but . . . ," which is a way of alerting the new employees to let them know they should be bored.) If you find yourself apologizing for your new employee program—change it!

- Many companies have multiple facilitators of the new employee onboarding program and process, so the responsibility for facilitating the program is shared. This helps prevent the burn-out effect that can occur if only one person is responsible for the onboarding process.

- Consider making the role of the New Employee Leader a rotating role for high-potential employees (from any business unit, not just within Human Resources). Each person could take on the role for six to twelve months and then pass the torch on to the next person. This allows top-talent employees across the entire organization to experience a Human Resources role, and to learn to mentor new employees from multiple business units.

- Review the program to determine if there are any aspects of the content that can be delivered in another way. Can any of the content be moved online? Should any of the content be delivered to the employee in another way before the employee's first day with the organization? Should any of the content be handled by department managers rather than by the corporate HR office?

- Consider bringing in Subject Matter Experts (SMEs) to present part of the content of the new employee program. As another alternative, ask employees with experience and tenure in the organization (who have done well in their careers there) to come and speak with the employees about what it is like to work in the company, and how their own career has progressed in the company

■ Another challenge for the leader of the onboarding program is keeping the materials current with the ever-changing names on the organizational charts, changing benefits and policies, etc. One way to make this job easier is to use some fill-in-the-blank spaces in any onboarding materials you provide, for employees to fill in during the onboarding program (whether the content is delivered live or online). Not only does this save you from having to update details constantly, but it also helps keep the attention of the employees, as they are listening for the information to fill in the blanks. Also, it adds a kinesthetic component to the program, so that the employees are now seeing, hearing and writing the information, which means their retention of the information also increases.

My hope is that this book has brought new ideas, new tools, and new resources to your attention, and that these will help enhance your new employee program, increase your own excitement and energy about designing and delivering the program, and increase the ROI of your new employee onboarding process. Congratulations on your role as the CEO of New Employee First Impressions—go forth and orient others!

Index

ABOUT THE AUTHOR

Doris Sims, SPHR, is the founder and president of Succession Builders, LLC, a leading talent management, succession planning, and onboarding consulting firm. She is also the author of *Building Tomorrow's Talent, The 30-Minute Guide to Talent and Succession Management, Creative New Employee Orientation Programs,* and *The Talent Review Meeting Facilitator's Guide.* For more information, go to www. SuccessionBuilders.com.

LINCOLN CHRISTIAN UNIVERSITY